FIELDS OF RESISTANCE

FIELDS OF RESISTANCE

THE STRUGGLE OF FLORIDA'S FARMWORKERS FOR JUSTICE

SILVIA GIAGNONI

Haymarket Books
Chicago, Illinois

First published by Haymarket Books in 2011.
© 2011 Silvia Giagnoni

Haymarket Books
P.O. Box 180165
Chicago, IL 60618
773-583-7884
info@haymarketbooks.org
www.haymarketbooks.org

ISBN: 978-1 60846-093-9

Trade distribution:
In the US through Consortium Book Sales and Distribution, www.cbsd.com
In Canada, Publishers Group Canada, www.pgcbooks.ca
In the UK, Turnaround Publisher Services, www.turnaround-uk.com
In Australia, Palgrave Macmillan, www.palgravemacmillan.com.au
All other countries, Publishers Group Worldwide, www.pgw.com

Cover design by Amy Balkin. Cover image by Luis M. Alvarez, Associated Press.

Special discounts are available for bulk purchases by organizations and institutions.
Please contact Haymarket Books for more information at 773-583-7884 or
info@haymarketbooks.org.

This book was published with the generous support of Lannan Foundation and
the Wallace Global Fund.

Printed by union labor in Canada on recycled paper containing 100 percent
postconsumer waste in accordance with the guidelines of the Green Press Initiative,
www.greenpressinitiative.org.

Library of Congress CIP Data is available.

2 4 6 8 10 9 7 5 3 1

100%

For the people of Immokalee,
and migrant communities everywhere

We write to taste life twice, in the moment, and in retrospection.

Anaïs Nin

We are all sovereigns. It's no longer the time of alms but of choices.

—"Letter to a Teacher," School of Barbiana
(my translation from Italian)

The migrants have no lobby. Only an enlightened, aroused and per-
haps angered public opinion can do anything about the migrants.
The[y]...have the strength to harvest your fruit and vegetables. They
do not have the strength to influence legislation. Maybe we do. Good
night, and good luck.

—Edward R. Murrow, *Harvest of Shame*

CONTENTS

Sign welcoming visitors to Immokalee, Florida

INTRODUCTION

Invisible. In the office buildings at night, in the hotels during the early afternoon, or in the kitchens all day long: they are janitors, dishwashers, service workers—low-wage workers, many of whom are immigrants. They're hidden. As are the farmworkers, dispersed along infinite fields from dusk to dawn.

Invisible, so they can be more easily dehumanized.

"Welcome to Immokalee 'My Home'": so reads the sign marking the entrance to this far-removed community in Southwest Florida, home to many farmworkers. The words frame an idyllic sunset on a lake with a cornucopia of fruits and vegetables in the foreground to signify the abundance of the land. Immokalee's position, in the middle of acres of cultivated fields, is what entices people from impoverished communities of Central America to come here. In Immokalee, there is work.

Fields of Resistance: The Struggle of Florida's Farmworkers for Justice chronicles a seven-month period (between November 2007 and May 2008), the length of the harvest in this part of the country, during which I regularly visited Immokalee and which coincided with crucial moments of the Coalition of Immokalee Workers' Burger King Campaign. The book revolves around seasons as well as holidays and other celebrations of special significance to the community. The narrative unfolds as I meet and interview farmworkers and their families, activists, religious people, and social workers. The book provides a personal account of these encounters, the "everyday life" moments I shared with the people of Immokalee, but also attempts to provide historical and social background to better situate the events. This is, inevitably, a partial account. For this reason, it doesn't aim to be an all-encompassing work about Immokalee or the CIW, nor is it a book about immigration.

This work seeks to show the various cultural and social realities that coexist today in this part of Florida: the migrant community, the Seminole reservation, and Ave Maria town. The geographical proximity of these three realities, which, one might say, represent the present, past, and future of this part of Florida, is another aspect that renders Immokalee and its surroundings such a fascinating yet contradictory place.

Low-income Latino immigrants, who make up most of today's farmworking population, are all too often demonized in public discourses. Labels like "illegal aliens" or "illegal immigrants" have the effect of dehumanizing real people who might not have citizen rights yet, but surely deserve to be respected as human beings and recognized, if anything, for their economic contribution to the wealth of the nation. They are often mistreated and robbed, and, increasingly, victims of hate crimes and racial profiling.

In addition, even in the supposedly post-racial era of the Obama presidency, we as a society need to confront the issue of racism in the food chain. Who are the people who harvest, clean, and package our food? And moreover: do *they* have access to clean and healthy food? To raise these and other questions means to address issues of power.

While sentiments of compassion may lead to volunteering and charitable work, both of which are of great help in communities like the one in Immokalee, they are not enough. Many well-intended, good-hearted people are doing so much to make Immokalee a better place. Yet, without an understanding rooted in social criticism—of why the immigrants are here; why they have been forced to migrate from their communities in Mexico, Haiti, Guatemala, and Honduras; why slavery still exists in America; why workers' rights are human rights and why they should be improved if we are to create a just society; why corporate accountability is key; why the free market is not really free in the world of seed patents; why cheap is not really cheap given the high external-ized cost of produce; why food can't be sustainable without being fair—we won't be able to create social change. This book does not purport to provide thorough answers to these questions or to analyze these issues exhaustively. However, it intends to invite reflection. Because it is upon places like Immokalee and the people who live and work there that the U.S. (and global) economy relies: places where human rights are rou-tinely violated; places that remain invisible. Until we as a society realize and act upon this simple truth, there won't be real change.

Altar at the CIW headquarters for El Día de los Muertos

One

EL DÍA DE LOS MUERTOS

Soup Kitchen

It's a sunny Friday morning when I arrive at the soup kitchen of the Guadalupe Center of Immokalee. It's November 2, *el Día de los Muertos*, a special day in Mexican culture.[1] Tricia receives me with her incredible smile. She offers to give me a tour of the center before the first round of lunch begins.

"Today it's pretty slow," she sighs, pausing. Then she concedes: "Well, it's better this way. It means that there is work."

Following the harvest means living a life ruled by the seasons and the daily vagaries of climate and weather—even in the Sunshine State, where winters are usually mild and summers begin in April and die out in November.

Several crops are grown in the fields that surround the town of Immokalee: cucumbers, peppers, watermelons, squashes, potatoes, oranges and, more than anything else, tomatoes. During the winter months, farmworkers here handpick 90 percent of the tomatoes consumed in the entire country.[2] Agriculture is the second-largest industry in the state of Florida after tourism with more than 47,000 farms and an annual production of seven billion dollars.[3]

Tricia shows me the tables loaded with food: these are the daily donations of bread and pastries that come from the local supermarket, she explains.

"Here at the soup kitchen we serve our clients," Tricia says with pride. "Every day we have different groups of volunteers, primarily seniors, who have decided to dedicate their time to help those in need."

The Guadalupe Center serves soup at lunchtime every workday. For many of the farmworkers, this is the only warm meal they get to eat; quite often, there are no kitchens in the trailers where they live. The center generally feeds more than a hundred people a day, although sometimes up to four hundred are served, including many children who come when the schools are closed and their lunch services are not running. The most critical periods for the center (and the community) are during the coldest parts of winter and in midsummer when there are few volunteers—many flee the hot and humid South Florida weather. Whenever a freeze hits the crops, many are left without work. Some end up wandering the desolate streets of Immokalee with no food or shelter.

The soup kitchen has been in operation since 1982. The idea came from Father Richard Sanders, "a priest of the people" who encouraged the migrant workers to rebel against the injustices perpetrated by their bosses and to fight for their rights. Soon after the Guadalupe Center was established, Father Sanders suddenly passed away. He now rests here, buried in the courtyard between the church and the soup kitchen; his grave lies in front of a flower-adorned statue of the Virgin of Guadalupe, the patron saint of Latin America to whom the parish is dedicated.

◆

I drove two hours from Boca Raton to get to Immokalee. I met Tricia a few weeks earlier in Miami. She told me about this community and its people, and invited me to visit.

Tricia has been working here for six months now. She originally came to Immokalee to visit her mother. Back in Iowa City she ran a taxi service company with her now ex-husband. After she worked for some days as a volunteer at the Guadalupe Center, they asked her to stay, offering her a full-time job.

"As a woman and a single mother, I feel like an outcast too, in a way," Tricia says while hugging her tattooed shoulders. "It's easy for me to empathize with the people here."

Tricia says that even though she holds a college degree, she had problems finding work in Iowa City, where many young people are un-employed, and more often than not end up accepting any job to make ends meet. She had to deal with some pretty difficult situations, too, she notes—not hard to imagine, when you picture an attractive young woman driving cabs at night in a college town like Iowa City.

"I need to get off early this afternoon. Madi is sick," she says refer-ring to her five-year-old daughter. "She got a high fever." Tricia lives in Fort Myers, on the west coast, an hour from here. She has been think-ing about moving to Immokalee though. "I like this place. And I'd rather drive an hour to go to the beach than have to commute five times a week."

She shows me the dining room crowded with plastic tables and folding chairs, and then the kitchen where the soup is simmering in a huge, steaming pot. We walk through the center to the shower room where the "clients"—as Tricia insists on calling the people who come here looking for help—can take care of their basic hygiene needs. Then, she walks me to the clothing room.

"The Guadalupe Center dresses over five thousand individuals every year," Tricia says, emphasizing the number.

Some of the volunteers are the same people who regularly receive help from the center. "That's Carla," Tricia says, nodding at a woman folding clothes. Carla reciprocates with a smile.

"One of her sons is in our after-school program," Tricia continues. "In exchange for her help, she gets free clothes for her kids. She lives with her family here in Immokalee, but they are thinking of moving north and doing something else. There's just not enough work here in the summer."

"I need a cigarette," Tricia whispers to me under her breath, while smiling at Carla.

On the way out, we run into a volunteer whom Tricia seems to know: a white woman in her sixties, her eyes sit uncommonly close to each other. She is carrying several large, empty plastic bags in her hand. "My husband has been dead for two years now," the woman says. She explains how she was able to finally get rid of her spouse's clothes. "At first, I had moved them to the closet in the other room. Then, they stayed for an entire summer in the garage. The other day, when you told me that you needed men's wear, those clothes I kept moving from one room to another came to my mind..." She breaks into a smile, somewhat relieved.

Another woman walks toward us: short, dark-skinned, her face reveals her Mayan origins. She is holding a young girl's hand. The child has big, black eyes, and a small, colorful backpack on her shoulders.

"¿*Tiene un cochecito de bebé?*" (Do you have a baby carriage?) the woman asks Tricia.

Tricia shakes her head. Then she reaches over to the door of the clothing room, opens it and, holding on to it, repeats the question inside, just to make sure. Then she turns back around. She finally says,

"No pero por favor venga el lunes a ver si tenemos uno a ese tiempo." (No, I'm sorry; try again on Monday.)

The woman thanks Tricia and leaves, now holding the child tight to her chest.

In Immokalee, there is no room for half measures, no room for apathy, no room for enjoying "the good life" as they do in Naples, to the west, or in Boca Raton, to the east. Here the hawks soaring overhead silently observe the work of the women and men below—never judging, never intervening—but they see it all. And the people of Immokalee seem to know it.

Meeting Paco*

"This is Paco. He'll be your guide today," Tricia says.

A lean, dark-skinned young man comes forward. His small, round glasses would make him look like Spike Lee if it weren't for the translucent purple shirt he is wearing, along with a matching tie with diagonal stripes.

The watermelon harvest had just ended in August when Paco was hired by the Guadalupe Center. Paco "Paquito" Gonzalez has worked the fields every summer since he was a teenager. When there was school, he would help his mother in the afternoon at the local produce market, doing his homework while selling overripe fruit. In a sense, Paco is the living example of what the Guadalupe Center aims to achieve: to break the cycle of poverty through education. He, too, is the son of migrant workers who came from Mexico to have a better life.

---

* Names marked with an asterisk in the text have been changed to protect the privacy of those individuals.

Like other migrant workers from the numerous Mexican communities in southern Texas, Paco's parents relocated in Immokalee in the early seventies. Angela,* Paco's mother, had come to the United States with her family, leaving behind an impoverished community in the Mexican state of Guanajuato. Juan Diego,* Paco's father, from the region of San Luis Potosí, arrived in the States by himself, and soon joined the struggle of the United Farm Workers of America (UFW) led by César Chávez. Once relocated in Immokalee, he continued to fight for better working conditions along with Juan Alberto Velásquez, founder of Migrantes Unidos.

Like Juan Diego, most of the migrants who live here came from rural areas; they were campesinos in their country of origin. "Immokalee became popular," Paco says, "because here the harvest lasts longer...like in California." Migrant workers tend to linger in Immokalee and sometimes end up settling in for the long run—like the Gonzalez family.

Later that night, I would get to know Angela, Paco's mom, a tired woman who never liked Immokalee, and yet ended up spending most of her adult life here. Paco, on the other hand, came back to Immokalee. He had left for college, but after graduation, he was here again to help his family, to live where he was born and raised, and where he keeps fighting to obtain better working and living conditions with the members of the Coalition of Immokalee Workers (CIW).

◆

Paco takes me to the preschool of the Guadalupe Center: an ultramodern, red-and-white building with a trapezoidal entrance, boasting a large American flag. The preschool was built with the donations of the local wealthy.

"Have you ever been to Naples?" Paco asks. "Well, it's a very rich community," he adds.

According to the U.S. Census, the city of Naples has a per capita income of more than $79,000 (the national figure is $27,400), with only 36 percent of the population in the labor force (versus the 65.2 percent national figure). Indeed, Naples features one of the highest concentrations of CEO retirees: this is their warm, "hard-earned" paradise on the Gulf of Mexico.

Immokalee's per capita income is estimated to be around $8,500.[4] Yet, Immokalee doesn't have its own municipality; it is part of Collier County, as is Naples.[5]

"There are 125 children from six weeks to five years old, with 350 more on the waiting list," Paco continues. The population of Immokalee, he points out, is very young; most of them were born here. They are U.S. citizens.

The preschool opens very early in the morning to meet the needs of the rural community. Most parents are indeed farmworkers who wake up to go work before the sun rises. Almost all the instructors here are bilingual and the center has a more advanced program than other preschools; they teach the children how to read and write, in an effort to compensate for the language gap they will face once in elementary school. Eighty percent don't speak English at home, and approximately 65 percent of the children drop out before finishing high school.[6]

It is here that I first briefly meet Angela, Paco's mother. A short but sturdy woman with deep black eyes, her hair is tied in two tiny ponytails like a little girl. She has come to bring lunch to her son. Paco shows me around, walking with the plate in his hand; in his office, he introduces me to the two interns who work with him. Then we leave, to continue the tour.

The streets of Immokalee are punctuated by overhanging power poles, whose height dwarfs the already low-lying rundown trailers and shacks. The town spreads along three major routes: Main Street, into which I-29 flows; New Market Road, which gets its name from the produce market situated there; and Immokalee Road, which here becomes First Street, before proceeding down to Naples.

In a friendly gesture as my host, Paco takes me to eat at La Paleteria on New Market Road; the store sells homemade ice cream, *aguas frescas*, tacos, *tortas*, and other typical Mexican sandwiches. Paco's lunch, the one that his mother brought to him, has remained on his office desk. Once we finish eating, we resume our tour.

We drive past many convenience stores and churches that look more like trailers than houses of worship.[7] We pass Six L's, Immokalee's biggest packinghouse, and La Favorita bakery, with its fifty-cent pastries and their exquisite Latin American flavors. Finally, we pass La Azteca supermarket on Main Street as we enter the area between First and Ninth Streets. This is Immokalee's most densely populated neighborhood— and its poorest.

Paco points to the side of the road. Over there, he says, are the rundown mobile homes. The workers live in terrible unsanitary conditions. Multiple trailers often share the same bathroom. The sewage system is inadequate and very old. Paco pauses. Up to fifteen people live in one trailer. They often sleep on the floor, without even a mattress, "stuck next to each other like sardines," as Paco puts it. To have this space and live in these conditions, some workers pay as much as $300 per month.

"I grew up nearby..." he says. "They say it's the worst part of town...And it's true...to some extent. I have seen many bad things happening here. Most of the time, the victims were the newcomers. In the eighties and nineties, it was the Guatemalans, who were coming to the States to escape genocide. Then it was the Haitians...They run away from one hell to find another one here," Paco remarks angrily. "They (the newcomers) get hired by contractors...they don't know anyone here. They get exploited, robbed, and up to some years ago, they were even murdered by their bosses, their corpses thrown in the ditches. Some were found in land clearings south of Immokalee..."

I'm about to make a left turn when Paco suddenly stops me, raising his arm.

"Watch out!" he yells. Two pedestrians are crossing the street. "In Immokalee you need to be extra careful when you drive," Paco warns me. "Many people here just walk or ride their bicycles."

We are by now nearing the bus station where the farmworkers get picked up to go to work.

The Pantry

Here we are, in the middle of Immokalee's labor pool. The hub of this community is a broad, dusty parking lot, known to many here, especially the older residents, as "the Pantry," from the former name of the 24-hour convenience store (once "The Pantry Shelf," now the sign reads "La Fiesta 3") located just across the street.

The farmworkers—men and women primarily from Mexico, Guatemala, and Haiti—must arrive early in the morning if they want to secure a seat on one of the yellow schoolbuses that will take them to the fields. Sometimes, they get here as early as five in the morning, even though they won't start picking until nine. The fields where they will end up working might be up to one hundred miles away, but it is here at the Pantry that the agricultural workforce of southwestern Florida is recruited.

The fields that extend all around Immokalee along I-29 seem to exist in a parallel reality, physically separated from the town—they can only be reached by private means of transportation, and yet they are a constant presence in the daily lives of the people here.

Once in the fields, the workers must wait for the dew to dry; picking when the plants are still wet would ruin the tomatoes. The farmworkers are paid by piece rate and they need to be fast: in order to earn $50 a day, they must pick *four thousand* pounds of tomatoes. However, it depends on the time of the year and the quantity of the harvest whether or not this may be possible. In addition, whereas wages have remained the same since the late seventies,[8] the cost of living has risen, and rent, especially, has soared in Immokalee. Rent for a dilapidated apartment close to the Pantry can be up to $850.[9]

"A lot of things have happened here..." Paco begins as he stares at the power poles that cross Immokalee's blue sky. "There are stories that have taken on a legendary significance for Immokalee." Paco recalls one event in particular that led over five hundred people to spontaneously march to the front of the ranch of a *contratista* (crew leader).

It was back in the mid-nineties, around Christmastime. One evening, a seventeen-year-old Guatemalan farmworker entered what then was just a storefront housing a young Coalition of Immokalee Workers. A dozen migrant workers accompanied the boy: extremely agitated, he was holding in his hands a shirt soaked with blood. The people who had gathered there for a meeting came up to him, and inquired about what had happened. The young man started to relate his story: it was very hot, and he asked for some water. Then the farm supervisor had yelled at him: "You came here to work, not to drink!"

When he asked again, the boss beat him up. The crew leader was then invited by the coalition to come to the center and discuss what had happened and present his side of the story. The crew leader showed up with bodyguards and dismissed the farmworker's account; in any case, he finally said, the whole matter was irrelevant to him. A few nights later, two hundred people gathered in front of the community center and, in the heart of the night, marched toward the house of the contratista. Hundreds of other citizens joined the march along the way, chanting "¡Golpear a uno es golpear a todos!" (To beat one of us is to beat us all!) and waving the bloody shirt.[10]

"It was a nonviolent protest," Paco recalls. "I was just a boy but I remember that day as if it were yesterday." That night marked the beginning of the end of guaranteed impunity for ruthless crew leaders and bosses in Immokalee.[11]

We enter the small trailer that hosts Radio Conciencia, the local station run by the Coalition of Immokalee Workers and located near the Pantry.[12] As Paco explains, Radio Conciencia was extremely helpful before and after Hurricane Wilma. In the aftermath of the storm, Immokalee remained completely isolated; it was impossible to communicate with the centralized emergency units located in Naples. Radio Conciencia offered an important service to the community by broadcasting emergency information not only in Spanish and Creole, but also in Zapotecan, Mam, and Kanjobal, the most common indigenous languages spoken exclusively by many in Immokalee.

In the radio's control room sits Gerardo Reyes Chavez, member of the Coalition of Immokalee Workers. Mexican by birth, Gerardo is a tall young man with a goatee and a friendly, open face. He is wearing a dark blue T-shirt with the CIW logo. His one o'clock shift at the radio station has just started.

"We are all volunteers here, farmworkers and other members of the community," Gerardo says. He tells me about the CIW. Created in 1993, the organization is involved in providing information about farmworkers' rights—basic human rights, like the one, in fact, to have drinkable water in the fields.

The National Labor Relations Act (1935) didn't include farmworkers who, to this day, cannot unionize. In 1966, thanks to the efforts of César Chávez and the United Farm Workers (UFW), some farmworkers were included in the Fair Labor Standards Act, and thus received minimum wage coverage. At that time, the UFW was an influential pressure group due to its large base, primarily located in California and in the Southwest.[13]

In Florida, however, the UFW failed to organize the workers against the citrus industry in a boycott against Coca-Cola during the early seventies.[14] Today, farmworkers still don't have the right to organize, and, in Florida, they are more vulnerable than elsewhere. Before the CIW was formed, other attempts to defend workers' rights were isolated and unorganized.

With the support of activist groups, churches, grassroots organizations, and hundreds of individuals—including many political personalities like former president Jimmy Carter—the CIW has spearheaded the Campaign for Fair Food since April 2001, when it called for a nationwide consumer boycott of Taco Bell. This change in strategy came after several protests and other actions to pressure local farmers for more humane conditions in the workplace.[15]

In this era of globalization and branding, the Coalition of Immokalee Workers soon identified its prime target: large American fast food chains. These companies prefer to buy tomatoes grown in Florida, whose consistency makes them easier to slice and, therefore, perfect for hamburgers. Although both the United States and Canada import tomatoes from Mexico, where the harvest never stops during the year, those fruits are actually too juicy, and often are ruined by the time they reach their destination. The CIW also understands that in today's global market, the agricultural and food industries are increasingly integrated, making it easier for them to exploit the workforce in order to maximize profit.

The efforts of the coalition are paying off. After the historic agreement with Taco Bell achieved in March 2005, the CIW signed a similar accord with McDonald's in 2007[16]: the companies agreed to pay the Immokalee workers one cent more per pound of tomatoes.[17]

"The target is now Burger King," Gerardo continues as he puts on some Mexican music. "So far, they have refused to sign a similar agreement."

CIW members work until late at night and into the weekend, earning about four hundred dollars a week, the average pay of a tomato picker when there is work. Similar wages are received by young members of the Student/Farmworker Alliance (SFA) stationed in Immokalee; the organization brings the cause of the farmworkers to schools and universities and raises awareness around the issues of labor, environmental, and food justice, and has been pivotal to the success of the CIW campaigns.

CIW and SFA members know that speaking to the people is the starting point in the fight against exploitation. They provide instruction on what it means to be treated humanely and not abused: receiving a fair wage for your work, living in a clean, sanitary environment, etc. One of the main CIW programs focuses on what they call "*educación popular*"—a method also theorized by Paulo Freire in *The Pedagogy of the Oppressed*—rooted in a collective necessity: the continuous turnover of the workers that leave Immokalee to follow the harvest or just abandon the fields as soon as they find a better job. Therefore, CIW members go door-to-door to speak with the newcomers, inviting them to stop by the coalition offices, just around the corner from the Pantry, to learn more about the CIW and its activities. Membership costs only $10.[18] Despite this structural disadvantage, the CIW has managed to expand the basis of its organization and counts today more than 3,500 members. "We are all leaders," Paco says. "We don't have representatives; we are all representatives. Our slogan is, 'Consciouness + Commitment = Change.' It's important to raise consciousness, but it's only with commitment that change can occur."

Radio Conciencia has been a vital instrument in keeping the community informed about the CIW campaigns. "Most of the people here tune in to 107.9," Gerardo says while taking off his headphones and launching a public service announcement against domestic violence, a significant problem in impoverished communities like Immokalee.[19]

I ask Gerardo if he has some data on listenership. "It's difficult to quantify," he says smiling optimistically. "But the radio station has a big following in the community because we adapt the programming to the routines of the farmworkers."

"Also, people here don't like mainstream radio stations, especially the music." Gerardo continues, "We play traditional Mexican and Guatemalan music...For instance, we have a program dedicated to *marimba*...Do you know marimba?"

Radio Conciencia connects to the California-based Radio Bilingue through the Web. "They have this program, 'Linea Abierta,' where they talk about issues such as immigration, free market, Mexican politics..." Gerardo says.

"Once we had the satellite dish, you know...but the hurricane took it away," he murmurs.

A Hidden History

"Up until not long ago, Immokalee wasn't even on the map," Paco says as we drive by Immokalee High School. "The school mascot is an Indian," he continues. "But it looks like it came out of the comics…do you know what I mean? It's not…it's not *real*."

Immokalee hosts one of the six reservations of the Florida Seminoles. It is located in the southern part of the town, outside the city limits. Once only the Seminoles inhabited the savannah that surrounds Immokalee. Before the Mexicans, before the African Americans, they were the ones who worked this land.

The Seminoles, too, had been forced to migrate. For them, like for today's farmworkers, it was a matter of survival. Members of the Creek Nation of Alabama fled south after the war launched against them by future president Andrew Jackson and they mingled with the people who lived in Florida at the time. The Seminoles were renowned for their inclusiveness: they welcomed runaway slaves and outlaws—a fact that surely did not help their relations with the U.S. government. A mixed tribe, their members came to be united through their common refusal to be dominated by the white man.

"The Seminoles are the only Native American tribe that never signed a peace treaty with the U.S. government," Paco continues. The Seminoles actually defeated the U.S. Army, even though the American government eventually declared victory over the tribe. During the Second Seminole War (1835–1842), medicine man Abiaka used his magical potions to fill his warriors with ardor, while legendary war chief Osceola led his people to victory, in spite of the numeric disadvantage, by virtue of his knowledge of the territory and sophisticated guerrilla tactics.

In 1872, the whites came to settle in the inland part of southwestern Florida and domesticated the animals by fencing them in—a practice that the Seminoles found absurd. Later on, corrals were also built for this indigenous people, as the government created reservations.

Paco, who wants to become a history teacher, laments the racism of the school system. "Who really knows the history of the Seminoles? They don't teach it in schools!" Paco says. "Everybody thinks *Immokalee* means 'my home'?!"

According to the official interpretation, Immokalee translates as "my home," and so reads the sign that welcomes visitors to town. In the Mikasuki language, one of the two indigenous languages still spoken by some Seminoles, "A-Muglé" translates into "my home" whereas "I-Muglé" is "my cage," or "my corral." The fact is, Mikasuki is an exclusively oral language and the meaning of its words depends on how they are pronounced.

"As with everything else in Florida, you want to make the tourists happy. So Immokalee becomes 'my home,' and the rest of the story remains untold," Paco comments bitterly.[20]

In Immokalee, mixed marriages between Mexicans, often also belonging to indigenous groups, and Seminoles are frequent. Still, Paco laments the fact that there are not local policies in place that work toward the integration of these two communities. "After all, they (the Seminoles) too were poor until they had the opportunity to make money with the casinos..."

The Seminole tribe is not poor anymore. For some tribal council members, at least, quite the opposite is true. Some say they have transferred their military genius into entrepreneurship. The Seminole's economic fortunes began to improve in 1977 with the opening of the first "smoke shop." The license to sell tax-free tobacco and cigarettes allowed them to make money quickly. It was with the casino business, though, that a considerable amount of cash started flowing in: one billion dollars a year, tax free, thanks to the fiscal statutes of the tribe. Under the direction of James Billie, the Bingo Hall in Hollywood opened on December 14, 1979; it was the first Native American gambling facility in the States. By the end of 2006, the Seminole tribe of Florida had completed the acquisition of Hard Rock International, thus also becoming the first Native American people to own an international corporation.

"Everything begins with knowledge," Paco insists. "That's why it's important to study history."

"I come from a family with a strong political consciousness. My folks even ended up in prison because they rebelled against their bosses. They were protesting in order to have better conditions in the fields and stop the abuses that were being perpetrated there, especially against women." Though highly unreported for fear of retribution, sexual harassment is still a reality in agriculture.[21]

Paco gets serious when he talks about these things, and he suddenly seems very wise: Paco, who moves like a fifteen-year-old boy, despite the tie and his small, round glasses.

While we are heading back to the Guadalupe Center, Paco tells me about the death of his father. Juan Diego had become ill with cancer because of his exposure to pesticides in the fields. Paco was just a boy at the time. Within a few months, Juan Diego passed away, leaving behind his wife and three children.

Back at the center, we find Tricia. She had wanted to go home earlier but is still here. The group of kids from Gulf Coast High School has not yet arrived. They just called, saying they had traffic delays.

"Let's wait," she says to Paco. "You might have the opportunity to change one of these kids' lives today."

Finally, at around five thirty, two minivans arrive. Their trunks are loaded with donations. On Halloween, these students walked around their neighborhood and knocked on peoples' doors. Instead of trick-or-treating for candy, they collected canned food for the Guadalupe Center.

At the CIW:"El Poeta" and Felipe

In the evening, right next to the Pantry, there is a festival organized by the Farmworkers Association of Florida. Food is free for all. Before Mass celebration begins, bright, colorful costumes move quickly in time to the Aztec music. On the ground lays a smoking lamp, infusing incense into the night air.

We enter the headquarters of the Coalition of Immokalee Workers, a large hall furnished with several sofas, an armchair, and three desks covered with flyers, photocopies, and other informative material. The very existence of the CIW is celebrated here. The walls are papered with posters and pictures reflecting struggles, past and current. The images depict the women and men who have been part of these struggles along with the individuals who inspire them. Colorful murals have phrases in English, Spanish, and Creole. Photographs abound: male and female workers in the fields, all equally bent in the act of picking tomatoes; women in the packinghouses, sitting elbow to elbow, in the act of selecting tomatoes, staring at the belt conveyor. The CIW logo— reminiscent of the old IWW one—is plastered all over the walls.

Hypnotized by their computer screens, the members of the Student/Farmworker Alliance are working, despite the ongoing celebration outside for el Día de los Muertos. They are getting ready for the big march that will take place in Miami at the end of the month. Only a few of them lift their heads as we enter. What welcomes us instead is a rather unusual altar decorated with fruits, *pan de muerto*,[22] and many flowers; at its center stands the Virgin who appeared in 1521 to Juan Diego, the indigenous American who converted to Catholicism: *Nuestra Señora de Guadalupe*. Positioned at the top of the altar, from her glass frame she looks down on Pancho Villa, Che Guevara, Martin Luther King Jr. with his wife Coretta, and all the other revolutionary heroes below.

The Virgin of Guadalupe holds a central, sacred place in Mexican culture. A symbol of syncretism, she came to represent nationalist pride during the war of Independence (1810–1821), deepening its roots in the indigenous culture. If most Mexicans are Catholic, they say, all Mexicans are *Guadalupanos*.[23]

At the festival, I met "El Poeta." The name was given to him during the Taco Bell Truth Tour: from that time on, everyone has referred to him this way. Indeed, he prefers not to reveal his real name. He doesn't speak any English, and Paco offers to interpret for us. El Poeta comes from Chiapas. He is short, his shoulders are curved, his irregular face brush-stroked with a brief moustache. We sit down; no one seems to pay attention to us. As we start with the interview, El Poeta begins to recite his verses, quietly.

"*Los tomates de Immokalee nacieron verdes/Los hombres al piscar se ponen verdes/Y el comprador nunca pierde...*" (Immokalee's tomatoes were born green/The men at the time of picking turn green/But the buyer never loses anything...)

El Poeta has lived in the States for four years. Like many immigrants, he contributes a large portion of his earnings to his family in Chiapas. Here in Immokalee, he lives in a mobile home with fifteen other people. "Yes, we have a bathroom at the house, but sometimes we find snakes, frogs, lizards..." El Poeta laughs softly.

To live there, they each are charged forty-five dollars a week. I ask him if he has ever left Immokalee. "Three years ago I went to Ohio. I was tired of working in the fields...I was a painter there...but then I came back."

Felipe* comes from Guatemala, and now works full time for the Coalition of Immokalee Workers. In the summer, he goes up north near Tallahassee to pick watermelons with the CIW cooperative. "We all work the same hours...fourteen a day, and at the end of the week we divide whatever the farmer pays us." This way, they eliminated the contratistas, the middlemen between the growers and the farmworkers.

Before leaving, I ask both Felipe and El Poeta about their dreams.

"Dreams?" Felipe repeats, looking at Paco; then he turns to me and says assertively, "We dream of helping our families and giving them a better life. We need to work, but we are not willing to compromise our dignity."

El Poeta dreams of becoming a writer instead. He says he likes to read books "to expand his mind." He began to recite another poem, this one inspired by the Mexican Revolution and one of its heroes, Francisco Madero. Paco asks him if there is one writer that he particularly likes; El Poeta lowers his eyes and shakes his head, chuckling shyly. "Unfortunately," he finally says, "I don't have a lot of time to read. I have to work."

At Paco's House

Paco tells me I can stay at his house for the night. Our plan is to wake up early in the morning and go to the Pantry. We park in front of his place. In the distance, the lights of a football field illuminate the night. The school team is playing the last game of the season. On the same field, Cardinals running back Edgerrin James used to practice years ago. He was a student at Immokalee High School and only a promising player in the local football team then.

We enter the house, and Paco shows me the bedroom where I will sleep tonight. "We've always had guests at my house," Paco says, seeming to read my mind. I wasn't expecting to have a room all to myself.

"Only recently we've been alone…me and my mom," Paco adds.

We begin to listen to the recording of the poem El Poeta recited for us earlier. Paco promised to transcribe it and then translate it into English. He goes to close the screen door, but leaves the other one open to allow the cool air to come in. We hear the echo of the cheering crowd and the marching band music that fills in when there is a break in the game.

"Do you want to go to the game?" I ask Paco. "We can do this some other time."

"No, let's listen to it again," Paco says gravely.

Only now do I realize that today is not just any other day for Paco and his mother. Mexicans commemorate the deceased on November 2, and the ghost of Paco's father, who died of cancer at only forty-five, is still very present in the Gonzalez house.

It's difficult to understand the quiet words of El Poeta as he recites his verses of proletarian struggle. We go outside for a smoke. The smell of the jasmine catches me unprepared, and I feel the sudden urge to put out my cigarette.

It's chilly, and Paco, wearing only a thin T-shirt, keeps moving from one foot to the other. The din is gone and the football game must be over, too. Suddenly, Paco throws away his cigarette and starts fanning with his hand. Angela has just pulled in.

"My mom doesn't want me to smoke," Paco whispers.

Once in the house, Angela starts doing the dishes that have piled up in the sink. She looks very tired. "Let's sit on the couch," she says after a while. Paco is nowhere in sight. We begin to talk. Angela tells me how she came to Immokalee; then suddenly she asks me whether I've found a fiancé here in the States. "It's hard to find the right person," Angela begins. She says she never liked American men. One day, when Angela was still living in Texas with her family, one of her cousins told her she had invited a young Mexican man over; she knew Angela would like him. It was love at first sight. The two of them started seeing each other but only when Angela's father was around, according to traditional custom. Later on, they returned to Mexico to get married.

Angela briefly mentions her husband's illness. "I am going blind too," she adds, "because of the pesticides." That's why she had to quit working in the fields. She can't even work as a hairdresser anymore, the job she loved when they lived in Mexico. Then she stops.

"I want to show you something," she says before disappearing into the other room. Angela comes back with a leopard-jacketed photo album. She hands it to me. I start turning the pages, expecting to finally see Juan Diego. I haven't been able to find him in any of the many portraits displayed all around the house. But Juan Diego is not in here either, only more pictures of her nieces and nephews and of her three children: Alberto, Serena, and the youngest one, the twenty-five-year-old Paco.

"You've got to read this," Angela says, pointing to a written sheet of paper. From the last page of the album, she takes out a couple of sheets, carefully laminated for protection. It is an assignment that her daughter recently wrote for an online English class. In it, Serena talks about her relationship with her father. She remembers when he would come back from work, how he was stinking because of the pesticides; she remembers his energy, the joy he would bring to the house with his music. Juan Diego became ill right after his daughter's *quinceañera.*[24] Soon after his death, both Serena and Alberto joined the army.

"Juan Diego came from a family of musicians," Angela recalls. "It was incredible. He could play any type of instrument. He would come home every night always carrying his guitar over his shoulder…"

At that very moment, Paco reappears. He has a small guitar in his hands, a *jaraña.* He sits down and starts playing. "This is actually supposed to be a duet," Paco says quietly, as he begins to sing. Angela listens, staring off into space.

Workers and families in line to get their
Thanksgiving meal at Immokalee Airport Park

Two

THANKSGIVING

Turkey for All

It's noon when I get to Immokalee Airport Park. Volunteers are about to start serving lunch. A long line winds through the park and continues far past the exit. It's hot, really hot. When peeping through the clouds, the sun hits hard.

Traditional Mexican music coming from the stage contributes to the festive mood of this late November day. From the large concrete windows of the building situated at the center of the park, apron-equipped middle-aged women and a couple of tall, skinny men serve turkey with cranberry sauce, sweet potatoes, mashed potatoes, stuffing, pumpkin pie, apple pie, cherry pie, and pecan pie: the typical Thanksgiving meal that millions of Americans consume today around the United States. In Immokalee, tortillas are served as well, to meet the tastes of the local population.

Through the crowd, I catch a glimpse of Paco. He's standing by the Guadalupe Center booth. I get near him to say hello. He introduces me to Barbara, his boss at the center. Paco appears visibly worried. "I think I messed up," he says in a low voice as soon as Barbara goes away. He has just done an on-camera interview for a local TV station.

How does it feel to serve the Thanksgiving meal knowing that some of these people here are illegal immigrants? The journalist had asked him something like that, Paco claims, still troubled by the question, which is obviously absurd to him. Paco remembers what he answered very well though. Thinking he had said the right thing, he relayed to Barbara:

"Thanksgiving is a holiday for everybody. Did the Native Americans ask the Europeans for their green cards when they came here?" Barbara's eyes had popped out.

There is a certain degree of historical irony in celebrating Thanksgiving in Immokalee. The town is now home to many Latino immigrants, a number of whom are undocumented and thus, according to some, have no right to take part in this celebration.

It is the day that Americans give thanks—to Squanto, the Native American who spoke English and initiated the settlers to agricultural life in the New World.[1] According to tradition, thanks go to him, and, symbolically, to the Native peoples of the Americas…but also, figuratively and more conveniently, to God, for having "conceded" these lands to the pilgrims.[2]

Thanksgiving is a day of celebration for everybody here, Paco says, because, contrary to Christmas or Hannukkah, *this* is the American holiday par excellence. Indeed, Thanksgiving was originally a sacred Native American ceremony, a festival to celebrate the harvest and give thanks for it.[3] According to this tradition, what better place to honor this holiday than Immokalee, home of the Seminoles and so many other indigenous peoples of the Americas?

In typical all-American fashion, however, Thanksgiving has been reinvented and today, more than anything else, it means consumerism.

There is another truly American tradition: the Presidential Turkey Pardon. Every year, more than fifty million turkeys get slaughtered to celebrate Thanksgiving. Since George H. W. Bush inaugurated it in 1989, one turkey gets spared during an official ceremony held at the White House on Thanksgiving eve. This lucky turkey—it will be named by the time it meets the president—gets a second chance in America, and is flown to California to the dream world of Disneyland where it will serve as honorary marshal of the Thanksgiving Day Parade. The turkey then spends the rest of its life at a Disneyland ranch with the other surviving turkeys spared in the previous years.[4]

As Arundhati Roy pointed out, this is a great allegory for New Racism. Who can, in fact, say that turkeys are against Thanksgiving if some of them receive such treatment from corporate agribusiness?[5]

"Thanksgiving in the Park" is celebrating its twenty-fifth anniversary today, so one could say that for Immokalee this one, too, has become tradition. The local paper reads: "Volunteers spread holiday treats with those less fortunate."[6] But in Immokalee nothing can be taken for granted, not even tradition. Let alone charity.

Later in the afternoon I will witness a conversation between Tricia and Paco, sparked by the short interview Paco gave to the local TV network. Tricia, tired but happy about the success of the event, tells Paco that there are indeed people who would like to eliminate the soup kitchen from the Guadalupe Center programs. The motivation? It also feeds undocumented immigrants.

◆

I hug Tricia and say hello as she is running toward the stage to make an announcement; she is wearing a white shirt decorated with pink and black flowers whose colors match the lotus tattoo that adorns her chest. As a representative for client services at the Guadalupe Center, Tricia thanks everyone (in Spanish, English, and Creole) who has worked hard to make Thanksgiving in the Park possible.

Paco still looks pensive. He is now wandering around the park; he often stops by the playgrounds to check on the children. His task today as a volunteer is to monitor the kids and make sure no one gets hurt.

The incident with the local TV network will trouble Paco for the rest of the day. Tricia will try to cheer him up, in her way, to make him understand that his has been a political mistake, not a mistake of the heart. Since he was speaking on behalf of the Guadalupe Center, such a statement might compromise the considerable donations that the wealthy yet conservative families in Naples make to the center, Tricia explains the both of us.

"You have your own ideas, and rightly so. You're also free to express them but then you need to be clear. 'I speak as Paco Gonzalez, not as a representative of the center. This is my personal opinion.'"

Paco listens carefully, in silence. He didn't mean to cause any problems for the Guadalupe Center. After all, he is "el cuervo," his nickname at the radio station, because of all birds, he says, the crow is the smartest. You can even teach him how to speak.

As we walk toward the offices of the CIW, the words of Chaplain Julian Griggs come to my mind. They are from *Harvest of Shame*, the documentary aired by CBS the day after Thanksgiving, forty-seven years ago.[7] The documentary reported on the deplorable living and working conditions of the migrant workers of that time. The cameras came also to Immokalee, whose labor force back then was largely made up of African Americans and poor whites. Chaplain Griggs, who was traveling with the farmworkers, asked the cameras (and thus the nation):

"Is it possible to have love without justice? Is it possible that we are into much…in terms of charity, in giving away Thanksgiving baskets, in terms of Christmas baskets, and not enough into eliminating poverty ?" (*sic*)[8]

CIW members are preparing for the big protest scheduled for November 30; a non-working day like today is a great opportunity to reach out to the community and invite everyone to participate in the 2007 March on Burger King.

In front of the coalition's headquarters, I meet Veronica, a sweet and vulnerable smile on her face. She sells rice, milk, fruit, corn, and homemade food she takes out from the trunk of her car. Veronica works as a paint scraper. "It's hard," she says smilingly, as she catches me looking at her tiny body. "I also work as a waitress," she adds. Veronica is twenty years old and has a one-year-old child; her husband works at the coalition, she says. I will later find out that she is the wife of Lucas Benitez, one of the most visible spokespersons of the CIW.

In the afternoon, a raffle is held in the lot between the CIW building and the Pantry. They are giving out bicycles, invaluable possessions here in Immokalee. But there is also a far more significant initiative: the CIW is collecting old work boots to bring to the Burger King headquarters in Miami. The idea is to show how worn-out the shoes of the workers can get.

This initiative emerged in response to Burger King's claims that intend to deny farmworkers' poverty. Drawing on a study commissioned by McDonald's and dating back to before the CIW agreements, Burger King has falsely claimed that Florida tomato pickers earned an average of $14 per hour, with the fastest pickers earning upwards of more than $18 per hour.[9] The CIW message was: "Walk in our shoes before you tell us who we are and what we earn."

"We Don't Call Them Slaves No More"

Laura, Lucas, and Greg are in London to receive the Antislavery Award the CIW has just won for its work in fighting modern-day slavery.[10] To this day, the organization has uncovered, exposed, and brought to justice six operations in which hundreds of farmworkers were being kept captive somewhere in the endless fields of Florida.[11]

The first case was in 1997:[12] Miguel Flores and Sebastian Gomez were sentenced to fifteen years each in federal prison. The charges were slavery, extortion, immigration violations, and illegal possession of firearms, among others. Flores and Gomez had their operations in the fields of Florida and South Carolina. Four hundred men and women had been forced to pick vegetables and citrus for ten to twelve hours a day under the constant surveillance of armed guards for a little bit more than twenty dollars a week. The ones who tried to escape were violently beaten. The testimony of escaped workers and a five-year-long investigation by CIW members brought the case to justice.

Other times, contractors made use of drugs and alcohol to keep workers in servitude, like Michael Lee, who was condemned to four years in prison and three years of supervised release in 2001. For his operation, Lee used to recruit homeless people, all U.S. citizens, and then drag them into dependence and debt. Workers were forced to buy food, cigarettes, alcohol, and even cocaine from the company store. Drugs were given away for free until the workers developed an addiction; then, they were sold to them at high prices.

Agribusiness often turns a blind eye to this system of exploitation by either pretending these severe violations of human rights never occur and/or claiming they are exaggerations. Confronted by the CIW, most food retailers have initially professed that it's not up to them to get involved in labor disputes between the farmers and the workers.[13] The growers, on the other hand, often claim to have a relationship with the crew leader, not with the workers, and, thus, to be unaware of what is happening on their own properties. The crew leaders, they say, are responsible for the supply of labor. As the Southern Poverty Law Center (SPLC) report on guestworker programs in the United States shows,[14] the use of subcontractors undermines workers' basic rights by absolving employers of responsibility and making the very enforcement of the legal protections provided by the H-2A program very difficult. On the other hand, undocumented workers (and many legal immigrants, too) cannot be represented by federally funded legal services, making these individuals even more prone to be exploited.[15] Produce corporations, however, have been held responsible for what is happening in the fields in a court of law. The successful class action lawsuit filed in 2006 against Del Monte on behalf of farmworkers is a case in point.[16]

To add insult to injury, some growers even rehired convicted crew leaders once they got out of prison. Michael Lee, for instance, went back to work for a citrus company located around Fort Pierce on the east coast of Florida. Abel Cuello Jr., a contractor for Manley Farms North Inc., had been sentenced to thirty-three months in prison in 1999 for having held more than thirty workers as slaves in two trailers and forcing them to work under armed surveillance. Cuello even mowed down with his SUV one of the workers who had managed to escape from his camp.[17] Once out of prison, Cuello started E&B Harvesting & Trucking Inc., got his Farm Labor Contractor license renewed,[18] and went back to provide work for Ag-Mart Farms.[19]

Ramiro and Juan Ramos, sentenced in 2004 to fifteen years in prison and the payment of three million dollars in assets, had supervised more than seven hundred people and coerced them to pick citrus under armed surveillance. Workers were forced to purchase food at La

Guadalupana, the convenience store run by Alicia Barajas, Ramiro's wife; quite significantly, La Guadalupana was situated only one block away from the local police station. The workers also had to sign back their paychecks to Ramiro Ramos, known to many as *El Diablo*. The hearsay among the captives at the camp was that one worker had his knees busted with a hammer and got thrown out of a car going 60 miles an hour by a Barajas. The man had attempted to escape the property.[20]

In 1997, a van driver, Ariosto Roblero, was found dead. Somebody had shot him in the back of the head and left him lying in a pool of blood next to his vehicle. The circumstances strongly resembled the ones of the attack on another van driver, Juan Martinez. Once again, there was no evidence. Everybody knew about the abuses, everybody knew "El Diablo" had killed Roblero. Something had to be done about the situation. The CIW's undercover operation was carried out by nineteen-year-old member Romeo Ramirez. Romeo volunteered for the job; he approached the Ramos brothers and asked for work. He went to live at La Piñita camp. He did it *"indigena* style," pretending to be very naive and not to know anything about anything. Thanks to the courage of this young Guatemalan, a CIW team helped four captives escape the Lake Placid–based barracks. After Ramirez and other es-capees testified, FBI and INS agents raided the camp while driving with a strikingly unassuming "INS Deportation Service" sign on their van. Eventually, the Ramoses were charged, but the FBI's and INS's sloppiness allowed the crew leaders to hide most of the captive workers in the orange groves. (Roblero's murder was never solved.) The Ramoses used to work for Consolidated Citrus and Lykes Brothers, the two major citrus companies operating in South Florida,[21] but when questioned by the Ramoses' defense attorneys regarding the farm-workers who picked fruit under their clients, Richard Hetherton, director of human resources for Lykes Brothers in Tampa, said: "These are not our employees."[22]

In 2007, Ron Evans, just like Lee and the Ramoses, was imprisoned on charges of drug conspiracy, financial reconstructing, and witness tampering charges, among others. Evans held women and men, most of whom were African American, in a perpetual debt cycle in the East Palatka labor camp in Florida and in Newton Grove in North Carolina. Here, also, the company store sold crack, tax-free beer, and cigarettes. Purchases were directly deducted from the workers' paychecks. Evans, too, like Lee, recruited American citizens in homeless shelters in Tampa, Miami, and New Orleans. Evans harvested on behalf of farmer Frank Johns, 2004 chairman of the Florida Fruit and Vegetables Association (FFVA, a lobbying branch of Florida agribusiness), and up to 2007, president of the FFVA Budget and Finance Commission.[23]

◆

In the United States, President Lincoln abolished slavery and involuntary servitude with the passing of the 13th Amendment (1865). However, as Douglas Blackmon illustrated recently and most notably, state-sanctioned slavery continued for many years after it had been outlawed.[24] After the Civil War, states and counties made liberal use of the convict-lease system to deploy workers in the fields and in the mines. The prisoners' working and living conditions were inhuman. Florida and Alabama remained the last states to abolish the exploitation of convicts in 1923. Debt peonage was also widely practiced in the South. In the 1920s, the public's growing demand for fresh fruits and vegetables led to the expansion of large-scale agricultural operations that required a labor force willing to work seasonally and then move along the Atlantic Coast to follow the harvest. Farmworkers were excluded from collective bargaining and other important New Deal–era workplace protections, thus leaving untouched a sector already prone to exploitation. More than half a million Mexican workers were forcibly deported in response to the lessened demand for foreign labor during the Great Depression.[25] However, a few years later, big U.S. growers claimed a scarcity of workers due to the war and pressured the federal government to create an "Emergency Farm Labor Supply Program." For U.S. farmers this agreement (also known at the bracero program) and successive guest worker programs resulted in a twofold advantage: domestic-born workers were no longer able to negotiate higher wages, and foreign workers could easily be repatriated and replaced. As a result a more subjugated labor force was created and exploitation in the fields continued.[26] In 1942, four managers of the U.S. Sugar Corporation were indicted for holding workers against their will in the Everglades.[27] The appalling conditions of the migrant workers once again reached national attention in the sixties with the broadcast of *Harvest of Shame*. Still, in 1986, more than three hundred sugar cane cutters (Caribbean laborers on guest worker visas) went on strike as the owners of the plantation, the Fanjul family, had started paying them a rate lower than what was written in their contract. The police stood by the Fanjuls and used arms and dogs against the strikers, who eventually got deported. The dispute became known as the Dog Wars.[28]

The guest worker program was reformed with the passing of the 1986 Immigration Reform and Control Act (popularly known as "Amnesty") and is now divided into the H-2A agricultural program and the H-2B non-agricultural program. The "Amnesty" eventually granted 2.7 million green cards to undocumented immigrants who had continuously resided in the United States since before January 1, 1982, or who had been employed in seasonal agricultural work prior to May 1986.

Whereas there are only five thousand green cards available for less-skilled workers (hotel workers, landscapers, and construction workers),[29] there are no numerical limitations for H-2A visas. In 2005, the United States issued 121,000 guest worker visas under the H-2 program to supply the national demand for seasonal labor, 32,000 of which were for agricultural work (H-2A).[30] Three-quarters of the H-2 visas are allotted to Mexicans.[31] Although the current guest worker program has numerous provisions that are supposed to protect both seasonal foreign *and* U.S. workers, the H-2 guest worker program is still flawed, mainly since it ties laborers to a single employer;[32] thus, migrant workers have no or little ability to enforce their rights. Furthermore, employers, who are required to petition the Department of Labor on behalf of foreign laborers, frequently rely on recruiters who invariably charge high fees (often thousands of dollars) to the workers for their travel, visas, lodging, et cetera. Lack of employer's accountability, little enforcement of labor and human rights, and, ultimately, unawareness of the existent legal protections available to temporary, unskilled workers make the foreign labor force easily exploitable. As a result, near slavery conditions are still widespread in agriculture as in other sectors of the national economy (i.e., forestry, landscaping, meat-packing, seafood processing, construction).

For a nation that grounds its foreign policy rhetoric on exporting and fostering democracy—an idea of democracy based on liberty and individualism—it remains a shocking fact that within its territory, human beings are still being held as slaves, or, at best, are denied the most fundamental protection of a free labor market.

According to Kevin Bales, author of *Disposable People*, there are between 100,000 and 150,000 slaves in the United States. Around 20,000 are human trafficking victims,[33] illegally brought to the United States from Southeast Asia to work as prostitutes in the many "spas" across the country, or from Mexico and Central America to work in the fields.[34]

In 2000, Congress passed an important piece of legislation—the Victims of Trafficking and Violence Protection Act—intended to protect those who denounce their persecutors and prevent victims from being deported as a result of their actions. The implementation of the law, however, hasn't been simple so far. U visas, for instance, grant crime victims temporary legal status and work eligibility up to four years and thus also protect victims who are cooperating with a police.[35] But as of November 2007, not even one U visa has been issued.[36] Furthermore, many low-income immigrants are not aware of this legislation and/or tend not to rely on institutions, especially the police. As a result, even though Latino immigrants are often targets of hate crimes and robberies, they rarely report them.[37]

Undocumented immigrants are notably discouraged from collaborating with the police especially after 287(g) agreements have extended the power to local police to enforce immigration law by cross-designating officers.[38] Latino legal residents also may not report crimes since they fear harassment or retaliation against their families and communities that host undocumented individuals.[39]

Finally, this distrust also has social and cultural roots; in their countries of origin, Latinos tend not to trust law enforcement agencies in general. Police are often corrupt and have been deployed as an instrument of oppression of the campesinos with the backing of the U.S. government; like in Guatemala, where the expropriation of lands has served the interests of the multinational corporations with the sanction of the local government.[40] As a consequence, once in the States, low-income immigrants have reason not to trust the "gringos" and people not from their community, especially if they are public officials.

Herein lies the crucial role played by the CIW, comprised exclusively of farmworkers, many of whom were campesinos actively involved in popular education programs in their countries of origin. Immigrant workers feel they can trust the CIW because the CIW is like them. The organization has indeed cooperated with the U.S. Department of Justice in the investigation and uncovering of the cases of modern-day slavery. Unfortunately, FBI agents are often not fully equipped to do the job or are not deployed to their fullest potential: indeed, once they gain the necessary expertise, they often get transferred to other assignments, making it difficult for others to use the information and knowledge they were able to acquire on the ground. CIW member Romeo Ramirez, who bravely went undercover to expose the Ramoses' operation, was a much better fit for the job.

Slavery has taken on different forms today. Unlike the system of chattel slavery in the United States, modern-day slavery is no longer a matter of ownership of people—although insane megalomaniacs like Abel Cuello Jr. might think so—but of total control over people's lives as Bales points out. In fact, it takes years to uncover and bring to justice slavery cases because coercion has taken on new, more deceptive forms. Many times there are no chains or locked doors, only isolated places in the middle of the fields where alienated human beings live under the constant threat of beatings.

The privation of individual liberty is deployed with the primary objective of obtaining profit. The estimated annual contribution by slaves to the global economy is thirteen billion dollars—a relatively small amount, whose indirect value is, however, much greater.[41] As the enslaved individuals become no longer productive—whether by age or injury—they simply get replaced. In addition, the labor force that is willing to work for a minimum salary has grown globally. In a sixty-five-year span, the world population has grown from two to six billion, and with it, the gap between the very wealthy and the very poor has skyrocketed. Millions of disenfranchised people have flooded the world's labor markets, thus "destroying the social rules and traditional bonds of responsibility that might have protected potential slaves."[42] Poor farmers, for instance, have been dispossessed due to the advent of modernized agriculture and disastrous free trade agreements, which have forced them to migrate and, thus, become vulnerable to enslavement.

Everywhere in the world, slavery is illegal today; this is the stated heritage of the Universal Declaration of Human Rights (1948) for the advancement of humanity. Whoever practices modern-day slavery is thus forced to hide or deny it. A common denominator for slavery is extreme poverty, often combined, in the United States, with the corollary of those enslaved being unaware of social and cultural norms and, most significantly, their basic, legally protected human rights.

As Bales notes, modern-day slavery doesn't need an ideological justification and race is no longer a determinant factor as it once was.[43] Profit alone is enough to justify exploitation.[44] However, if one looks at who exploits whom and where, this phenomenon is positively grounded in new manifestations of racism and patriarchal systems.[45]

The State Department has estimated recently that there are twelve million slaves disseminated around the world.[46] According to Kevin Bales and his coauthor Ron Soodalter, there are actually twenty-seven million people who are held captive throughout the world. Slavery "is thought to be the third most profitable criminal enterprise of our time, following only drugs and guns."[47]

In realities driven only by profit, social injustice thrives, and exploitation often occurs; here, there is fertile ground for the proliferation of hidden, dispersed, isolated places, where individuals lose their uniqueness and end up becoming beasts, once again. Victims are primarily concentrated in the Global South: India (despite its restrictive laws against slavery), Brazil (in most of the Amazon and in the west of the country, despite President Lula da Silva's much-publicized campaign against slavery right after taking office), Pakistan, Bangladesh, Nepal, Southeast Asia (Thailand, Burma, Laos, and Cambodia), and northern and western Africa (that is, Mauritania) where slavery conditions are the norm.[48] These are faraway territories with names that are often unpronounceable to Westerners.

Immokalee, Florida, in the United States is also one of these places: hard to pronounce, hard to make sense of, metaphorically and physically, and hard to locate on the cognitive map of most Americans.

By the Fire, the Starry Sky Above

Paco and I stop at a local homeless shelter called the Friendship House. Monica, the person in charge, is not there. I call her and make an appointment for the day after. She makes it clear on the phone: she wants to be present when I interview the guests of the shelter. We proceed to walk on Main Street. We pass in front of the Rollason Center, which houses the child care facilities of the Redlands Christian Migrant Association (RCMA), where the children of many farmworkers go to kindergarten. Paco, too, went here. A long mosaic covers the middle section of the walls depicting the tomato pickers and their daily lives. Below are tiles with the names of the donors of the Rollason Center.

In the evening, we go to Tina's. Tina* and Angela are best friends. Her husband, Carl,* works as a nurse and health educator in Immokalee.

Today, they are having a twenty-first-year birthday party for Gabriela,* one of Tina and Carl's children. There are indeed a lot of kids, friends of Gabriela and Sara,* their youngest daughter, and a jovial yet intimate atmosphere. The kitchen's bulb sheds some timid light in the living room where we are gathered. In Immokalee, people try to conserve electricity if they can, and at night they talk.

Carl and I sit at the children's table and begin to converse softly, the semidarkness acting as our facilitator. Carl is a very thin guy who wears small, round glasses. He props his arms on his knees and lets his long hands swing. As a health educator, Carl informs the local population about the risk of diabetes, quite a widespread problem here in Immokalee.

"As you may know, African Americans and Native Americans tend to have diabetes. And the people who come from Central America, who knows why…" Carl wonders sarcastically, "after a few years of living in the United States…also get diabetes…"

There is no hospital in Immokalee. Carl works at a medical center: his patients cannot spend the night at the facility. The nearest hospital is in Lehigh, twenty miles away. Carl also holds classes on family planning, on the various contraceptive methods (sterilization included), on the prevention of breast tumors, on sexually transmitted diseases, and on prenatal and postpartum care. When women give birth, they are all brought to Lehigh Hospital. "If they don't have documents," he says, "the government still pays for the expenses related to childbirth since this is considered a life-or-death type of emergency."[49]

Carl has lived in Immokalee for twenty-three years. He met Tina in Paraguay while serving in the Peace Corps. Originally from Connecticut, when Carl's parents moved to St. Augustine, the young couple decided to relocate to the Sunshine State, to be close to Carl's family.

"But I also wanted to work with the migrants and back then the only place was in Immokalee," Carl continues. "So we moved down here and I started working as a nurse."

And it's in Immokalee that Carl, who is fluent in Spanish, learned to speak Creole. He now gives lessons on the risks of diabetes and high blood pressure in the language spoken in Haiti.

The kids have lit a fire outside. It's pitch dark by now and it's getting cool. Behind Carl and Tina's house, a vast swamp stretches. There are extra-sweet *bananitas* hidden like small golden treasures and, where the slow waters of the creek bed reach, alligators.

"You cannot build on this land…" Carl begins to explain, his foot suspended between the doorsteps. He is looking toward the swamp, now as black as oil. Carl has stopped talking as if he were surprised by how suddenly the night has fallen on his surroundings. "But we have to fight every day to keep it this way," he finally says as if regaining his train of thought.

Carl daily strives to set some limits to the expansionistic projects of the developers. Only 25 percent of Collier County is zoned for building. The remaining 75 percent contains swamps and savannah—a pristine habitat to be preserved as they are host to endangered animal species and thousand of plants, like the many varieties of orchids.

"You see, back in the eighties we were able to buy a house…*this house*," Carl continues while going back inside. "But times have changed, even for Immokalee…It was easier back then, for farmworkers. They could afford to buy a car and even a house if they conscientiously saved."

Carl reappears with two lawn chairs. We join the others sitting around the fire. Meghan and Damara of the Student/Farmworker Alliance are here now, too. Meghan and Damara are two beautiful, tall, slim young women with clean faces. Meghan is slightly older than twenty, blonde, with an athletic physique. Damara, from California, is in her thirties and has long brunette hair; her first wrinkles bracket her smile.

We drink beer and make jokes. Damara begins to tell stories from the Taco Bell Truth Tour. She remembers the 230-mile march the CIW organized from Fort Myers to Orlando. Damara had arrived in Immokalee at the end of the nineties, as a Sister of Humility volunteer. She came here with the idea of spending only a few weeks in Immokalee, and ended up staying seven years working on the CIW campaigns. She now lives in Oakland, California, but she has come back to Immokalee to help the coalition organize the protest action against Burger King.

"Paco is acting strange," Damara says out loud. "Look at him, he pretends he doesn't even know me..." she adds teasingly. She glimpses at Paco. He understands he's got to get up now and hug her, and so he does. Paco later tells me that Damara lived for one year at his mom's house when she first arrived in Immokalee.

Damara seems happy tonight. For her, this is a trip down memory lane. She is reliving the beautiful times she once spent here, remembering the many struggles she has fought side by side with the people of Immokalee.

"Do you remember the dangling arm of Lady Liberty?" she asks, recalling her memories of that long march. A young woman from Miami, Kat Rodriguez, came up with the idea, and, along with other SFA and CIW members, built a huge papier-mâché Lady Liberty for the march toward Orlando. "Lady Liberty was wonderful," Damara explains, "She had a brown face and was holding this bucket full of tomatoes...Instead of the torch, there was a huge tomato!"

Damara invites those who participated in that long demonstration to remember, and her laughter is contagious as she recalls that during the two-week march Lady Liberty's arm (and thus the tomato) kept falling down, and how finally arriving in Orlando, Lady Liberty showed wear and tear from the journey for economic justice.

The papier-mâché statue is now part of a collection of the Smithsonian Museums in Washington D.C. The curators thought it was an artifact that deserved preservation. The statue hasn't been exhibited to the public yet; it's locked in a warehouse waiting until History recognizes the importance of the struggles of the Florida farmworkers.

We talk about the possibility of going to the Carnival. It's a big deal when the *carnis* come to Immokalee, Paco told me. But it feels too good to stay here and just talk, with the starry sky above and the peacefully still air. More wood gets thrown in to revive the fire.

On the other hand, I would like to go see the casino of the Seminoles. Everyone is tired but eventually, Gerardo—who has joined us in the meantime—Paco, Damara, Meghan, and I jump in my car, as if we were a bunch of old friends.

We take Immokalee Road and turn left into the semi-deserted parking lot of the casino. Paco is carrying a camera over his shoulders and gets stopped by one of the security guards. No pictures inside the casino. We get in after leaving the camera in the car. Once inside, I regret having dragged everybody here. Casinos in America, small or big, all look the same. A place where it is always night, people drink for free, and smoking is still allowed. The same annoying background noise: orchestral instruments that are tuning up before the concert begins, only here the concert never begins and the conflicting sounds turn out to come from nothing else but the slot machines.

Today, there are only a few tourists and some "snowbirds," the most assiduous clientele of the casino here. People spend Thanksgiving with their families in America. Ironically, too busy interviewing, I have forgotten to eat and now I am starving. The kitchen is closed, says Manuel, a Mexican guy that Damara knows who now works here. The two of them begin to talk, and I start wandering around.

Still, there are people that today have shut themselves in to play at the Seminole casino. A couple of poker tables are populated by weary players. Hung on the wall by the entrance, the serious-looking portraits of the tribal council members of the Seminoles stand out; but in the Casino, there are no traces of the Seminoles tonight. Rather, endless touch-screen slot machines are lined up like mechanical rows of vines crowded by annoyingly noisy birds.

The old slot machines, the ones with the lever on the side, are nowhere to be found; now it's all electronic, push-button, which makes the experience incredibly aseptic to me. It feels like one is neither losing nor winning.

I observe the people play, their eyes lost in the whirling of the slot machines, long red fingernails touching the bright screens. Manuel leaves to go have his Thanksgiving dinner with his colleagues. We depart too, bored, in search of food because I, at the steering wheel, am hungry. But everything looks closed this long Thanksgiving night.

Eventually, I come out of a convenience store with a Starbucks frappuccino. That's all right, the casino made me lose my appetite anyway. Paco and I drop off the others and go home. I get ready for bed. I look for Paco to say goodnight. From the kitchen window, I see my friend lying in the hammock, under the mango tree. He has fallen asleep.

Friendship House

The morning after, I wake up early. I lay for a while staring at the neon-pink wall, standing out even in the darkness of the room. Paco and his mom are sleeping. I leave a note for Paco: *8 a.m. I'm going to the Friendship House.*

The building of the Friendship House looks like a huge mountain refuge, with a sloping gray roof and yellow-ochre walls. It's a medium-sized building, modestly furnished inside: couches, beds, and bookshelves have all been donated.

Founded twenty years ago, the Friendship House was created as a temporary shelter for the homeless, specifically for Immokalee's farmworkers. The center was established for those migrants who found themselves without a place to stay; it allows them to get accustomed to the town, and maybe save some money while benefiting from free lodging and meals for a few days.

Monica gives me a tour of the shelter; she shows me the section of the Friendship House where families and women sleep. When they can, they try to accommodate the entire family in one room, she says. "We have women who are victims of domestic violence, or families that found themselves without a place to stay because their house had caught on fire," Monica explains. "This unfortunately happens quite often in Immokalee since homes have very old and faulty wiring systems."

But there are other reasons why someone may be homeless: for instance, because of suddenly losing a job—perhaps being let go due to a bad harvest season or for a dispute with a crew leader. In general, living paycheck to paycheck doesn't allow workers to save for emergencies.

"The shelter is open 24/7," Monica says while showing me the large room where the men sleep. "As the person in charge here, they can always reach me," she says patting the pager on her belt.

Monica is originally from Indianapolis, and has worked in Immokalee for the last three and a half years. Just like Paco told me in advance, she is as tiny as she is strong-willed.

"We have plenty of volunteer opportunities here," explains Monica. "Although what we'd really need is *skilled* volunteers," she says with a sigh.

The Friendship House participates in the "Alternative Break Program" initiative: kids from colleges dispersed all over the country come to Immokalee to volunteer during their Spring Break. Instead of going to guzzle beer and cruise along the Gulf Coast drives of Panama City Beach, they take the opportunity to get to know the town, and, maybe, fall for it.

"Today the soup kitchen at the Guadalupe Center is closed because of the Thanksgiving holiday, so we'll probably have more people than usual at lunch," Monica says.

We enter the room where donations (canned food, books, blankets) are collected and where meetings and classes (Alcoholics Anonymous and health education courses) are held.

"This is a mess!" Monica says opening her arms. On the floor, sleeping bags and mats testify to the recent presence of those who took shelter here last night. Monica looks embarrassed, as would someone who finds herself showing a modest and untidy home to an unexpected guest.

"Fact is, Friendship House has a capacity of thirty-four in total but right now we actually host thirty-one men…" Monica explains. "Since we don't allow men in the area reserved for families, some of them have to sleep here on the floor…"

The majority of the guests are farmworkers, most of whom are convalescents, people who have some sort of illness that prevents them from working, or people who just arrived in Immokalee and are looking for work.

"Would you like to do some interviews now?" Monica gently asks. "If you don't mind, I'd like to stay."

"It's important to protect the privacy of these people," Monica continues. "We don't want them to feel in danger or judged in any way. We do whatever we can so that they can feel safe here. That's why we also work with the local police," Monica says pointing at the police station located right across the shelter.

There are many reasons why people find themselves broke and without a place to sleep in America. Poverty, however, is the common denominator, and it leads many to Immokalee.

Pamela*

"Maybe you could talk to Pamela…" Monica says weighing her own words. "Wait here. I'll be right back."

On the bookshelf by the entrance a series of Bibles sit, one next to the other.

Monica reappears followed by a big, blonde young woman. We introduce ourselves and go sit in the little living room of the center. Monica had informed me that Pamela is expecting twins. She also suffers from asthma and epilepsy. She lived for a while in her father's apartment but he has Alzheimer's, and at one point he kicked Pamela and her husband out of his place. He convinced himself that they were stealing from him Pamela has told her.

Monica sits next to Pamela; she smiles at her, as if to reassure the woman that all is well. Pamela begins her story: she and her husband ended up in Naples, broke and with no place to sleep at night. Since the St. Matthews House (the homeless shelter in Naples) was full, she says while nibbling her lip, they sent her to Immokalee.

"Where is your husband?" I ask.

"In jail," Pamela says promptly as if she sensed my question was coming. "And I have no intention of saying anything else about this," she adds, resolutely lowering her eyes.

Monica informed me that when the couple got to the Friendship House, they ran a background check. As it turned out, there was a warrant in the husband's name. They had to call the police.

Pamela is now looking for a job. "It's not easy, though," she says. Pamela can speak a little bit of Spanish, "but here in Immokalee," she continues, "if you don't know it, well, they won't hire you...Not even to work in the kitchen." Moreover, she is a resident of another state: she doesn't have a Florida driver's license, nor does she have any intention to move here, which makes things even more difficult for her. Pamela is three months pregnant with twins: she will give birth to her babies in June, then she will try to go back to California, where the rest of her family lives. There, it will be easier to find a job, and she could rely on a support system to look after her children.

"Pamela is helping me write the thank-you notes for the donations we have received for Thanksgiving," Monica injects, trying to break a long silence, "She's doing a great job." Pamela nods her head, and finally breaks into a smile.

Juan*

Juan is originally from Texas but, as he puts it, "he has lived all over." He worked as a welder for more than twenty years, many of which were in Houston for Kellogg Brown & Root, Inc. He was in the union, too: he was getting paid well, up to $25 an hour.

Juan doesn't say how he ended up in Immokalee. He is a man consumed by a life of hard work. And, recently by illness. Juan has liver cancer. He got diagnosed a year and half ago. When Juan tells me his age (he is fifty-three), I can hardly hide my disbelief. His face is plowed with wrinkles, and his tired and sick eyes make him look at least twenty years older—a testament to the ravages of alcoholism.

As he talks, Juan keeps moving his hands around his face, his black-edged fingernails in the foreground. It's hard for him to focus: his thoughts are too quick to capture, he says, as he keeps bringing up chunks of his life. He has kids, somewhere. He got married very young, at sixteen…his wife was only fourteen. From what Juan says, I understand that they had separated at one point, and that he hasn't seen his daughters in years.

Juan receives a $150-a-month pension. He has been staying at the Friendship House for several days now, and I will find him here again a couple of weeks later. It is here that Juan has his medicine delivered. As Monica explains, sometimes guests stay longer than allowed, or, like Juan, they can leave for a few days and then get readmitted.

Juan was waiting for a new liver, but at the hospital in Houston the doctors said the cancer had spread all over, so they took him off the list. They had given him two months.

"When was it?" I ask.

"Three…four months ago," he says. But that doesn't seem to make a difference. He looks at me with his extinguished eyes and shakes his head.

"I am just here waiting…waiting to make room for somebody else."

John*

We sit with John outside, on the bench by the entrance. The morning sun has begun to bake Main Street. John has been in Immokalee for a week now. He was in Naples for a while but the St. Matthews shelter was full, so he was sent to the Friendship House.

John is a blonde guy who wears Bono Vox–style sunglasses and a page-boy haircut, which is quite uncommon for anyone past the age of ten. John, thirty-six, is originally from Oregon but has worked in restaurants and bars all over the country.

"I know how to deal with people," John says proudly.

Years ago, John lived in Miami Beach. He was working as a bartender.

"I was making a lot of money, even $600 a night…with the tips and everything," he says. "A friend of mine was able to buy a car and a house, while working at the bar." John continues. "I've always liked to party, so I've never been able to save and put some dough aside. My bad."

I ask him how he ended up in Naples. "I took a Greyhound in New York," he begins. "I wanted a change of scenery. That's the way I am. I'm a little bit crazy," he says laughingly.

> I like to feel free, that's it. Generally, I don't have problems finding a job because I have twenty years of experience in the business. But this time things went wrong and I ran out of money, so I found myself in the street…I couldn't even go to Miami where I have friends because I didn't have the thirty dollars for the bus ride. So I started wandering around, as many do. Tired of carrying my suitcase, I found a cart…an Office Depot cart. I thought: "That's exactly what I need!" I put my stuff in there, found a nice, clean spot without bugs or ants, and lay down to get some rest.
>
> Somebody must have called the police because at eight in the morning with sirens wailing a squad arrived and two cops started asking me all these questions as if I were a criminal or something. They put me in jail for twenty-five days. Can you imagine? I didn't even have my pocket knife on me anymore! I'd thrown it away along with the other stuff because I had too many things to carry. Guess what the charge was? "Illegal possession of private property!" All because of a

freaking shopping cart!? I had even thought, I'd be doing them a favor. I'll return the cart closer to Home Depot. Because the cart wasn't in front of the store when I'd found it…It was somewhere on a sidewalk!

How is it possible to spend twenty-five days in jail for having borrowed a shopping cart? I don't know if John has a clean record. He probably does not. Still, the story he told me, as shocking as it is, is not uncommon. That morning in Naples, John was trying to satisfy a basic human need: the one to rest. His mere presence in a public space landed him in jail. Streets need to be clean.

A few days after my visit in Immokalee, I came upon a similar case. Just behind my apartment in Boca Raton, a retailer had called the police because there was a homeless person sleeping in the back of his store.

My friend Mike, a Cuban American activist in Miami, spent a night in jail because he got stopped while riding his bike at night. He was wearing a Che Guevara T-shirt. They ran a background check and found out he hadn't paid two tickets he received for driving without a valid license. He still had to spend the night in jail. "They give you food with a tin ladle, taking it from buckets, as they would do with beasts," he told me. In court, a few days before Christmas, he was found not guilty.

◆

"Do you really wanna know what the most lucrative business in Florida is today?" Jim asks. "You might think it is tourism, right? Nahhh. I'm telling you what it is: incarcerating people!"

I meet Jim at the bar where he works in Delray Beach, on the east coast. He tells me that he had spent eighty-four days in jail with four different charges. Eventually, all of them were dropped.

"When you cannot afford a lawyer, they give you a public defendant, also known as 'public pretender,'" Jim says. "These are young inexperienced lawyers who are poorly paid and so they're easily corruptible and ready to do everything that would advance their careers."

"There was this guy in jail," Jim continues. "He would spend most of his days in a corner making imaginary calls. So I went up to one of the guards one day and told him what he was doing. 'That man needs some help,' I said. "And what did the guard do? He just pretended not to hear. 'OK, I said, but now that I've told you, you know and you can't say you didn't.'"

Incarceration has become a big business in America. Prisons can request additional federal funds to cover the expenses of the growing jail population; therefore, this system has triggered a vicious mechanism that favors the imprisonment of people and keeps detainees in jail longer under dubious pretexts. The 2008 Pew Center report on the Public Safety Performance Project highlights the shocking statistic in its title, *One in 100: Behind Bars in America 2008*. One American out of one hundred is in jail.[50]

More than two million adults were incarcerated in 2007. The most worrying data concerns the young African American male population, which speaks volumes about the persistent racism of the system: between the ages twenty and thirty-four, one Black man out of nine is in prison. The figure is one out of thirty men overall.[51]

In 1987, the federal government spent a third of what it invested in higher education in detention facilities; in 2007, the ratio was 60 percent, which means that in twenty years the cost of the prison system in relation to the educational one doubled. The total state spending for corrections was estimated to be $52 billion (in 2008).[52]

In the state of Florida, the jail population grew from 53,000 to 97,000 between 1993 and 2007. The Sunshine State set the sad record of the highest prison growth rates, with a 2007 General Fund Corrections Spending of $2.7 billion that placed Florida only after California ($8.8) and Texas ($3.3).[53] Experts agree that this is the result of correctional policies and other practices that have been adopted by the state in the last few years. In fact, this is *not* caused by an increase in criminal activities. As detailed in the Pew report, legislation abolished "good time" credits and discretionary release along with the mandatory extension of the time prisoners spent in jail to 85 percent of their sentence regardless of their prior record. Subsequently, there were the "zero tolerance" policies and other measures that extend the time spent in prison for "technical violations." Furthermore, these harsh law enforcement–only policies disregard the recommendations of the International Association of Chiefs of Police.[54] "Without a change of direction," according to the Pew report, "Florida is expected to reach a peak of nearly 125,000 inmates by 2013."

Jim was absolutely right: this is a business more lucrative than tourism.

If one is to understand the deprivation of the sovereignty over one's body as a human rights issue, it's worth noticing that this becomes problematic only when it's about arbitrary imprisonment, as in the case of slavery or torture, whereas the type of captivity perpetrated by institutions (incarceration) or the very elimination of one's body (with the death penalty) seems to be socially accepted and thus rarely questioned.[55] Most notably, activist and author Angela Davis has long advocated the abolishment of the prison-industrial complex, as it reproduces class, racial, and gender injustices.[56]

The people I met at the Friendship House on November 23 were all U.S. citizens: they were only guilty of being old and ill, displaced, or pregnant and with an incarcerated husband. All of them happened to be poor at that point in time.

In any case, anyone who roams the streets without having taken a shower in three days automatically becomes a "bum," a loser in American society, and if these streets are ones in Naples (or Boca Raton), the "garbage" needs to be taken away, as quickly as possible.

It's not good for business. Urban beautification mandates the removal of everything that is dirty, imperfect, or ill because it is considered ugly, and thus, in contrast with the surrounding, allegedly "beautified" landscape. It's gentrification, the new form of segregation that operates not only and primarily on the basis of race—although the color of the skin is still an important discriminator—but on class as well.

Naples is not a place for low-income immigrants from Mexico, Guatemala, the Dominican Republic, or Haiti, but as Oannes will illustrate to me at length, these are exactly the people that keep this big boat called the United States of America afloat.

The Unconquered Seminoles

Paco and I decide to go to the Seminole reservation. To get there, we drive outside the city limits of Immokalee, pass the casino, and stay on First Street for another mile.

The Seminole administration building lies at the end of a now-deserted parking lot. On the other side of the street, half-hidden by trees, is the Immokalee Jail Center, Paco tells me, seemingly unconcerned with the anomalous proximity.

We get out of the car and walk toward the entrance, but it's all too evident that the offices are closed today. On the right, some kids are playing in the streets of the reservation. I look up toward the monumental construction in front of me, and I notice the symbol of the Tribal Council: a "chickee," home in the Mikasuki language, a small hut with a palmetto-frond roof arranged on a cypress wooden frame-work. Below, a fire, there to represent what once was the center of Seminole life. The illustration is framed by the words "In God We Trust," chased by the inscription "Seminole Tribe of Florida."

I pick up a copy of the *Seminole Tribune*, the tribe's official paper whose subhead is "The Voice of the Unconquered," to signify the pride of this people who never surrendered to the U.S. military.

The first settlements in the southeastern territories of the United States date back twelve thousand years. The word *cimarrones* ("free people") was first used in 1771 in reference to those indigenous popu-lations who had separated from the Creek Confederation.[57] Indeed, the Seminoles were never a homogenous group. They descended from the Muskogee, the so-called Creek Indians, those native peoples first recognized as "civilized"[58] by early colonizers because they established good relations with the Europeans and soon incorporated much of the colonizers' culture into their own.

Yet, establishing relations with the colonizers marked the begin-ning of the separation of the Seminoles from the Creek Confederation. After Congress passed the Indian Removal Act (1830), thousands of Seminoles were forced to move west of the Mississippi, thus opening up twenty-five million acres of land to colonial settlement and slavery.

The operation, motivated by the expansionist drives of the federal government of Andrew Jackson under the false pretenses of preserving the populations that lived in the southern territories, resulted in the "Trail of Tears," the forced resettlement of the "civilized" natives in what is now Oklahoma. During that journey, the Native peoples suffered from bad weather, diseases, and hunger—many of them didn't make it. The ones who survived the long march arrived in very bad shape.

The federal government forced the evacuation of thousands of Native Americans, sometimes after having set fire to trees and sugarcane fields. So, the ancestors of the Florida Seminoles, compelled to leave the lands of Georgia and Alabama, kept moving southward until they found shelter in the Everglades. It was during this time that the Seminoles refined their ability to fabricate chickees: homes quick to build and quick to destroy without leaving a trace. Runaway slaves and outlaws found refuge with the tribe; a fact that further worsened their relations with the federal government, which ended up declaring war against the Florida Seminoles.

The federal government engaged in three conflicts in the attempt to defeat the Seminoles:[59] from the first fusillade of November 21, 1817, until Colonel Gustavus Loomis declared the third war over on May 8, 1858. In the forty-one years of intermittent hostilities, billions of dollars were spent and more than 1,500 American soldiers lost their lives.[60]

Legendary Indian warrior Osceola led the memorable defense. Even though numerically disadvantaged—it has been estimated that no more than four thousand warriors had fought against the federal troops—the Seminoles, aided by their detailed knowledge of the swampy territories, managed to outlast the U.S. troops. No peace treaty was ever signed. The government, however, declared victory.

The Seminoles who settled in Florida brought with them two Muskogean languages: Creek and Mikasuki. A group of Creek-speaking Seminoles found refuge near Lake Okeechobee, while most of the Mikasuki-speaking Seminoles—later divided politically into the Seminole and Miccosukee Tribes—settled further south, in the Everglades. Through most of the twentieth century, they lived deep in Florida's wilds, isolated from the surrounding, burgeoning communities.

◆

"Do you want to take a walk in the reservation?" Paco asks.

A man stands almost suspended on a ladder put against the wall of a house. We ask him about the reservation, but he shakes his head. He doesn't know anything about it, he says in English with a strong Spanish accent. "I'm just finishing fixing this roof," he adds. After a few minutes, he leaves.

We begin to stroll around the community of the Seminoles. The kids have disappeared. These streets don't look any different from ones in any other American, middle-class neighborhoods during a workday: the same protruding mailboxes, the same well-kept yards. Modest homes. The only recurring element: the ever-present pickup truck parked in the driveway, a testimony to a lifestyle in contact with a wilder, rural environment.

Just as February is the month dedicated to African American culture, November is American Indian Heritage Month; these days, institutional America celebrates its most invisible minority, its original sin. For this reason, the timing of the exposé by the *South Florida Sun-Sentinel,* one of the major newspapers in the area, on the alleged financial squandering and fiscal non-fulfillment by certain leaders of the Seminole Tribe of Florida, is noteworthy, to say the least.[61]

Specifically, the report exposes the villas built on reservation land by David Cypress, Tribal Council representative for the Big Cypress reservation (about six hundred residents) and Mitchell Cypress, current chairman of the Tribal Council. According to the Indian Gaming Regulatory Act (1988), the law that regulates the revenues from gambling, the casino proceeds should be spent on tribal government programs that are geared toward the well-being of its members and its economic development. Also, the profits used for housing must be equally available to all the Seminoles.

Among other things, the articles point to the hundreds of thousands of dollars Hollywood Tribal Council representative Max B. Osceola Jr., owes the federal government. According to what the *Sun-Sentinel* reports, he has a debt of $958,308 with the IRS, and another of $227,000 with the tribe, the latter accrued in the nineties with the opening of his smoke shops in Hollywood.

Massive tax evasion? "I don't think Native Americans even had the word tax in their language," Osceola declared to the South Florida paper.[62] And he seems to amuse himself when he cites the late Seminole Billy Cypress: "You know taxes, it's kind of like the federal government stole our land and now they want you to pay for it." (Afterwards, as if to reassure the journalist and the readers, he stated that he does pay taxes, "just like every other citizen of the United States.")[63]

Two thousand seven marks the fiftieth anniversary of the ratification of the Constitution of the Tribal Council of the Seminoles of Florida. When Roosevelt signed the Indian New Deal (or Indian Reorganization Act) in 1934, the right to self-government was finally granted to Native Americans. The Seminoles, distrustful of the white man's government, did not take advantage of the new law until 1957 when they had to face (once again) the possibility of their own annihilation—not literally as during the wars, but in terms of recognition from the federal government.

In the aftermath of the Second World War, the U.S. government drastically reduced public expenses and began the so-called termination policy. The reasoning of Arthur Watkins—one of Utah's senators and proponent of the legislation that made termination the new Indian policy (1953–1962)—was that while the United States was spending tons of money fighting communism, it was promoting socialism on Indian reservations by supporting costly programs. Watkins's cause was helped by the mismanagement of federal funds by some tribes in the face of their persistent poverty. Claiming that Native Americans would be better off if individually assimilated into American society, the federal government tried to terminate its special relations with the smaller tribes and began the new "Indian Freedom Program." Among the most significant cuts were the funds allocated to the Bureau of Indian Affairs, the federal agency that administers programs to Indian tribes. In 1953, a congressional resolution (HCR 108) mandated the abolition of reservations all across the country. Congress compiled a list of tribes to be considered for possible termination. The Florida Seminoles were on it.[64]

At the time, council meetings were taking place under a big oak tree located in Hollywood, south of Fort Lauderdale, since then designated as the "Council Oak." Under the shade of the thick, spreading branches, members began to discuss and make decisions about the future of their communities. By this time, most Seminoles were still living the simple life in their chickees, and only a few inhabited concrete blockhouses.

In 1957, the tribe filed a petition with the United States for a settlement to cover the territories the Seminoles had lost because of the many aggressions perpetrated by the federal government. Forty-five years later, in 2002, the United States paid a multimillion-dollar settlement to the Seminoles.

"Council Oak" is today a luxurious "Steak and Seafood" restaurant in the new Seminole Hard Rock Hotel & Casino, located only a few miles from that original oak tree, right behind the stately headquarters of the Seminole Tribe of Florida.

In December 2006, the Seminoles completed the acquisition of Hard Rock International from the Rank Group, Plc. for $965 million.[65] In February of 2007, the media spotlight was on the Hard Rock in Hollywood. In one of its rooms, celebrity Anna Nicole Smith was found unconscious. The mix of sedatives and painkillers she had ingested would later turn out to be fatal.[66]

In 2005, during Hurricane Frances, the Seminole Hard Rock Hotel & Casino was used as a shelter for the Seminoles. According to the *Sun-Sentinel,* the Seminole guests occupied more than 150 rooms. The bill for a dinner of one tribal member at the Council Oak topped $645. The tribe then submitted a bill of $123,130 to the Federal Emergency Management Agency (FEMA). FEMA initially rejected the claim but then made the funds available to the Seminole Tribe once they indicated that the casino/resort was listed among the evacuation temporary shelters.[67] After several requests of further documentation, FEMA agreed to pay $103,864 of the bill. The agency, which is supposed to reimburse only $31 a day per person in meals, eventually turned a blind eye to the Seminoles.

Many lament the continuation of disbursement of public funding in the face of the wealth of the Seminole Council members. But Osceola replies to the critics: the tribes are entitled to funds, regardless of their financial situation.[68]

Oannes Pritzker

"You have to meet Oannes," Paco said.

Oannes Pritzker belongs to the Wabanaki tribe. He's originally from Maine but has lived and worked in southwestern Florida for over twenty years.

Unlike many Native Americans, Oannes has a high level of education; he is a biologist and an adviser to the Center for Environmental Sustainability Education at Florida Gulf Coast University. Most importantly, he is an activist and a long-time supporter of the struggles of the CIW. Like many Native Americans, Oannes has diabetes. That's why, as he will point out, he wasn't able to participate in the event organized by the CIW on Thanksgiving Day.

Oannes lives halfway between Immokalee and Naples. I travel south on Immokalee Road for about twenty miles until I turn onto a long, straight road that divides a sparse cypress forest. Oannes receives me at his doorstep. He wears a red bandanna that covers his thin gray hair. He makes way for me into the house, maneuvering with ease the wheelchair he is forced to use due to his illness. Oannes's body is extremely swollen because of diabetes; his neck, in particular, overflows onto his chest.

We move into his office. The room is of modest dimensions and the two high bookshelves delimiting the walls make it seem even smaller. Oannes invites me to sit on a low couch between his desk and the door while he positions himself in front of his 26-inch-wide computer screen. It is from here that Oannes broadcasts his online program on Radio for Peace International called "Honoring Mother Earth/Indigenous Voices." And I can tell that it is in this room that Oannes spends most of his time.

"I belong to the *people* of Wabanaki," he specifies right away. "I come from that part of North America that today they call Maine..." Oannes explains, reformulating my question in his own terms. I have used the word "tribe" and Oannes, evidently, doesn't like it (like many others, as I will soon find out).[69] Then *he* begins to ask questions: where I'm from, what I'm doing in Florida, what I'm writing about. I say to myself: every interview is, first of all, a mutual encounter, and this is his way of checking you out…

Suddenly Oannes stops talking and deliberates. "You absolutely have to listen to this interview I had with Bryan Payne, one of the founders of the Student/Farmworker Alliance," he says, getting closer to the computer. "He is white and young as you are. He was born and raised in Arcadia, a small farming community in Florida that was once part of the segregationist South," he continues, while operating his mouse in search of the audio file. "Bryan lived in Immokalee for four years. I'm sure you'll appreciate his point of view on things…"

"I'd love to…Perhaps later though…after the interview," I finally manage to say, somewhat embarrassed. So the listening session gets postponed, but trying to resist and start with *my* list of questions is pointless. Oannes hasn't exhausted his yet.

Oannes has in store for me the story of the construction of the Vatican Advanced Technology Telescope (VATT) located on Mount Graham, eighty miles from Tucson, Arizona, at a height of over a thousand feet. The VATT depends on the Vatican Observatory Research Group (VORG), which is hosted by the Steward Observatory at the University of Arizona. It works in close collaboration with the Vatican Observatory, where the Jesuit astronomers of the Center of Castel Gandolfo operate. The construction of the observatory was a case that spurred a lot of controversy in the nineties because of its collocation in the Coronado National Forest.

"The huge telescope is located in the territories of the indigenous populations of what is now called Arizona," Oannes continues. The Apache of San Carlos, indeed, tried in vain to stop the building of the observatory and sued the center, even after Congress had approved its construction. "This is one of the most tragic examples of desecration of spiritual places and of colonization in its most tangible form," Oannes says. "A representative of the Vatican...I can't recall his name, got to the point of saying that the Apaches don't have a religion, so it doesn't really matter...Something like that. Now, this is one of the most racist, pseudo-Nazi, I would say, statements I've ever heard."

"As a matter of fact, the Apaches were not even totally against the construction of the observatory," Oannes continues. "They had suggested a different, better collocation: another mountain on which it would have made more sense to place a telescope."

"According to what the chief of the Arizona Apaches says, the observatory doesn't even work properly where it is now because of the very collocation of that mountain," Oannes explains. "The reason why I told you this anecdote is to explain to our listeners—*Oannes speaks as if we were recording a radio program*—the attitude of the Roman Catholic Church against the Native Americans..."

I understand now. In Oannes's eyes, growing up in a place like Italy, which hosts the Vatican, is no different than growing up in the backward and racist South of the United States, where Bryan was raised and "where the Ku Klux Klan still recruits its followers," as Oannes puts it.

"More than once, the indigenous peoples of the western hemisphere have asked the Catholic Church for an apology for the five-hundred-plus years of colonization and for all the brutalities committed in the name of Christianity..."

Oannes unexpectedly stops and asks, catching me unprepared: "But you want to talk about the subject of your research, right? You want to talk about Immokalee..." he says, staring at me with his lash-less eyes.

I nod my head, sighing. I ask him about the origins of the name Immokalee. But conciseness is definitely not one of Oannes's qualities...

He begins by pointing out that, again, he does not belong to the Seminoles, so he cannot speak *for* them. He adds, though, that he's a close friend of their representatives. "I only have positive things to say about the Seminole community in general."

Yet, Oannes hasn't always agreed with the choices made by the tribal council. He says, for instance, that he was in disagreement with them regarding certain positions they have taken regarding the energy operations development in the Everglades region.

"The Seminoles were indeed interested in a partnership with Florida Power Light (FPL) that intended to build a coal power plant on one of their territories..." Oannes explains. "I don't want to say where exactly because that is their land," he adds. "Legislators were making it seem as if it was about the right to self-government and auto-determination but that was hogwash. They were using the issue of Seminole self-determination to better serve the interests of this big corporation. I can say that we of the Yat Kitischee Native Center,[70] together with a coalition of environmentalists, were able to stop that operation with the S.I.N.G. (*Save It Now, Glades!*) campaign."

Oannes is referring to the victory won by a group of environmentalists who prevented the construction of two 980-megawatt coal power plants in the middle of the Everglades. In May 2006, the Florida Public Service Commission denied the permit to build the so-called Glades Power Park by resolving that the proposed plants did not represent the most efficient alternative at the moment.[71]

Oannes pauses, so I ask him another question: What does he have to say about the relations between the people of Immokalee and the Seminoles? Oannes continues as if he hasn't been interrupted and has actually read my mind, showing me that *there* was exactly where he was going with his reasoning.

"All of us, regardless of where we happen to live, have the responsibility not only to take care of Mother Earth but also of our own communities. It's what I call 'Earth Justice' and it comprises the right of *every* form of life. Pollution and the poisoning of Mother Earth from farmers with the use of fertilizers and pesticides, for instance, is first an economic, social, political, and then an environmental, problem."

Oannes is indeed highly critical of certain kinds of environmentalism. "We love to save whales and wolves and eagles and I agree as a Native American because I consider animals as part of my family, but I'm also very angry, because after thirty years of environmentalism the vast majority of promoters of the preservation of Nature, which are mostly white, do not support the struggles for economic and social justice. They cannot see the link between the CIW struggles and the ones of the environmentalist movements. That's why in the nineties we worked to develop a national environmental justice movement."

Oannes's commitment to farmworkers' rights is also rooted in his past as a blueberry and cranberry picker in Maine. "The cranberry flower is a medicinal plant sacred to the Native Americans," Oannes continues. "But with the coming of agribusiness and the mass production of cranberry sauce, especially during Thanksgiving…well, things have changed, and for the worst." Oannes also believes that the exposure to pesticide used in blueberry farms contributed to his illness.

"There's a lack of accountability. That's the real problem. And this is often at the origin of the disconnection between indigenous communities and the rest of the population."

"When I arrived here, over twenty years ago, a good part of the labor force was made up of Seminole and Miccosukee Indians. In the last few years, we have seen enormous economic and political progress for the Indian nation. Thanks to the casino, the Seminoles have been able to get out of poverty: they have built modern houses and bought fancy cars. Their conditions have got better...At least on the material level."

"However, indigenous people should fight together..." Oannes says, finally getting to his main point. "Would you like to take a ride to Naples?" Oannes asks without pausing. "It's only half an hour from here." He wants to show me the change in scenery, and, maybe, get out of the house for a little.

Before leaving, I ask Oannes whether the necklace he wears has any particular meaning. It's crafted artfully with a green turtle as a pendant. "We call this part of the Earth...the northern American continent," he begins.

"The Great Turtle Island" to indicate the sacredness of this place and of our native lands...We, the indigenous people of North America, have many stories about the creation of this region of the world. One of these has to do with the Great Spirit. Sky Woman was falling from the sky and the aquatic animals offered to bring up the mud so that she would have had a place to land. The turtle said they could put mud on her shell. And that's how this part of the world, North America, was born.

The turtle represents the spiritual life. It's a very intelligent animal, often stupidly mocked by people because of its slowness. Turtles actually think about the consequences of their actions before they make a move. That's the way we've been raised in our culture...with these types of values. The turtle represents the intelligence and the patience, the ability to learn to think before making a decision. We've been taught to consider the effects that our actions and thoughts can have on the following seven generations...So the turtle teaches us not to be motivated by anger or selfishness or jealousy when we make a decision.

Oannes finishes speaking, finally displaying his toothless smile.

Apartheid South Florida

I help Oannes get into the car. We make it, though with some difficulty. I close the door and, instructed by Oannes, begin to steer the wheelchair back to the doorstep.

"That's alright. Thanks!" Oannes yells from the car.

We drive back to Immokalee Road, turn left, and pass 951, Collier Boulevard. Suddenly, just like Oannes warned me, the landscape radically changes: gone are the cheap motels, the half-deserted gas stations, the tall cypress trees, and the derelict buildings; a series of residential communities, country clubs, and golf courses with names like Stonebridge and Pelican have now replaced them. The gated communities get more and more luxurious as we drive west, and so do the entrances, which get more monumental the further they get from the homes dispersed along the endless labyrinthian drives.

"It's like a science fiction movie, don't you think?" Oannes remarks. "It's like going from one world to another."

"At six in the morning you see the buses leave Immokalee to come to Naples," he continues. "They stop at the corner of these fabulous villas or at the entrance of one of these gated communities. Then you see the women, primarily Hispanic, but also Black, African American, and Haitian, get out of the buses and go work as housemaids..." Oannes says.

"And the men in landscaping," Oannes adds as he waves to a bunch of workers who are mowing grass on the side of the road.

"Then around five o'clock you see these people, the ones I call 'the servants,' lining up at the bus stop, waiting for their ride back to Immokalee. God forbid by any chance the police find them at night in downtown Naples! To me it's similar to what was happening in South

Africa when the Black people were leaving the bantustan to go work for the Whites. That's why I call this area 'apartheid South Florida.'"

We enter Pelican Bay and drive by the Philharmonic Center for the Arts, the new theater hosting the best ballets and concerts in town. We slow down while passing the building to admire its structure, and a traffic policeman yells at us and waves his arms to move, *quickly, quickly,* and it seems to me that he is so irritated for no other apparent reason than the fact that I am driving a fourteen-year-old Honda Civic that has lost most of its paint because of the unmerciful Florida sun.

We finally get to Fifth Avenue, the heart of Naples, with all its pricey stores, bars, and restaurants. Oannes shows me the art gallery where his wife works. He invites me to look at the people who are walking on the sidewalk, the ones sitting at the tables all equipped with wide umbrellas to protect them from the blinding sun.

"They are *all* white. The 'colored,'" Oannes points out with sarcasm, "are hidden in the kitchens."

"The only ones with the authority to say who can stay legally or not in North America are my people!" Oannes erupts. "It's time that we start passing out green cards to the ones that *we* believe are eligible to stay in the American territories! All the others should be deported...to the other side of the ocean!" Then he pauses. "I'm kidding...obviously," says Oannes, now all serious. "But this whole idea of the 'illegal aliens' and the border between so-called Latin America and North America is another example of unbelievable racism."

"The so-called border between the United States and Mexico is land of the indigenous people, just like Guatemala and the territories between Guatemala and Mexico. That border, too, is just another invention of colonialism! And all those white supremacists, like the

Minutemen, are the ones that one time persecuted Native Americans and now are after the immigrants from Central and Latin America."

Oannes illustrates his theories, jumping from one topic to another, getting lost in historical details and anecdotes, yet I can now recognize the rigorousness of his reasoning. Oannes keeps talking into my tape recorder and for a while I have the feeling that something revolutionary is actually happening in this car. Oannes speaks on:

> Plus, these migratory waves have been caused by disastrous policies, especially during the Reagan administration, supported by the United States in Central and Latin America. And [because of] the brutalities of the military dictatorships that the United States has helped reach and maintain the power there. The School of the Americas (SOA) is an example of this strategy, just like the 'corporativization' of the territories that once belonged to the campesinos by multinationals, most of which are North American.[72] Or treaties like NAFTA, signed in 1994, or the Central America Free Trade Agreement, or the Free Trade Agreement of the Andes...These are all cases in point of this ongoing colonization that today they call globalization...The poor people in Immokalee come from Guatemala, Mexico, and the other regions south of the Rio Grande. They are here as a result of the longtime warfare waged by the United States against the indigenous peoples.

Or maybe not. Maybe Oannes is just an idealist suffering from a plague widespread among his people, so ill that he can't even get out of the car since we haven't brought the wheelchair with us. He can't help but keep talking about social justice, solidarity among indigenous people, and the protection of Mother Nature to an imaginary audience in the free and unlimited space of the Internet.

Even if so, I look at the setting sun, and want to believe that not everything is lost because *there are* people listening to Oannes,[73] like the many young minds he inspired with his words and presence at the Encuentros organized annually by the Student/Farmworker Alliance.[74]

Horizon Village

The next day, I decide to go visit the Horizon Village, the housing complex Monica told me about. It's there that the male guests from the Friendship House are sent once their stay limit is up at the temporary homeless shelter.

To reach the Horizon Village is not an easy enterprise. Located behind the subsidiary sheriff station, the building is not visible from any of the main roads. Nonetheless, its construction had to comply with the standards of urban decor of Collier County; as a result, the housing complex cost more than intended, landing the Housing Authority in debt. Ironically so, in a town like Immokalee, one just needs to walk across the road from the Horizon Village to find the urban decay that is ever present downtown.

Juan and Dan, two filmmakers in town shooting a documentary, have some time off and offer to drive me to the Horizon. We take Immokalee Road (here called First Street), and then turn into the housing projects, primarily inhabited by Haitians. There are people sitting outside, playing cards. They look at us suspiciously as we drive slowly through the unpaved road that skirts the building. Once we get to the end, Dan speeds up to make it over the crest of the curve; "It's the only way I know," he tells me, hanging out the window of his car.

I accelerate, too, until I get back to the paved road leading into the parking lot of the Horizon Village that I now see in all its longitude, a yellow cathedral standing out against the Floridian, cerulean backdrop.

Two stocky, dirty white columns support the yellow lintel and the vault above it and lead visitors to the housing complex's waiting room. But here, too, offices are closed today because of the Thanksgiving holiday—so say two men standing in front of the Horizon. I try to communicate with them in Spanish, but I'm having a hard time until Juan, who is Colombian, comes nearer and offers to translate for me.

The younger of the two men, Francisco,* is an eighteen-year-old Mexican. He smiles a lot and speaks softly. The other one, Jorge,* is in his forties. He is a short, sturdy man with a friendly round face. Jorge comes from Hidalgo, Mexico, and makes up for Francisco's shyness.

There is lot of excitement in Immokalee in anticipation of the march on Burger King, so I ask the men if they intend to participate. Francisco says he reserved his seat on the bus already. Last year he went to Chicago to participate in the CIW march on McDonald's. He's been in town for three years; he picks tomatoes, watermelons, and sweet potatoes. Jorge doesn't know anybody here. He arrived in Immokalee only three weeks ago. He just met Francisco…right here. Jorge has been waiting for his roommate actually…since he forgot his badge and got locked out. "I have to talk to my boss Friday, he owes me money," Jorge says. Then he begins to complain about the work in Immokalee. "It's too hard," he says. "We don't just have to pick tomatoes here," Jorge adds, "but also clean them, get rid of the stems and everything, and the buckets always have to be bulging with tomatoes."

Jorge hasn't worked for the last four days. "I don't have money to go to the march," he finally says. I tell him that it is free: the CIW will provide for meals and lodging. But he shakes his head. "I have to talk to my boss Friday." Jorge says. "Plus, I haven't sent any money home in three weeks." Jorge usually goes to the Mexican store here in Immokalee: he pays twelve dollars in commission for every five hundred that he sends to Mexico, fifteen for one hundred. Not bad, he says. Stores like this are associated with money transfer companies like Western Union and generally offer rather dependable services.

Back in Mexico, Jorge has a wife and three children. The region where they live, Hidalgo, is very poor. The local economy is based on agriculture: they grow lettuce, tomatoes, and other produce. Last year, he says proudly, the cameras got to Hidalgo…Some American filmmakers…

Jorge won't stop talking while I'd like to involve Francisco in the conversation; the young man has moved away from us, his back against the wall of the Horizon. When Jorge announces that in the last ten years he has crossed the border five times, he immediately recaptures our attention, perhaps knowingly so.

"I have been lucky, because they have never caught me. Last time I gave $1,800 to the *coyote* but he abandoned me in the desert…the first time, in 2005, I had paid 1,300." Jorge has worked all over the Southeast (Florida, the Carolinas, and Missouri), where he has harvested pineapples, watermelons, and even tobacco. Jorge tells us he's never been to a protest.

"I don't know anybody," he says. "I always stay in one place not long enough to make friends. Plus, if I go to the march, I miss a day of work. I pay $56 a week for lodging and another fifty to eat. If I don't work enough, I can't send money home." The other reason, the obvious one he doesn't yet express in words, is fear.

Fear of repercussions.

In fact, Jorge, most likely to justify the grounding of his fears, recounts an anecdote: "Once I was in North Carolina for work. I was on the side of the road along with other migrant workers. We were all waiting for a truck to take us to the fields. At one point, a container truck pulled over. The driver asks if we wanted to work. Then he invited us to jump on the truck. But we didn't because we didn't trust him."

Jorge pauses.

"There was something that didn't convince us about that container truck and those people…something was strange. It turned out that they were ICE agents[75] in disguise and they were trying to arrest us," he says.

Jorge doesn't say how they found out they were ICE agents and not contractors. "They were strange," he keeps repeating. Jorge just wants us to understand that if you don't have legal documents to work here, you always need to be cautious of *la migra*, which can take different forms, and one could very well be disguised as a farmworker like you, or an activist. That's why Jorge learned to be self-sufficient, and not to trust anybody. Yet, he says repeatedly, "As long as I'm capable, I keep traveling to the States to provide for my family."

Francisco came to the United States when he was fifteen. The coyote didn't even cross all the way with him: he left the boy in the middle of the Arizona desert. Francisco walked at night until he arrived in Phoenix. With his first five weeks of work, he paid off his debt to the coyote.

Francisco is sitting on the floor, stuck to the wall. As he tells his story in bits and pieces, he rolls into a ball, closer and closer to the wall as if to seek refuge in there. His uncle knew the coyote and was able to make a guarantee for him. Francisco could cross the border by himself, without running the risk of becoming an indentured slave for unscrupulous crew leaders as too often happens to young, vulnerable, undocumented immigrants like him.

At the Carnival

I eventually decide to drop by the carnival. Traditionally, the "carnis" come to Immokalee for the Thanksgiving weekend bringing much-needed entertainment for kids and grown-ups alike, and giving everybody an excuse to keep celebrating until Sunday. The carnival is being held in the wide space behind the Guadalupe Church, in the large field where young boys and men usually play soccer.

Outside the carnival, vendors sell tamales.[76] From the open trunk, whole kernel corn topped with grated cheese and butter are also sold in white plastic cups. Most of the sellers are women who cooked the food at home in an effort to make some extra income.

Entire families stroll around the unpaved ways of the carnival, getting lost and finding themselves again. The rides are many and placed too close to each other; music, voices, and brazen sounds overlap almost completely, making a babel of underlying languages.

A guy with an annoying voice gets my attention and apparently the attention of many others. A crowd has indeed gathered in front of the attraction and seems amused. The performer is on top of a yellow slide: protected by a net, and speaking into his super-loud microphone. He invites the participants to hit the red target behind him. When they do, he falls down into the water. To tease the paying pitchers to throw harder, the showman makes fun of them with his croaking voice.

"Hey, *chink!* Can't you get me? Do you want me to call Jackie Chan to help?" he now addresses an Asian-looking guy. The audience seems entertained, while the participant attempts a smile—as if to say "I am cool, it's just a game"—while red-faced, he violently launches the ball in the effort to hit the target.

It's time to go to bed.

I stopped by the CIW; I know Paco is there. My friend comes out sipping his matè with a *bombilla,* the typical steeled straw. He walks me home.

"I have to go back though," he says. As we walk the short distance to his house, Paco tells me that there is an important meeting at the

CIW: they are discussing a new case of slavery some members have discovered recently.[77]

We get home. Paco holds the door for me, and hands me the matè. Then he jumps on his bike and disappears into the night.

Leonel, a member of CIW and the band Son del Centro, taking part in the march on Burger King in Miami, November 30, 2007

Three

LUCHANDO POR COMIDA JUSTA

Immokalee farmworkers won't obtain their raises before Christmas. At the beginning of November, the Florida Tomato Growers Exchange (FTGE), which represents 90 percent of the state's farmers, threatened to fine up to $100,000 any member of the organization who agreed to pay the pickers one cent more per pound and thus complied with the agreements signed by Taco Bell and McDonald's. In the meantime, the CIW and the corporations have jointly created an escrow account to collect the extra money earned by the pickers as a result of the agreements until it can be dispersed to the workers. The FTGE decision not only prevents laborers from getting the raise but also further reveals the close ties of the local growers with Burger King. Hence, the Coalition of Immokalee Workers decided to center its actions in Florida this time. Burger King headquarters is located in Miami, and the interests of the fast food giant are deeply rooted in local economic politics.

After the liberalization of the North American market with NAFTA, U.S. growers have coped with rising operating costs (i.e., gas for transportation) and increased competition from Mexican farmers (by keeping workers' wages low). On the other hand, fast food chains' demand for cheap tomatoes has put additional pressure on the growers. Thus, the idea of paying more for labor, even just one cent more per pound, seems like a blasphemy. It's "Un-American," according to Reggie Brown, vice executive president of the FTGE. The arrangement, however, would result in almost doubling the workers' wages: from 45 to 77 cents per bucket of tomatoes.

"Why would [growers] allow anyone other than their own management to set wage rates?" Brown added.[1] Perhaps because the bonuses of top executives of Goldman Sachs, the primary bank holding company subsidizing Burger King, exceeded $200 million in 2006. Twice as much the amount ten thousand tomato pickers collectively earned in South Florida during the same year.[2]

The irony is that the famous one cent per pound is not even coming out of the farmers' pocket; the world's largest fast food restaurant company Yum! Brands—which controls Taco Bell—and McDonald's are paying for the increase. The collaboration of the growers, however, is crucial to the implementation of the program—in the end, *they* are the ones who will sign the checks to the workers.

Regardless of their status, whether they are American citizens or seasonal workers on H-2A visas or undocumented immigrants, Florida farmworkers still earn sub-poverty wages and have no right to overtime compensation, health insurance, or paid vacation. To begin with, they are asking for fairer wages. In essence, they are asking the American people to consider who harvests the food that ends up on their tables.

Burger King gave in to the requests of animal rights groups and recently changed its policies regarding the use of pork and eggs in its products, thus getting ahead of the competition in terms of animal welfare standards.[3] Burger King's decision came after a nine-month-long "Murder King" campaign led by People for the Ethical Treatment of Animals (PETA). Yet, the fast food chain has repeatedly refused to sit down with the CIW and discuss its demand to address basic workers' rights, human rights.

Conversely, Burger King has questioned the migrants' poverty by claiming tomato pickers earn up to $18 per hour if they are fast.[4] Two days before the protest, Burger King's nonprofit branch, Have It Your Way Foundation, donated $25,000 to the Redlands Christian Migrant Association (RCMA), the childcare and education center located on Main Street in Immokalee. (I guess you can always count on charity when it's motivated by a guilty conscience.)

A few months earlier, the fast food chain had offered to send its representatives to Immokalee to recruit labor to work in Burger King's restaurants.[5] Lucas Benitez, member and spokesperson of the CIW, rejected the proposal as "an obviously unworkable, and frankly pretty ridiculous idea."[6]

Eliminating farmworkers to eliminate poverty in the end is the same logic governing the all-American tradition of the "turkey pardoning": sparing a few to justify the slaughter of the many. Reggie Brown might be right after all: CIW's ways *are* un-American.

Miami Stops to Listen to Immokalee
Friday, November 30, 2007

It's only nine in the morning but the sun is shining high already. It looks like it's going to be a very hot day. The hurricane season is officially over today, the radio reminds Floridians. For the second consecutive year, the Sunshine State has been spared by this often-devastating force of nature.

I'm driving down to Miami when NPR announces that the supporters of the Coalition of Immokalee Workers will take over the streets of the city...

A thousand migrant farmworkers will march nine miles to the doorstep of Burger King's headquarters in Miami. They're demanding a raise: a penny per pound of the tomatoes they harvest. It doesn't sound like much, but Burger King is still putting up a fight. From our America's Desk at WLRN, Dan Grech reports.[7]

I arrive at Bayfront on Biscayne Boulevard—downtown Miami, the financial center of the city. It's 10 o'clock by now, and a cheerful crowd has gathered in front of the Florida headquarters of Goldman Sachs. The yellow T-shirts of the Fair Food Campaign are being distributed to the participants: they display a parody of the logo of the fast food chain. The word "Burger" has been substituted with "Exploitation," so it reads "Exploitation King." Below, "Burger King Exploits Farmworkers" is restated. Nearby, the Intercontinental Hotel is being invaded by hordes of yellow-clad protesters in search of restroom facilities before the beginning of the march. I go too, moved by a similar need, and jump into the carousel of the hotel's doors. Intercontinental staff members, all clad in a stiff livery, follow our moves half-surprised and half-wary, unsure about how to handle the massive influx of visitors.

Representatives of several unions, and political and religious organizations that support the CIW are getting on the stage, which is set up on the back of a big truck that will lead the march.

They deliver their speeches before the march begins. Among them are Eliseo Medina, vice executive president of the Service Employees International Union (SEIU); Lucas Benitez, spokesperson of the

CIW; and Noelle D'Amico, pastor of the Presbyterian Church U.S.A. (PCUSA) and national coordinator of PCUSA's Fair Food Campaign.

There's a lot of excitement in the air: the big day has come. Around three hundred people have gathered in front of the stage to listen. By the time we get to the Burger King headquarters, more than two thousand individuals and group members representing various grassroots organizations from the Miami area and beyond will have joined and flowed into the river of the march.

We start walking. The marchers pass by the Torch of Friendship, the monument erected in 1960 by John F. Kennedy to celebrate the special relationship between Miami and Central and Latin American countries.

The perpetual flame is burning for every nation, each one of them remembered with a medallion on the concave wall that surrounds the short obelisk located in the middle: the Dominican Republic, Jamaica, Haiti, Panama, Nicaragua, Honduras, Costa Rica, Mexico, Guatemala, Guyana, Suriname, Colombia, Ecuador, Peru, Chile, Argentina, Uruguay, Paraguay, and Brazil. All the Central and Latin American countries but one: Cuba. Cuba occupies a special place in the consciousness of the United States, particularly Miami's.

Biscayne Boulevard. The palm trees stand sentinel along our way, and the music begins to play beside the festive marchers. I catch a glimpse, behind the convex skyscrapers, of the Freedom Tower, the building modeled after the Giralda, the Gothic-Baroque cathedral of Seville. Today, the Freedom Tower is the property of the Miami-Dade Cuban American National Foundation. In the sixties, the federal government established the reception center for Cuban refugees here. Once the refugees arrived in Miami, they received health insurance and other benefits, and were instructed about the quick and easy process of integration into American society—a treatment the U.S.

government specially reserved for them, unthinkable for any other Latino immigrant.

As we pass by, I notice two flags, the American and the Cuban, affixed on the sides of the building, there to reaffirm the anomalous rapport with the nearby Caribbean island and to represent the sentiments of the many anti-Castro Cuban residents of Miami. So the imposing Freedom Tower oddly compensates for the absence of Cuba among the countries listed on the wall that surrounds the Torch of Friendship and reaffirms the partial union, marked, to this day, by a profound ideological rift with the Cuban government.

Photographers and camera operators in search of the most panoramic shot invade the staircase of the American Airlines Arena. We marched past the belittling, brand-new, electric blue skyscrapers. Ahead, from an elevated scaffold, the workers have stopped and are looking down on the march. Some of them timidly begin to wave at us, more soon join: the enthusiasm of the crowd below is too contagious, and, energized, we wave back with double cheerfulness. We're walking through the underpass now, and the resounding drums and choruses are giving me goose bumps.

Justicia Ahora! Justicia Ahora! Justicia Ahora! (Justice now! Justice now! Justice now!) We pass the brand-new Carnival Center and the Ziff Ballet Opera House. We approach the first Burger King and the march begins with a new chorus.

Some of the police in vehicles who have been escorting us speed up and are now guarding the fast food store. But the march is absolutely peaceful. We turn onto Twentieth Street and the scenery dramatically changes. The street is desolate, and the buildings on the side are crumbling.

Big trees provide the first real shade since the start of the march. We are now in the neighborhood called Wynwood—also known as Little San Juan or El Barrio—historically inhabited by a largely Puerto Rican population that is now relocating to wealthier neighborhoods, leaving room for the newcomers: poorer immigrants from Central America.

We continue our walk north on Twentieth. We get to the African American neighborhood of Overtown, one of the poorest communities in Miami but also one of the oldest. Its development dates back to the end of the eighteenth century when workers who were building the railroad envisioned by developer Henry Flagler populated the area.

During the era of legal segregation, Color Town, which later became Overtown, was created. At one time, it was a commercially and culturally vibrant community: African American artists, musicians, intellectuals, and writers the likes of Billy Holiday, Ella Fitzgerald, W. E. B. Du Bois, and Zora Neale Hurston stayed here while in Miami. Today, Overtown counts a population of ten thousand with an annual median household income of $13,000.[8]

In the sixties, the area got divided in two by the construction of the highway (I-95): another tale of racist and anti-poor urban policies similar to Robert Moses's development plan that resulted in the construction in New York City of the Cross Bronx Expressway (1948–1972). In New York, the construction of the expressway worsened the decay of the South Bronx and forced many Blacks to relocate elsewhere.

The neighborhood organization Power U has been fighting Crosswinds Condos, the gentrification project named after the Michigan development company that intends to transform this neighborhood of Miami into an upscale residential area by building on publicly owned land—just like the upscale Crosswinds Communities in Detroit.[9]

Power U and the people of Overtown welcome the marchers with a banner that encourages the protesters who have come from all over the United States in support of the CIW and its struggle against Burger King.

Here is where I meet Camilo Mejía. Camilo tells me that he's an Iraq war veteran, the first who resisted and refused to go back there and fight for a war he has never endorsed. He was then declared a deserter and spent nine months in the military jail in Fort Sill, Oklahoma. Camilo tells me that he wrote a book, a memoir.[10] He believes that the movement against the war should be closely linked to the one against any form of social injustice. The so-called war on terror is anything but a war for natural resources, he will explain the day after at the workshop on war. (Camilo, who lives in Miami, was the chairperson of the board of directors of Iraq Veterans Against the War and represented them at the march here in support of the struggle of the Coalition of Immokalee Workers.)

A young woman asks me to hold the banner with the sign "Power U Is on Your Side" and then disappears. I'm left with Camilo to hold the banner until the march dries up. The yellow cordon winds throughout the neighborhoods of this capital of social injustice where the divide between rich and poor is among the highest in the country, pooling Miami in with so many other Latin American metropolises. I leave Camilo to rejoin the march.

We go through the colorful "*la veinte y la veinte*"—the neighborhood so called because it covers the area between Twentieth Street and Twentieth Avenue. Here the road widens; on the sides, several 99 cent stores still survive, spaced out by mechanics' garages and some ethnic supermarkets.

We pass by the firefighters' station, and again the screams and encouraging greetings of the people lined up on the sidewalks, just like an audience at a bike race, strengthen the purpose and cheer the spirits of the marchers.

I have goose bumps, despite the increasingly suffocating heat. The cars stop at the traffic lights, and CIW members take the opportunity to hand out informational material on the struggles of the workers and the reasons for this march against Burger King. Some drivers ask questions, leaning out the windows; they want to know more, and so Lionel, Roberto, or Cruz of the CIW along with Marc, Meghan, and others of the Student/Farmworker Alliance stop and provide explanations, brief yet to the point. "Burger King exploits the farmworkers." "Florida farmworkers are still getting paid like in 1978." Then they joined the march again, running on the side to catch up with their original group.

I begin walking with Candera. Candera comes from Kenya and arrived in the United States in 1992 to study; she lives in Gainesville, Florida, where she now manages Dorothy's Café, named after Dorothy Day, the journalist and activist who in 1933 founded in New York the Catholic Worker Movement.

In Gainesville, too, Candera says, there is a recruiting point where laborers wait; this one not exclusively for the workforce in agriculture. Every Sunday, at three in the morning, volunteers from Dorothy's Café bring fresh-baked bread to the workers (who gather, I imagine, in a place not that different from Immokalee's Pantry) waiting for someone to pick them up for work.

A beautiful young woman, Dominique, smiles and asks me kindly if I can hold her big banner. Dominique is dressed in a rather extravagant manner, with plumes and flowers, so it doesn't surprise me when she says that she studies theater. She is part of the Students for a Democratic Society at the University of Central Florida in Orlando. She says that they recently organized a sit-in in front of the Burger King on the campus.

It's twelve thirty. We stop for lunch at Jerry Curtis Park. It's here that I see the shoes, lined up in the trailer that the truck spearheading the march will pull when we resume. The CIW collected the old shoes from Immokalee workers to bring them to the Burger King headquarters for the company's executives to see. "Doubt Our Poverty? Walk in Our Shoes/*No Crees in Nuestra Pobreza? Camina en Nuestros Zapatos*," proclaim the signs over the hundreds of boots set up on the truck's trailer.

Tables covered with sandwiches and sodas are arrayed on the basketball court of the park. People sit on the grass, many looking for the well-deserved shade. I see Eliseo Medina of the SEIU. Medina, currently SEIU's executive vice president, was once a grape-picker. Young Medina participated in the historic United Farm Workers' strike in Delano, California, and for over thirteen years worked with César Chávez, becoming United Farm Workers' national vice president.

I take advantage of the lunch break to ask Medina some questions regarding the tactics adopted by the CIW in its struggle for workers' rights. Eliseo wears a blue SEIU T-shirt with the unequivocal question *What Would Rosa Parks Do?* over a long-sleeved, periwinkle shirt. Sitting on the grass, knees bent up to the chest, Eliseo begins to explain. The lack of a federal law allows agricultural workers to bring forward their requests to a third party as the CIW did: with Taco Bell first, and McDonald's after, and now with Burger King. Since farmworkers are not covered by the National Labor Relations Act (1935),[11] the UFW was able to carry out a secondary boycott against grocery chains selling boycotted grapes and lettuce in the 1970s.[12]

In the CIW's case, since the workers have an ongoing dispute with their primary employers, and not specifically with the fast food chains over their pay, they have the freedom to attack Burger King and possibly invite customers to boycott it—as happened with Taco Bell.[13]

Unions like the SEIU couldn't do this because "secondary boy-cotts" have been outlawed since 1947 (the Taft-Hartley Act) with the motivation that they would represent "coercive" practices as the economic repercussions would fall on other subjects, different from the ones with whom the union has been negotiating. [14]

"On the other hand," Medina continues, "at the end of the eighteenth century, the boycott of a third party was quite a common practice in the United States."

In 1947, the Taft-Hartley Act defined this course of action adopted by the unions as among "unfair labor practices," thus contributing to further weakening the effective capability of American unions to pressure the employers. The legal definition of boycott, however, is quite unclear, and the same U.S. workers' organizations have got around it sometimes.

"Reality is far more alarming," Medina adds. "Things have gotten worse for the unions. Fact is, workers' rights have been eroded so much in the last few years and the unions have lost most of their negotiating power. Besides, the law now protects more the employers than the workers. If a worker gets fired for union activity," Eliseo continues, "It takes years to obtain a trial. And if the employers are eventually found guilty, the penalty is minimal. So for them this doesn't work as a deterrent...In other words, it doesn't stop them from firing the workers who organize."[15]

From this disadvantaged position, the CIW made a virtue of necessity, and capitalized on the increased freedom of action that the law allowed agricultural workers. In Immokalee, the high turnover of the labor force renders the adoption of traditional forms of workers' organization practically impossible. SEIU itself, Medina continues, makes sparing use today of the National Labor Relations Act.

In the seventies, as a UFW Florida director, Medina managed to sign a contract for 1,200 citrus grove workers with Coca-Cola (owner of Minute Maid) but the resistance of the Florida Farm Bureau and its members nullified the attempts to establish a strong UFW presence in Florida.[16] Medina was one of the main organizers of the service workers' strike that in April 2000 resulted in the highest raise in the history of the Justice for Janitors Campaign led by the SEIU.[17]

"That campaign, too," Eliseo continues, "was based on protests geared toward popular mobilization to pressure the employers. It was not so different from the CIW's tactics. In the years to come, unless the law changes, these are the types of actions that will prove more effective. So it is still better to rely on mobilizing people than on the National Labor Relations Board."

I finally see Paco. He's wearing the orange vest of people volunteering to help the CIW with security. His job this morning has been picking up the last of the speakers at the airport. Indeed, Paco says, he hasn't been able to really enjoy the march yet. But he's happy to see that more and more people are joining. He apologizes, in his way, for not returning my calls. He has been going through some problems at work: there've been cuts at the Guadalupe Center, and he is afraid they are going to fire him.

Before we start walking again, I meet Father Patrick, one of the priests of the Guadalupe Church in Immokalee. Father Patrick—or Padre Patricio, as many in Immokalee call him—has close set, blue eyes that he is forced to squint because of the strong sun; he has a round, ruddy face that makes him seem younger than he is. He introduces me to Tequila, his big, black dog, "a chocolate Labrador Retriever."

We start off again and approach the Twenty-Seventh Avenue Bridge. Father Patrick sets the pace, fast. He begins to converse, extremely jovially, as if he has known me for years, and asks me a lot of questions. His laugh resonates loud and high. He says he is trying to catch up with some friends or parishioners, or both, I don't understand, as he speeds up his pace even more. (*We are almost running now.*)

As we walk briskly over the bridge, and the warm wind ruffles our hair, Father Patrick invites me to go visit him in Immokalee.

"Take a look at the website," he says. "But remember the right address," he screams. Tequila is running ahead now. "There are so many 'Guadalupe Churches' on the Internet!" says Padre Patricio, bursting into a loud laugh, which gets immediately lost in the wind and leaves me just with his red, smiling face. I ask him, screaming myself, to repeat the name of the website, now holding my little notebook. Father Patrick gets nearer and begins to write as he proceeds quickly to avoid losing even more ground.

I join a group of middle-aged women. They are here to represent the Saint Moritz Church in Hollywood, south of Fort Lauderdale. They joined the march only at the park, which explains why they look so rested. Meanwhile, I'm getting tired, despite the pleasant wind.

We begin to chat as we enter the area called Miami Central, between southwest Miami and Hialeah. There are more colorful stores with only Spanish signs around. On the left, we skirt the Flagler Dog Track and the opposite big square that hosts the flea market on the weekends. On the right, there is a women's hair salon: a bunch of cheerful, curious, curler-ed ladies have crowded on the sidewalk to wave and encourage the marchers.

We pass in front of more Burger Kings and the choruses intensify, while the bewildered customers emerge to check out the march. "They started giving out free burgers here," one guy says. "I got one myself but now that I know about your struggle, I won't eat there anymore!" At another Burger King, employees have started handing out water bottles to the protesters. The marchers commend the gesture of solidarity.

We find a McDonald's and the protesters clap their hands. (*Since McDonald's conceded to the CIW requests, it made it to the good list.*) We turn onto Seventh Street and new groups join the march, like the Bolivarian Youth with its chairman Michael Martinez, waiting in front of the organization's headquarters, Radio Miami.

A hippie-looking girl smiles at me. She's holding a stick of white sage: her sister told her to diffuse it in the air. She couldn't make it to the march, but the sage she gave her will bring peacefulness. The sage produces a lovely aroma and the march goes on peacefully indeed: the cops escort us, even laughing and joking with the protesters at times.

I ask a guy how many people he thinks there are marching.

"I have no idea," he says. Steve (that's his name) is wearing a CIW hat; underneath, a T-shirt to soak up the sweat. We begin to talk and Steve turns out to be an attorney who has worked with the CIW since 1994. He lived for years in Latin America and now works in Washington as a managing attorney for the national Health Law Program, a law firm that works to provide health insurance for low-income people.

"My job with the CIW is limited. I only make sure that their actions are being brought forward within legality." He pauses. "The goal of all this," continues Steve, looking around, "It's not to change the law...but to mobilize the people."

Steve tells me about his trips to Latin America. Only now I realize that Steve walks with a limp. "I only got off the truck a hundred feet back...Motor accident," he says anticipating my question. Cars are honking at the march on this wide and busy road. It's four thirty by now, Friday afternoon, and Miami is getting ready for the weekend. We keep talking about Immokalee.

"So you belong to the second category…" Steve says at one point.

"What do you mean?" I ask.

"Well, you see…during the years, I've seen people having two very different reactions when they visit Immokalee. There are the ones who cannot wait to get the hell out and the ones who can't help but go back, always, as if that place has gotten into their blood."

By now we have reached the imposing building that hosts Burger King headquarters: a convex structure guarded by the palms below.

We mingle with the crowd. "What was your impression of Immokalee the first time you visited?" I ask Steve.

"It's almost like being in some small town in Costa Rica. Honestly, I wouldn't live there."

Steve greets Laura Germino, one of the people pivotal to the creation of the CIW, and he introduces me to her. Laura is a slender woman with severe features and sparse yet sweet smiles. She shakes my hand as she bends over a stroller, to give some water to her son. From behind the blue-stained glass windows of the building, silhouettes of Burger King personnel appear, probably made curious by the colorful gathering nestled at the feet of the headquarters.

I take out my notebook, and Steve gets immediately suspicious.

"I have to talk to Laura and Greg (Asbed) before I can release an interview. In the end, *they* are my clients," he says.

I tease Steve for a while; he's acting just like a lawyer right now, but I see that he is actually quite serious about it, so I don't insist. Meanwhile, on the stage, a series of emcees are inciting the crowd, hip-hop groups and traditional Mexican bands, all friends and supporters of the coalition.

They give the mike to more speakers, supporters of the CIW: Kerry Kennedy, here representing the Robert F. Kennedy Memorial

Center for Human Rights; Marleine Bastien (Haitian Women of Miami); Tony Romano (Miami Workers Center), and many more. Thousands of candles light up as the sun begins to turn pink in the Miami sky.

It's five o'clock. The Burger King employers leave the office, go down, unseen, to the garage, turn on the engines of their cars, and go home to eat a dinner that someone else probably prepared for them. Most likely, they will eat produce from around Immokalee.

Francisca Cortez and Gerardo Reyes pick up a couple of boots among the many ones that have been displayed along the flowerbed that surrounds the building. Mercedeses, Ferraris, and Lamborghinis pass by the area where the protesters have been fenced in, for "security reasons." In the distance, we see a blond woman taking the boots that Gerardo hands her. The crowd interprets the gesture as a victory sign and rejoices. Maybe Burger King agreed, metaphorically, to begin a dialogue with the CIW. But several months will pass and unimaginable things will happen before the CIW will be able to knock out the king of fast food.

Miami, Saturday, December 1, 2007

The day after the march provides an opportunity for reflection: CIW workers and members of the different organizations get together at the African Heritage Cultural Arts Center. The facility is located in the Black neighborhood of Liberty City where the Miami Workers Center also is, and where in June 2006, seven men (who soon became known as "the Liberty City 7") got arrested on charges of comprising the core of a terrorist organization that was planning an attack on the Sears Towers in Chicago and on the FBI building in Miami.[18]

A conference entitled Our World, Our Rights has been organized for the day to discuss problems posed by globalization, and come up with new strategies to promote social justice, peaceful cohabitation, and the rights of subaltern people.

Paco seems preoccupied as he sets up the booth where several copies of Naomi Klein's *The Shock Doctrine* are displayed. The writer and activist decided to donate to the Coalition of Immokalee Workers the profits from books sold today.

I ask Paco how he thinks the march went.

"Well...I think," he answers evasively. "I'm afraid that people did not understand *why* we were marching. There were representatives of other organizations handing out fliers along the route," he adds.

CIW worker and member Gerardo, however, is extremely pleased. He smiles while he's getting ready to chair the first roundtable of the day: "Organizing Ourselves: Low-Wage Workers Fighting Back."

"At one Burger King yesterday," Gerardo says, "they started giving out free burgers at one point. Can you believe it?!"

On the other hand, Gerardo is highly critical of those who wrote "Fuck Burger King" on a wall near the headquarters of the corporation. "This way they jeopardize the entire campaign," he will repeat in front of the audience.

Today is also a day of celebration. Paco plays his *jaraña*; he has joined his Californian friends of Son del Centro. "*La jaraña es mi fusil*" (the guitar is my rifle), is the title of their album. Together, they sing *son jarocho*[19] in the open space of the cultural center near a workshop on sweatshops and the militarization of the frontier, on neoliberalism and the resistance of indigenous peoples.

I see Oannes. He is here representing the Yat Kitischee Native Center and Radio for Peace International. He smiles at me with his toothless smile as I get near his wheelchair to give him a hug.

"How nice to be here!" he says. "It's like the fulfillment of the prophecy."

"Which prophecy?" I ask.

"Our ancestors used to say that a time would come, seven generations after the arrival of the conquistadores, when all the young people will rebel against the system of exploitation that is poisoning a big part of the world. This movement for cultural, economic, social, and environmental justice is the manifestation of that prophecy." Only through this coalition can we obtain what Oannes calls "social environmental justice."

"As Martin Luther King Jr. said: 'Injustice anywhere is a threat to justice everywhere,'" he adds.

African American, Asian, the Caribbean and Latino communities, the inhabitants of the Pacific Islands, the indigenous populations of the western hemisphere, all are rebelling against the Eurocentric model. The Coalition of Immokalee Workers has been able to gather so many different people, a true rainbow movement, as I call it. Here we have indeed the representatives of the five sacred colors of the human family: red, white, black, yellow and brown.

This prophecy is known as the one of "the eagle and the condor": the eagle comes from that part of the globe they now call North America and the condor comes from that part of the globe they now call South America. The two sacred birds bring their prayers to the Creator, the Great Spirit. All these people are here to create a better world for the great human family but also all those forms of life that are equally sacred: the animals and the plants, the birds, the fish, the water relatives, the grass, the nation of the insects, the rocks, what we call Nature or Ecology or Biosphere.

The CIW struggle is not just for fair food, human rights and dignified wages for farmworkers, all very important struggles, but it is also about deciding what is going to be of the Earth in the twenty-first

century, about who will control the world and the fight against the corporations that have become the enemy.

Oannes stops to say hi to his friend Melody and to a couple of CIW
members.

"It's a privilege for me as a Native American to be here with the
other brothers and sisters of the five sacred colors of the rainbow to create a better world," Oannes says while watching them mingle with the
rest of the crowd.

The Road to Immokalee

Marc Rodrigues (national coordinator for the Student/Farmworker Alliance)
Now we can talk, Marc says, his combat military cap held firm on his
head. Marc Rodrigues is a tall guy with large shoulders. A cynic might call
him a "do-gooder"; but Marc, and others like him in the Student/Farm-
worker Alliance, work daily to change this country, step by step.

A Portuguese New Yorker with two big, black eyes enlarged even
further by the lenses of his glasses, Marc has found what he was looking for in Immokalee, at least for now.

He was a student when he began to participate in the CIW actions
and joined the campaign against Taco Bell. At that time, he was looking at the CIW as an exemplary model of grassroots organizing, led by
the very workers it sought to organize, and centered on popular education and on the mobilization of the general public. He interned with
the Student/Farmworker Alliance, and upon finishing his studies,
found out that the SFA was looking for a national coordinator for its
campaigns. He interviewed and got the job. Since then, Marc has lived
in Immokalee.

Like most activists, Marc doesn't like to talk about himself. His re-
serve, however, is not just an acquired behavior rooted in the vocation
of activists who tend to take on the problems of others as if they were
their own; rather, his reserve comes from genuine shyness.

The SFA was born in the year 2000, Marc explains, when a group
of Florida students joined Immokalee workers in the 230-mile march
from Fort Myers to Orlando. Back then, the CIW was still trying to
start a dialogue directly with the Florida growers. Within a few years,
the SFA has spread its campaigns at the national level, raising awareness around the conditions of farmworkers and contributing to the development of the fair food movement. The primary goal of the student
organization has been, however, the education of young people about
their strategic role as major consumers of fast food, and, thus, a target
market of the industry.

"The biggest problem is apathy," Marc continues.

> People don't believe change is possible anymore. The challenge is to
> pass the message that it is, and that we can all work to make it happen.
>   In this country, in particular, where you go to school to get a
> diploma, find a good job and make a lot of money…What we need to
> educate young people about is that…Life is something more than
> that…And the corporations don't just exploit the workers, but *all of us*,
> though in a different way. They take advantage of the youngest with
> their advertising campaigns. They manipulate youth culture and then
> sell it back to us. Students need to realize that this is also their fight.
>   We generally have three or four people who live in Immokalee, in
> close contact with the community. We try to model after the farm-
> workers, get inspiration from them, be responsible to them, and not to
> do anything that might damage their interests. The struggle, also, has
> always been nonviolent, which means that we don't go throw rocks at
> Burger King.

I ask Marc what's so special about Immokalee.

"Well, there's something in this community…It's hard to find the words to say what it is. The very fact that for so long it was a place that no one had heard of, with no sign to show how to get there…The workers were exploited, even killed, if they created troubles or they were of no use anymore. But then the poor people got organized and things have changed. Now the bosses are the ones who fear the workers!"

Marc shakes my hand and takes leave with a brief yet warm smile. I will see him again at the concert; he's chasing a little kid, his long arms dangling. The boy laughs heartily. Marc makes faces, lifts him up, puts him on his shoulders, and disappears into the crowd.

Lupe "Lupita" Fernandez* (Coalition of Immokalee Workers)

Lupe "Lupita" Fernandez wanted to become a secretary. Her dream was to work in an office. That's what she wanted to do. After finishing high school, though, her father told her: If you go to the university, you will have to put everything into that, never fail an exam, and work over the weekend. I, too, will have to go to the States to work.

But for their oldest daughter of six, Lupita's parents would have done it. Lupita, though, didn't want to have her family go through all that; plus, it would have been too much pressure on her. So she decided she wouldn't go to the university. Her father, however, had to leave Mexico anyway. And at seventeen, along with her youngest sister, Lupita left Oaxaca and went to America.

But America for Lupita became Immokalee: not the big cities she had imagined, but endless fields and hard work under the burning sun.

"We would climb high ladders, carry huge, heavy baskets full of oranges…" Lupita says while she adjusts her glasses. Lupita remembers well when she first arrived in Immokalee. It was the end of the season, summer already. Lupita and her sister rested for a couple of days and then started to work harvesting tomatoes.

"The first day we got out at five and came back at eight [in the evening]...It was so hot, the clothes got stuck to your skin from the sweat," says Lupita, touching her arms and waist to better illustrate the effect of the heat.

> There were no trees, no shade...The school bus that took us to the fields had no air conditioning and the sodas were undrinkable...The food stank.

> We worked for ten hours. We got paid 37 dollars. I thought that was a lot of money, I was comparing that to Mexico. But my dad said: You can't buy anything with this money here.

> Meanwhile, my father would mysteriously disappear every Wednesday night. "I am going to a meeting," that's all he would say. One night my sister and I followed him...And so we found out that he was going to the CIW. We knew where the offices were, we had seen them during the daytime.

Lupita and her sister started attending the meetings, too.

> I remember that back then we were discussing the system called "one dime per bucket." Most workers were paid the minimum hourly wage...$3.85 or something, which was very low and then 10 cents more per bushel of tomatoes, which just was an incentive to work harder without a real gain for the workers. It just made you pick faster...

> I didn't become active with the CIW until we went to Tallahassee and marched up to the governor's house with our requests. Then, the Coalition was focusing its efforts at the regional level and looking for a dialogue with local politicians.

Lupita became part of the CIW staff on April 1, 2001, the day in which the "Boot the Bell" campaign was launched.

"At that point I was already going door-to-door and talking to the people in Immokalee, inviting the workers to join the CIW. Sure, at the beginning there was a lot of resistance because I'm a woman. I moderated debates, I was very strong-willed...My dad, too, stopped being skeptical only after we won against Taco Bell. Then he understood that what I was doing was right, and it was working, too!"

Lupita, now twenty-seven, has a little daughter. She hosts a daily program at Radio Conciencia.

Melody Gonzalez (national coordinator for the
Student/Farmworker Alliance and Interfaith Action)
Many are the reasons that led Melody Gonzalez to Immokalee. Melody's grandfather participated in the Bracero program, the labor agreement between the two North American countries that from 1942 to 1964 brought more than four million Mexicans to work in the fields and in the building of the railroad system all over the United States.

Melody's father, the oldest son in his family, started working in the fields when he was five years old; at eleven, he was forced to drop out of school, at eighteen to leave Guadalajara and go to America. He crossed the Sonora desert in Arizona where he and his grandfather were abandoned by the coyote. He had to drink his own urine in order to survive, until he was found by *la migra* and got deported. He crossed again: this time he didn't get caught. In California, he began to pick tomatoes and grapes. In the spring and summertime, he migrated to the states of Oregon and Washington to pick cucumbers, raspberries, and other produce. In the early eighties, he decided to go back to Mexico, but the economy was so bad that he resolved to leave again. He worked as a dishwasher in various restaurants for a few years, and then he was hired by the fiberglass factory in Santa Ana, California. There, in Santa Ana, where 75 percent of the population is Latino, Melody was born and raised.

Melody's mother has flown in from California to participate in the march organized by the CIW and to visit her daughter in Immokalee. We met yesterday at the park, during the lunch break. Like her husband, she didn't want to make a life for herself in the United States. Her sister, though, was married to the brother of Melody's father. That's how the two of them met and ended up staying in Santa Ana.

"My mom worked in a TDK factory for many years, and then at the Marriott Hotel," Melody says. "Now she is a cook at a Catholic high school."

Melody sits next to me on the couch, looks forward and moves her hands as she speaks; every once in a while she pulls back her hair.

> I remember well when my dad brought us kids to Oregon. It was spring, I was ten years old…We were traveling to the state of Washington but we stopped in the convent that helped the farmworkers. They picked raspberries; my father wanted us to realize what it meant to work in the fields all day along. So we got up at four and picked raspberries until sunset. We got to the convent that evening and we were so tired! And picking raspberries is not as hard as picking tomatoes! (laughing)
>
> We earned only enough to buy our sandwiches for lunch. We could not believe it!
>
> I bore that in mind and I remember that trip dearly, also because that was the last vacation I took with my little sister. She died only a few a months after, run over by a car.

Melody left home to go to college in Indiana at eighteen. She had to leave: the continuous tensions between her father and little brother were exhausting her. She went to the University of Notre Dame.

I was going very far from my family, but the scholarship I got was excellent: it waived almost all the university fees, so I accepted. The first year was terrible. The courses were really hard, even harder for me because I hadn't gone to a good high school. I had the opportunity to travel to the border though, to El Paso and Ciudad Juarez. The second year I went to Immokalee for spring break: with our group, we visited the CIW, the Guadalupe Center, the Six L's packinghouse.

One day we went to pick tomatoes and the same night we participated in one of the CIW meetings. I remember we were all exhausted whereas they, the farmworkers, who had also worked all day, were discussing excitedly, still full of energy.

It was the time of the Taco Bell boycott, and in Indiana we began to picket the Taco Bell on campus. Back then I wanted to get into politics because, I thought, that's the way things get changed.

So I left for Brazil to study at the Universidade de São Paulo. While there, I interned for an organization dedicated to the defense of human rights and visited the headquarters of the Movimento dos Trabalhadores Rurais Sem Terra (MST) and la Escola Nacional Florestan Fernandes that was still under construction.

The poverty I saw in Brazil and the contrast between the rich and the poor...the kids roaming the street with guns...all this had a profound influence on me.

While I was there, Lula won the elections. And they were all excited for that but I kept thinking, why do we have to wait for Lula to change things?[20]

Back in Indiana, Melody was ready to fight: she was full of energy now. It was then that she met Tony. Tony, too, came from California. He, too, was the son of migrant workers. He, too, listened to Rage Against the Machine. They became best friends and together they organized the protest to have the Notre Dame football team discontinue its sponsorship with Taco Bell. Tony began his hunger strike on March 31, 2004, on César Chávez's birthday, and Melody began to publicize his actions.

There were calls from the CIW headquarters for Tony.

"¿*Tienes hambre?*" (Are you hungry?) They were asking from Immokalee, and we replied defiantly in chorus: "¿*Que es eso?*" (What is it [hunger]?)

Tony starved for seven days. The students at the college began to answer positively to the initiative, to request the suspension of the contract.

"I remember it as a very happy period. Every night we would go pray in this grotto...It was magic," Melody reflected.

When the university ignored Tony's demands, students decided to do another hunger strike.

> Over a period of two weeks, 150 students fasted one to three days, and we even had a hunger strike headquarters. Meanwhile, we continued to do sit-ins outside the university president's office and collect petitions. Notre Dame is renowned for being a conservative university, the students don't usually protest and our action had a lot of clout. And the fact is, we won! That summer the university decided not to renew its contract with Taco Bell. Notre Dame was among the twenty-two colleges that joined the boycott during the "Boot the Bell" campaign.

Melody ended up writing her thesis on the CIW as a nontraditional model of workers' organizing.[21] "In the Coalition, there is this strong effort to keep the organization horizontal in structure. All decisions are made in groups, even though this takes more time," Melody says.

Once she finished school, Melody was asked by members of the "Immokalee crew" to join them, and in August 2005 became part of the staff of the Student/Farmworker Alliance. "I was the first person of color to be part of the SFA staff...Since then, I've represented the CIW in several international delegations. I had the opportunity to travel a lot, both in the States and abroad, to see places I never thought I would be able to see."

Melody participated in "La Otra Campaña" in Chiapas[22] and the World Social Forum in Venezuela in 2006. In 2007, she was in Israel and Palestine, where she met Arab workers who live in Israel and in the Gaza Strip.[23]

"Since I've traveled so much, in my family, many stories circulate about me...In Mexico, my grandparents are convinced that I work for the White House!" says Melody, laughing.

Melody will move back to California next year. She might take up a job in Southern California, probably with the Chiapas Media Project, the organization that educates the indigenous communities on how to produce documentaries. She wants to be back with her family for a while.

"They need me...It will be hard to leave Immokalee and its people, though. They have become such an important part of me."

Eduardo Salazar*

"*Me llamo Eduardo Salazar y soy Mexicano.*" (My name is Eduardo Salazar and I am Mexican.) Eduardo introduces himself to the participants of the roundtable on war, titled "From the War at Home to the War for Empire." He's wearing the yellow "Exploitation King" T-shirt. In the green room of the music hall, the space where the workshop is taking place, the chairs have been arranged in a circle. A young woman volunteers to translate Eduardo's account. She then moves her chair near him.

The roundtable is almost over. War resister Camilo Mejía has just finished talking about his experience in Iraq and in a military jail for refusing to go back to Iraq. He linked the antiwar movement to the global justice movement and stressed the need to fight "all imperialist wars." Before him, David Solnit, author of *An Army of None*, spoke of the false promises that the military makes to so many young men and women when they enroll, hoping to gain an economically secure future or the possibility to attend college without having to go into debt.

"I come from Chiapas," Eduardo continues. "And I have seen many innocent people die during the Zapatista revolution. I was in the Mexican military then..."

Eduardo begins his long and detailed account and his words are as low and continuous as a mantra: interruptions occur when the interpreter manages to capture Eduardo's attention, so he allows her time to translate.

"I enrolled in the army because they pay well...We always needed money at home. My uncle was in the military, too...I remember that some captains from Guatemala, those ones who had fought in the Highlands got sent to train us.[24] One time they had us kill a chicken and then drink its blood. It was still warm. Another time a dog, and we had to eat it, raw."

We all hang on Eduardo's words. Those who don't understand Spanish wait for the interpreter to render the meanings of his quiet words.

"We watched a video, years after, and I found out that these were the same training techniques used in the Schools of the Americas.[25] It was dehumanizing [for the soldiers]. I saw people lose their sense of judgment," says Eduardo, staring at an undefined spot in front of him. "I considered myself lucky. After all, I was able to get out of there. Now I'm here, in the United States..." Eduardo's big black eyes become watery. "But I still feel I'm in a war. But this time is a different struggle...a struggle against exploitation."

Eduardo gets up, showing his strong, towering body. Poseidon without his trident.

He shakes hands and then puts his backpack on his large shoulders. Eduardo is about to leave when I stop him. I would like to hear more about your story, I manage to say. He leans his head to listen to me. *Esta bien.*

Mike, from the Bolivarian Youth, attired as usual in his Che Guevara T-shirt, is happy to help me with the Spanish. Mike, too, participated in the roundtable and has been struck by Eduardo's testimony. We sit down at a table inside one of the large rooms at the center. Eduardo begins, seemingly from a random point of his life, and it is like getting into this man's mind or watching an adventure movie. As snapshots, the episodes he recounts materialize before me.

I restrain myself to merely interpreting the flux of his thoughts and maybe giving them order through my questioning, in the attempt to reconstruct, in a more or less chronological sequence, what has happened in the last few years of Eduardo's existence.

Immokalee is, in fact, just a stage in the life of this man with deep black eyes like a night with no stars. Eduardo, who is thirty-seven, works in landscaping in Felda, a small town ten miles north of Immokalee. He has a good salary now, Eduardo says, he can't complain. He makes up to $60 a day. When he got to Immokalee nearly two years ago, his boss was only paying him thirty. When there was work. At that time, he lived in a trailer with other men, slept on the floor, and paid sixty dollars a week in rent. Every evening the workers gave ten dollars for their dinner to the same boss.

"We didn't have water in the fields. Our lunch break was five minutes. The crew leaders had a fridge with some soda on the truck, but they kept it hidden. At lunchtime, they would take it out of the truck and charge us one dollar per soda."

I ask Eduardo why he is still part of the coalition. Now he has a good job as he stated himself.

"When you are part of a struggle," Eduardo answers determinedly, "you fight for everybody else's rights, not just for your own."

The CIW, Eduardo adds, wants him to be an example for all the workers, so that others will resist exploitation too.

"When I could, I always rebelled," Eduardo says with pride.

"When the war against the Zapatista revolt ended," Eduardo continues, "everyone was talking about human rights' violations in Chiapas. I didn't even know what human rights were…"

Eduardo's eyes get lost in the continuous movement of his thick hands.

"While we were in Lacandon to fight, we imprisoned people and then loaded them up on the helicopters. Then we would throw the prisoners out in the jungle, the famous *Selva Lacandona*…"

I ask Eduardo to tell me how he got to Immokalee.

"Everybody was saying that it was impossible to cross the border. I had my own hesitations at first…But then, in 2004, I put my fears aside and got on a bus north and I got to Mexicali, near the border."

I ask Eduardo how long it took him to get to the United States.

"That time…" Eduardo concentrates and begins to count. "Night and day, night and day, night and day…The first time I walked for three days and three nights along the railroad. I thought more than once to jump on the train, but it was too fast. Eventually, they found me and sent me back to Mexico, to Oaxaca.

"There I befriended this guy…he told me how *la migra* deported him as well as other people. My friend hid *under* a train car, but in the end they sought him out. Together, we decided to try again."

The janitors ask us to leave the room and Mike, Eduardo, and I go and sit down outside, on the steps of the patio yard.

"We arrived by the border with sixty Mexican dollars," Eduardo continues. "Hungry, dirty, wounded from the beatings we had got from *la migra*. We were six men, and a thirteen-year-old girl who was there with her father. We walked four nights and five days. We only had a little bit of water like…" Eduardo looks for a referent. When he finally finds it, "Like that one," he says, pointing at a small water bottle. "After we finished it, we started drinking from pools. Eating…We were eating cactuses. One day we found a big turtle. We lit a fire and began to cook it. Some didn't want to eat it at first, but when they saw we were eating it and liking it, they wanted some, too. (*laughing*) At that point they would have even eaten the shell!"

The first time I crossed I wasn't aware of all the dangers of the desert…We found vipers, rattlesnakes, coyotes, wolves…but we made it, except the father with the little girl. They were exhausted and didn't go on with us.

Once we crossed the border, I took a train to Coachella; there, I started working in the grape harvest. But right after that, I went back to Mexico. Fact is, I had a girl then and I wanted to bring her to the States. As I was in Mexicali, I sent her the money so she could join me. Together, we tried to cross again; they caught us, but they let us go and so we tried another time and they caught us again.

So the next time around, I paid a coyote. Two thousand five hundred dollars, but halfway *la migra* caught us again. Three days later we tried again and then they took us to Phoenix, Arizona. Then they deported us to Mexicali. While there, my girlfriend found out that her mother was really sick. She had got lung cancer, and my girlfriend wanted to go back home. She said, "You go," but I wanted to be close to her, so we both went back to Chiapas and for fourteen nights we took care of her mother until the day she died. We organized the vigil and the funeral; we arranged everything.

I began to work again in Chiapas but it was really hard; I sold fish at the market but I wasn't making enough money to survive. So I decided to try to cross once again...

This time I left by myself...She didn't want to go. It took me eight days. When I got to the border I paid a coyote...$700 right there, and the rest, after. We walked at night, in the desert.

The coyote left Eduardo in Phoenix. From there, a guy took him on his truck and drove him to Quincy, Florida, northwest of Tallahassee. The coyote knew a crew leader there: he could count on him to make Eduardo pay the remaining eight hundred dollars.

"When the season was over and I paid my debt, I went to Tennessee to pick tomatoes, zucchini, and beans. But the boss was stealing from me, so I decided to go back to Quincy. But there, too, they were taking advantage of us, and I was tired of being ordered around. I told the crew leader he could go to hell. That's when I came to Immokalee.

"It was during the campaign against McDonald's that I met Romeo [Ramirez, CIW representative]...

"Radio Conciencia was doing a program outside called 'Remote Control' from Campo Colorado, right outside of Immokalee. I was with some friends at a store nearby, we had just finished work when we heard the music. We went to check out what was going on. There was karaoke and they were giving away free T-shirts to whomever would sing a song.

So I mustered up the courage and sang a *ranchera*..."

Eduardo stops, trying to remember the title.

"Camino de Michuacan," he says eventually, glad to have recalled the name of the song.

Then Romeo invited him to go to the radio station.

"For a season I hosted a program at the radio station, from three to six in the morning. I loved to work there," he continues, "At that time, the people of Immokalee get up to go to work. Everybody is sleepy and I tried to instill some energy, so that they could better face the long day of work."

Eduardo hopes he will be able to have the same program next year.

The center is shutting down. We are the last ones left along with the cleaning personnel. The CIW bus is gone too, leaving behind Eduardo and his adventures. We get in the car to go to the concert at Bayfront. Eduardo continues to talk: he says that he now lives by himself. He might go back and work in the fields though, when there is no work in landscaping. Now the season is starting again and he knows a good crew leader for whom he could go back to work.

"He keeps asking me to go back and bring more people with me," he adds proudly. "But I will leave soon. I want to go north."

◆

We arrive at Bayfront. A stage has been set up in the amphitheater in front of the imposing Intercontinental Hotel, right where the march started yesterday. The hip-hop, Milwaukee-based band Kinto Sol is leaving the stage to the songs of justice and freedom of the Son del Centro. Their screaming song is a son jarocho. We settle on the side of the stage, by the booths of the booksellers and the CIW.

Eduardo continues his account as if he can't stop; now he speaks of the poverty of Mexican rural areas.

"You see, there are places where people are so poor that the children run in the street with no clothes and eat what they find on the ground...Even grass when they are really hungry..."

On the right, the big skyscrapers of Miami began to light up and impose their presence over the facing multicolored hill. Eduardo speaks of the bloody revolts in his country. Not only the Zapatistas', which he personally condemns, "since the operation of Comandante Marcos has brought death and hasn't been able to extend the protest."

"Comandante Marcos was not able to protect the people in the rural areas," Eduardo adds. "He attacked the capital to attract media attention, but he left the countryside 'unprotected.' That's why so many innocent people died, unnecessarily…"

But he also speaks of the teachers' revolt in Oaxaca. That protest, unlike the Zapatistas', extended to students, politicians, and unions.[26] The teachers protested against Governor Ulises Ruiz of the PRI[27] (in English, Institutional Revolutionary Party) for having rejected the requests to raise their salaries and to provide standardized, free books for all students.

"Out in the country…the teachers don't even get paid…" Eduardo comments bitterly.

Eduardo restates his rejection of violence and the necessity of a peaceful resistance, at least at the beginning. That's why he likes the CIW and joined its struggle.

I have quit taking notes by now. I look at Eduardo and the Biscayne Bay receding into the darkness behind him; the sky and the ocean soften in the same colors of the dusk. At this moment, I realize that Naomi Klein is on stage. She's now reminding the audience that the stockholders of Goldman Sachs received an exorbitant bonus last Christmas.

…*The profit of the corporation in 2006 was $2.23 billion. And Burger King refused to accept the CIW conditions that would cost the company not even $300,000 a year*…

The audience applauds Klein's exposure of Burger King's greed.

Eduardo is still telling his stories, but Mike has tuned out, too; he's no longer translating, he, too, is distracted by our surroundings.

I look up to the lit-up Goldman Sachs skyscraper and the electric blue one behind it. I turn to Eduardo again and meet his steely fighter's gaze. And I know we will win.

The oratory and nativity scene in Ave Maria, Florida

Four

DECEMBER 8—IMMACULATE CONCEPTION

Ave Maria Town

My friend Kathia agrees to go back to Immokalee with me. I've talked to her at length about the community with the result of stimulating her curiosity. Technically, I am the one who is accompanying her this time. My Haitian American friend has some books to give out: a storage trunk full of children's texts, both in Spanish and in English.

We set out for our trip. It's December 8, the Immaculate Conception, the day Catholics celebrate the virgin mother of Jesus Christ. It's almost noon when we get on SR-29. A few miles before Immokalee we find the sign for Ave Maria. I turn the steering wheel abruptly. A little deviation, I say to Kathia, as if to apologize for the risky maneuver. We drive five more miles south, during which I briefly explain to my friend what I know about Ave Maria town and its founder.

My curiosity in this place was stimulated by a film producer friend of mine; he had mentioned the existence of a recently built Catholic university near Immokalee called Ave Maria. "I want to do a documentary about its founder…Tom Monaghan," Daniel told me. "His story is incredible."

We drive by the orange groves, one after the other. The landscape changes at one point, though, and the landscape becomes the wild one of the Seminoles. Solitary cypresses and palm trees (some worn and small, others taller and thriving) seem to gang up on each other, lost in low clouds, indifferent to the bush population below.[1]

Monaghan is the founder of Domino's Pizza,[2] by virtue of which he became, in a twenty-year span, one of the wealthiest people in America.[3] Monaghan is an innovator—he made money betting on the idea of fast home delivery and maximizing the output during peak hours—and what one would call an authentic self-made man. His greatest regret, admittedly, was being kicked out of seminary—for pillow fights and talking during service.[4] Since he couldn't afford to go to college, he joined the Marine Corps; in the middle of the ocean, far from civilization, he started daydreaming…Fancy cars, yachts, penthouses.

Born in Ann Arbor, Michigan, Monaghan came from a very poor family; his mother, unable to provide for her children after the death of her husband, gave up custody of little Tom to the Polish Felician nuns. The experience in the orphanage of daily masses, frequent confession sessions, and prayers, along with the influence of his teacher, Sister Bernarda, a father *and* a mother in Tom's eyes, left an indelible mark on the founder of Domino's Pizza.[5]

Indeed, Monaghan professes he's always tried to be a good Catholic, but it was only in the eighties that he understood he had to get rid of his fortune—estimated to be over $900 million—to truly become one. "I want to die broke," he declared.[6]

That's all Daniel told me. A Franciscan vow of poverty, I thought in admiration. What Daniel didn't tell me was that Monaghan decided to donate most of his belongings to the Catholic Church. He became born again. A born again Catholic, while remaining an entrepreneur to the bone.[7]

A strong opponent of reproductive rights, Monaghan has been involved in campaigns to outlaw abortion since early on; for this reason, the National Organization for Women (NOW) organized in the eighties a boycott against Domino's Pizza. Monaghan, however, used the action to get further momentum for his cause. He also joined the presidential campaign of anti–abortion rights advocate Senator Sam Brownback, and supported other ultraconservative Republicans like Tom Coburn and Rick Santorum.[8] When he retired from his billion-dollar business in 1998, he expanded the scope of his donations and began to finance (with millions upon millions of dollars) the Catholic education system because: "There's a lot of philanthropy out there," he once stated. "A lot of people giving money to social causes like fighting poverty, or to medical research. These are all very good things, but I don't think they're as important as helping people get to heaven."[9] In Monaghan's view, this means expanding the Catholic influence in the culture and, thus, to proselytize, so that more people can be "saved."

Monaghan wants to contribute to the creation of the next generation of Catholic leaders in the United States (in Michigan before, and now in Florida) and in Central America (Honduras, Nicaragua). That's why he has invested so much in the Ave Maria School of Law.[10]

We turn right. The two-way road is separated by a traffic island, escorted by a series of recently planted palm trees. On the sides, well-kept meadows spread out. We are definitely in a rather different scenario. Kathia is excited. I know my friend: she is an adventurer. The sign *Welcome to Ave Maria est. 2007* confirms it: we've just entered a world of its own.[11]

All around Ave Maria University, a big residential complex is burgeoning. "A self-sustaining town," to quote one of the largest landowners in South Florida, Barron Collier Companies,[12] which donated one thousand acres for the building of the university. Monaghan contributed

$100 million, thus becoming fully involved in the project of developing the residential Ave Maria town.

So even before establishing the community government, the 50–50 private partnership called Ave Maria Development (Tom Monaghan and Barron Collier Companies) was created. The founder of Domino's Pizza is surely not the kind of person who donates money and then goes back to minding his own business...Ave Maria has its own zip code and, to unwary eyes, may seem to be just another town being built in the middle of nowhere to fill the wide spaces of America. However, the "tailor-made law"[13] that renders Ave Maria town a "special" district[14] allows landowners (read, Monaghan and Barron Collier) to take advantage of tax-free municipal bonds to finance the community projects that serve a public interest, thus also saving them millions of dollars thanks to the lower interest rates of said bonds.[15]

What did the state legislature do? Governor Jeb Bush (a converted Catholic) endorsed the project of Ave Maria town and university in November 2002, and then legalized the Ave Maria town government in June 2004. The Collier County Commission unanimously approved both Ave Maria development plans (June 14, 2005) and the special district government (October 28, 2003). One could say that policy makers just saw a business opportunity for an economically depressed area of the Sunshine State.

To be sure, Monaghan seems to have found his El Dorado in the Sunshine State's Southwest. "I've got swampland in Florida I'd like to sell you" was once a jokey phrase. The saying dates back to the time before the reclamation of the Florida swamps, the time of the big construction boom of the twenties during which the price of land continued to rise up to 1,000 percent a year. Then there was the so-called Big Miami Hurricane (1926), which, coupled with the successive economic crisis, ended the speculation. Since then, the flat land of Florida has been drained, canalled, paved, injected with pesticides, and taken over by more speculators and agribusiness. At Ave Maria, too, canals are the non-navigable arteries of the town, and the water here originated elsewhere.

The drives multiply as the signs become sparse. We cross a little bridge; then stop at the Information Center.

In front of a glass-protected, plastic-and-wooden model, the clerk, a blonde fellow in his twenties, is wearing a business suit and a tie. He diligently shows us the 6,000 acres of land over which the town will unfold in the next few years. The wooden Ave Maria Oratory dominates the center of the model. Fifty-four thousand square feet, the church has been erected to be the fulcrum of the community; in front of the building, the university campus extends.

Originally located in North Naples, the university began to hold classes at its permanent location here in Ave Maria town at the end of August 2007. Once the development project is completed, residents of the community will have a private chapel located within walking distance from their house. The oratory, once in operation, will celebrate Mass every hour starting at six in the morning.

All around, on the 5,000 acres of land of the town district,[16] a couple of restaurants, an elementary school, a golf course, a tennis court, and additional residential areas have been built—with the help of tax-free municipal bonds.

"...A fire station, a medical center with a helicopter for the emergency transportation in Lehigh...Various clubhouses," continues our static Cicero, slavishly showing us the structures in the model.

"Del Webb," for instance, the residential complex scheduled to open soon, will be a retirement community. Others are still under construction: the empty spaces without volume in the plastic-and-wooden model. The supermarket, the gas station, and the public school that, as our guide reassures us, will be built north of the private one operating already.

Kathia elbows me as our guide turns around; the receptionist requires his attention. Kathia whispers into my ear something about the school. In such a small community, the project of building a public school is intended to show concern for lower-income people. However, the school is not there yet. We look at each other, and wonder whether it will ever be built.

We get in the car and continue to drive toward the downtown area and the university. We arrive at the main square. The oratory stands out in the middle of what is called Annunciation Circle. Majestic, a declaration of principles. All around, Lilliputian buildings unfold: a couple of clothing shops, a jewelry store, the information center at the corner, and other colorful buildings still awaiting signs, all commercial entities whose management, as the rest of the real estate of Ave Maria town, has been entrusted exclusively to Monaghan and Barron Collier.

Ave Maria Oratory hasn't opened to the public yet, and until the bishop consecrates it according to Catholic rituals, it won't be able to rightly claim the name of "church." Once inaugurated, however, it will be the largest fixed-seating Catholic church of the country.[17]

The extendable arm of a crane supports a couple of men who are working on the cross hoisted at the top of the facade of the church.[18] In front of the oratory, a nativity has been arranged with two statues of Mary and Joseph; in the middle, the cradle waiting for Baby Jesus. We park in one of the many empty spots and approach the imposing building. On the lower right side of the facade, the date of construction has been engraved in Roman numbers: AD MMVI.

The church, designed by Monaghan himself—a would-be archi-tect, in addition to a would-be priest—is modeled after the one in Notre Dame, but the coarseness of the material—visible, especially upon a closer scrutiny—and the clear contrast with the flat, surrounding ce-ment reminds us that we are not in France, let alone Paris. Zooming out on Google Maps would confirm that we are in Southwest Florida in-stead, a stone's throw away from the Corkscrew Swamp Sanctuary, a re-serve of countless types of orchids and many endangered species like the bald cypress and the American stork, and yes, only a few miles from downtown Immokalee.

We pass again by the nativity. Joseph overshadows Mary: the im-maculate mother of Jesus looks even smaller, kneeled the way she is, arms close to her breast, her eyes upon the empty cradle.

◆

Ave Maria University was born from Monaghan's desire to invest a big chunk of his wealth in the promotion of the dogmas of the Roman Catholic Church. Upon making a fortune from his Domino's Pizza empire—and after buying and selling (but only once the team had won the World Series championship) the Detroit Tigers—Mon-aghan decided, indeed, "to die broke." He got his epiphany after reading *Mere Christianity* by C. S. Lewis, a Christian author quite popular among both Catholic and Protestant Evangelicals. The chapter that struck him was about "the great sin:" the one of pride.

"C. S. Lewis told me that it was pure pride," Monaghan once said. "You wanted to impress other people—impress them with a spectacular play, or you wanted to impress them with all your worldly goods and ac-complishments."[19] So Monaghan decided to get rid of his possessions—among which were a collection of antique cars, numerous paraphernalia of the much-admired architect Frank Lloyd Wright, a private jet, an island north of Michigan, and the Detroit Tigers. "Everything that was ostentatious," as he declared to CNN.[20]

The other sin he waged a war against was lust, the obsession par excellence of the Christian right. In his attempt to build an ultraconservative Catholic community modeled after the medieval citadel, Monaghan insisted on some restrictions—no access to pornography (not even via satellite), prohibitions on selling condoms and other contraceptive methods at Ave Maria—and made the national news, creating a big fuss and forcing both the founder of Domino's Pizza and Barron Collier to backpedal.

Although no one, as Monaghan himself has pointed out in interviews, would expect a young gay couple to move to a place with such a name, these rules appeared excessive to many, violating basic civil liberties, specifically the freedom of speech and the right to privacy.

So Monaghan had to give up: no citadel, for now. A defeat, but only a minor battle compared to the long war to overthrow *Roe v. Wade*. That war was undertaken on a new level with the creation of the Ave Maria School of Law and the founding of the Thomas More Center for Law and Justice, whose main goal is precisely to outlaw the practice of abortion. (Tom Monaghan is now seventy-one; however, he believes himself to be seventy-two, since he calculates age from the day of conception.)

The idea of Ave Maria University, however, wasn't born in southwestern Florida. Back in 1983, Monaghan, still a brilliant and unrepentant business man, created the Mater Christi Foundation, which soon became the headquarters of Ave Maria Foundation in his hometown of Ann Arbor, Michigan.

Ave Maria College was established in 1998 in nearby Ypsilanti, right where, along with his brother back in 1959, Monaghan had bought the first small pizza store, DomiNick's, for only $1,400, nine hundred of which he had borrowed. In 2000, Ave Maria School of Law was also created, and in 2005 accredited in record time by the American Bar Association.[21] The town of Ann Arbor, however, voted no to the construction of the university.[22]

In addition, Monaghan largely financed the construction of the cathedral of Managua in Nicaragua. In 1972, a 6.2-magnitude earthquake had killed five thousand residents, injured twenty thousand, and left over 250,000 homeless. It also destroyed their church.

Monaghan contracted the project to the renowned Mexican architect Ricardo Legorreta, who designed a $4.5 million cathedral.[23] Afterwards, Monaghan allied himself with the anti-Sandinista clergymen,[24] took over a small college and financed the only American university in the country: Ave Maria College of the Americas in San Marcos, one of the poorest communities in Nicaragua.

So the choice of Nicaragua—the only nation where liberation theology has been put into practice and revolution welcomed by the majority of the local clergy—was not accidental.[25] Monaghan believes in a doctrine that has become dominant in the United States due to the recent emergence of the cultural and political hegemony of neoconservatism. After he became born again, Monaghan met Michael Novak.

Novak, a major thinker of the Bush administration, was a resident scholar at the American Enterprise Institute for Social Policy Research. His political vision combines social conservatism and rampant neoliberalism. In sharp contrast with liberation theology, this doctrine proposes a development model through capitalism, deemed to be the best, proven-by-facts form of economic, social, and cultural progress—and as Novak maintains, rich soil for the expansion of human creativity.[26] After all, C. S. Lewis and Frank Lloyd Wright were raised and thrived in capitalist America.

Some say Ave Maria is a positive thing for Immokalee. By 2016, the town is planned to accommodate up to thirty thousand people—which means new jobs, new housing facilities available for the farmworkers, a new educational center for the young; at the time of writing though, these are only good ideas on paper. To begin with, Collier County Area Transit has no plan to develop a public transportation system between the two towns.[27]

◆

On a subsequent trip to Ave Maria, I had the opportunity to visit one of the model houses adjacent to the information center. Bryan welcomed me from behind the tall counter at the entrance, as if it were a hotel reception. As soon as he understood I was Italian, he began to speak in my native language. Bryan primarily lived in Norcia, Italy, where he ran a gift store within a monastery; he was enrolled in an Austrian university where, he explained, he studied Philosophy and Theology. Now he was in Florida because of his girlfriend (who attended Ave Maria University).

Bryan showed me the residential communities, this time on a map. The street names, he pointed out, somewhat amused, were Italian—Verona, Kathia, Fontana, Avellino. On the other hand, the logic behind the choices and the distribution of those specific names was as obscure to me as to Bryan. (*This was one of the many questions I would have liked to ask Mr. Monaghan if his entourage would have let me interview him.*)

"Vuoi vedere le case? Sono aperte..." ("Do you want to see the houses? They are open.") Bryan kindly said with a surprisingly slight American accent. He then left me in front of the Oakmont model. The driveway lights were on, even though the sun was pitilessly bright. I looked around, undecided on which property to visit first. Walking toward the Capri model, I saw a group of six or seven people, anxiously seeking their American Dream in the middle of the Floridian concrete of Ave Maria. I opted to visit Oakmont, by myself. From the outside, these houses all looked the same, with their sloping roofs and pastel colors. Only the Carlyle model, a two-story house located at the end of the street, seemed to be definitely bigger.

Inside, a fake fireplace was ominously on; in the adjacent dining room a table had been carefully set. Fake cookies adorned the kitchen counter. I looked up in the corners of the ceilings to check if there was closed circuit television. After all, Bryan hadn't even asked for my ID before he let me visit the properties. There were no cameras—or at least I did not see any, even though the feeling of being observed stayed strongly with me throughout the whole visit.

A huge plasma-screen TV had been placed over the fireplace in front of the cream leather couch. The house had a wide laundry room, a garage, and a guest room. There was also an indoor pool and a lanai, although these amenities were not included, as Bryan later pointed out, in the $315,000 Oakmont model.

Beyond the black screen that delimited the pool, I stared for a while at the bare Floridian plain. As I was walking toward the pool, I caught a glimpse of the bedroom on my right: table lamps on, a book by Ken Follett deliberately placed on the bedside table, and a pair of reading glasses likewise deliberately placed over it. I went past and then stopped again to gaze at the endless, sunny level land beyond the screen.

Back in the office, I asked Bryan if those five model houses would ever be occupied—a curiosity I had always had about model houses. No, he answered firmly. Well, not soon, at least. Then he conceded, elusively, "Perhaps one day..."

And I wondered...Had I had the privilege to meet Tom Monaghan, I would have told him that he is still stained by the sin of pride, that perhaps he doesn't know, but in one of his model houses, even in one of the smaller ones, a dozen farmworkers could comfortably live—those farmworkers who, instead, are ashamed even to ask for help at the Friendship House, so they sleep in the bushes, within spitting distance from here. That perhaps, one day, a rumor will spread in Immokalee that no one lives here, and then someone will try to go sleep in the Oakmont model, and the story will be splattered all over the local news.

On the contrary, these model houses are still empty and are destined to remain this way; museums erected to human indifference and its greatest sin: sloth. And before leaving, just to vent right to the end, I would have asked Monaghan this question: if he really believes he is not the smug billionaire he once was, why the hell did he have that monstrosity of a church built?

◆

Kathia and I stop to get ice cream at La Paleteria on New Market Road. We take a walk in the brief adjacent strip mall. My friend enters a second-hand store that presents itself under the guise of an antique store. My cell phone rings and I wait outside.

While on the phone, I observe the overcrowded shopping window of the store. A grayish flowered couch (priced at $60) and the statue of a ceramic tiger (no price) are displayed. My eyes linger on the tiger, I'm not sure whether it's because of the weird attack position in which the animal has been captured or the routine conversation I'm having on the phone, or both.

I hear Kathia laughing. I finally hang up and go inside. Kathia confidently introduces me to the woman who runs the store: from behind the counter, Rosa*, a large face painted with heavy makeup, stretches out her hand through dozens of statues, holy pictures, fake flowers, crosses, and the other paraphernalia that adorn her workspace.

Mucho gusto, I say.

On the counter, I spot a statue of John Paul II.

"A keepsake from his first apostolic trip to Mexico," says Rosa, sliding the figurine of the deceased pope closer to me.

I smilingly nod in appreciation.

"It's a cruet," adds Rosa, jeweled-glasses sitting on her breast.

"It contains liquor," Kathia whispers as Rosa disappears behind the counter.

The woman reemerges, a holy picture in her hand. On her right sits a smiling Buddha, a Christmas decoration on his neck and a small American flag stuck into his ear, on her left, a Madonna borne by a winged angel.

Rosa tells me that the figure wearing the New Orleans–style beads is the Virgin of Guadalupe, and, she quickly remarks, is not for sale. (I wonder whether the menacing tiger on display is.)

On December 12, Rosa reminds us, the people of Immokalee will celebrate Our Lady of Guadalupe, "a real event for the community." The procession begins at dawn and ends after walking through the main streets of Immokalee.

Today's event, however, is the Christmas parade. And everybody will be there.

The Christmas Parade

Main Street has been closed to traffic. In front of the CIW, I meet Paco. We chat for a little while; he asks me if I will stay for the parade.

"I saw your mom," I say. "She said she's going to be watching the parade from the Azteca (supermarket) with Tina." But Paco is not listening anymore, distracted by the talk of some friends that are now walking into the CIW offices.

Kathia and I head toward the Friendship House. Monica said to be back around six. I would be able to speak with other guests then.

Main Street. Strange to look at it, deserted and traffic-less as it is right now. Main Street. The major artery of Immokalee, the only one to have lighting. Past the sunset, the street lamps turn on, and the "happy holiday" banners underneath almost disappear into the imminent darkness. The clouds expand and grow gray over the people spread along the roadsides.

Lucas (Benitez) appears not to recognize me. London and the media spotlight are far away today. Now, after the preparation for the march in Miami, the CIW is back to work full time on the usual emergencies. Like the new case of slavery uncovered around Naples, which the coalition has been investigating along with the Florida Freedom Partnership.[28]

Lucas hoists his son on his shoulders and walks away, mingling with the swarm of people, a farmworker, as are the many others that today are taking their place on the side of Main Street, waiting for the passage of the parade. The people of Immokalee: entire families, and lots, lots of children, small and very small, climbing on shoulders or fastened in strollers. Some people sit on the edge of the sidewalk, some lean against the store walls. There are some who parked their red Christmas-adorned dune buggies at the gas station, now filled with kids excited for the upcoming parade.

The stores sell lemonade and iced tea. No one will be inside the Friendship House, I think. The entire town seems to be here, out on Main Street, in a festive mood.

But I am wrong. There is somebody in the homeless shelter. Even now.

Eliezer*

Eliezer is fifty-eight. He left Nassau, Haiti, when he was only a little boy.

"I come from North Carolina," he says. "That's what I call home."

Eliezer speaks softly while staring at the TV. There is an old episode of *Friends* on but the signal is bad; yet, Eliezer watches the show with his vacant eyes, almost ignoring us, but not out of rudeness. His mind just seems to be somewhere else.

Eliezer has curly hair, with distinct black and white strands, the stark contrast of which make it clear that there is no such thing as "gray" hair. He's short, and seems even shorter seated as he is on the couch, with his arms draped over his semi-opened legs, hands crossed forward.

Kathia has begun to talk to another frantic man. He continuously gets up and overwhelms my friend with questions, even though I can't understand in which language. I get distracted and almost annoyed by this presence that seems to want to capture my attention at all costs.

Eliezer is a farmworker. He used to pick fruit in North Carolina. The first time he came to Immokalee to work was during the harvest season of '74; at that time, he had a wife. She was waiting for him and he would go home regularly. Then, the convulsions started, so Eliezer had to quit working in the fields. He found a job in construction, driving a forklift, but that didn't last long either. Once he almost died on the job.[29]

Eliezer is staying at the Friendship House because he can't work at the moment. Last September he fell, dislocating his shoulder: he still takes painkillers because it still hurts. He won't be able to use that arm as he used to, the doctors said. He can't lift it anymore, Eliezer shows me. Besides, if the rumor that he suffers from convulsions spreads, it would get even more difficult to find somebody who would hire him. Too much responsibility. No employer wants to deal with a guy at risk of dropping dead on the work site.

"It's been years since I last talked to her," Eliezer says, abruptly referring to his wife. "She must think I'm dead."

Kathia finally introduces me and Javier,* the frantic one. She says that he, too, has a story to tell. Without giving Eliezer the impression that our conversation is over, I move to the chair closer to Javier.

Eliezer and Kathia begin to talk. Kathia says something in Creole and Eliezer smiles and seems to cheer up a little. He admits that he has problems with the language…Quite often the Haitians he meets do not consider him to be a Haitian. "They have this attitude…" he says. "'I'm better than you,' right?" Kathia nods her head. They both laugh. Finally, Eliezer has turned his eyes away from the TV. He now looks at us as he speaks.

Meanwhile, Javier calls for attention. He complains because he needs to get paid. He is Mexican and speaks Spanish but at points tries to communicate in English. It's hard to understand him and Kathia helps me with it. Javier has lived in Florida for twelve years now. He has a wife…She is Black, he says, she lives in North Carolina along with his son. He sends money home but he hasn't seen them in two years.

"There is a lot of work here: the tomato harvest, the oranges, the beans…or in landscaping," he says.

Javier has a punched card in his hand. It serves to take note of the hours worked in the fields. But I have trouble understanding how that works, and he's giving the impression he doesn't understand it very well, either. So the four of us gather around the punched card in an attempt to decipher it.

There's a grid with the months and hours; they refer to a certain farm, but it's impossible to read the name as the card is badly wrinkled. The hours have been punched ten times between the period of January and May. Since the pay is $2.50 per hour, the boss owes him $50. Or so we figured.

Javier almost rips the card apart as he pulls it away out of our reach; we manage to read the name on it. It's not Javier's, Kathia notices out loud. He has to withdraw some money on behalf of a friend, or his brother, he mutters. Or perhaps Javier simply found that card and is now trying to claim fifty bucks.

Someone calls him from the other room. Javier springs up and disappears without even saying bye. He has to cash out, Eliezer excuses him, as if he knew what the truth with Javier is. Eliezer looks much more relaxed now. In the end, we are a distraction for him, a welcome distraction. He seems to get bored a lot and have a desperate need for companionship. Still, he is not the type of guy that feels sorry for himself: he's grateful, he says, after having been spared so many times in his life, and he considers the possibility of sharing his emotions with somebody a gift.

We hear some noise coming from outside. The Christmas parade is passing by the Friendship House.

"I don't know when was the last time I have seen one," says Eliezer, still undecided whatever to go outside or not.

"Let's go, then!" Kathia encourages him.

It's gotten dark. Main Street is invaded by sparkling, colorful floats; the kids are not the only ones having fun as Shrek, Peter Pan, and Cinderella in her pumpkin carriage pass by. The floats set up by the Immokalee schools and other local organizations are on parade. Tradition is tradition again, and here in Immokalee it still seems to be meaningful to the community: it's a time of playfulness and sharing.

"I feel so lucky," says Eliezer, smiling as a child, and he repeats that he hasn't seen such a nice parade in years.

"You know, I believe in God. God is real," Eliezer adds at one point.

Kathia gets near him and asks Eliezer if she can pray with him. She takes his hand and puts her arm around his shoulders. Eyes on the ground, Kathia begins to pray as the last illuminated floats parade away. The people of Immokalee thin out slowly and go back to their homes. We hug Eliezer good-bye and set out onto the darkness of "Alligator Alley."

A line of FEMA trailers on the side of an unpaved road in Immokalee

Five

JANUARY

Padre Patricio

I tune to Radio Conciencia. I'm driving on SR-29, the roadway that vertically cuts southwestern Florida into two and on which Immokalee nestles. I left dreary weather on the east coast, but around the Big Cypress reservation the sky opened with a promise of a beautiful day.

I come back to Immokalee after the holidays. Father Patrick—Padre Patricio, as everybody calls him here—offered to be my guide and translator this weekend. We'll be visiting some of the families that live on Ninth Street, the ramshackle neighborhood located around the Guadalupe Church and the soup kitchen.

The priest helps the families as he can: driving the women to buy groceries, worrying about the most urgent needs as well as the daily ones. "I understood that everywhere I went the poorest people were among Latinos," Padre Patricio tells me as we're having lunch at El Ranchito, a Mexican restaurant on Main Street. That's why some years back the priest decided to learn Spanish.

"The vocation of the Church is to build a community among the ones who need it the most," he continues.

Padre Patricio arrived in Immokalee six months ago. "The principal of a school in Fort Myers is a very good friend of mine. At that time, I was serving in a small town in Brunswick County, North Carolina, that one, too, a community primarily inhabited by migrant workers. My friend knew I was thinking of moving to Mexico. So he said: 'Why don't you come to Immokalee?' After a little while, I received the official invitation from the bishop."

But Patricio opted not to accept the position of parish priest.

"I didn't know this community and at that time I wasn't even that fluent in Spanish," he says. Padre Patricio, who will turn forty this year, is a pretty laid-back churchman; one can tell by the very way he dresses. Today, for instance, he is wearing a T-shirt and a pair of shorts.

"People are going to talk now...'We saw Padre Patricio at El Ranchito with a beautiful girl!'" he says, teasingly; then he bursts into his unmistakable laughter.

Coming out of the restaurant, we run into the Garcia* family. Padre Patricio begins to talk with the father, Carlos, a Mexican man in his thirties. Carlos shakes the priest's hand and then mine. From the big, black pickup truck his wife, Sonia,* pops up as the darkened window slowly goes down. Sonia says hello to the priest while she rubs her eyes. "I was dozing off," she says to excuse her sleepiness. She is very tired, after a day of work in the field. I catch a glimpse of the kids in the car. Padre Patricio calls them up and introduces them to me: Aurelio,* nine, the oldest, Cristiano,* seven, and Juan,* four.

Padre Patricio tells the Garcias how last week he tried to go to work in the fields. No, he couldn't make it because he didn't have a farmworker card. Now he does, as he shows us. The card reads "Immokalee Agricultural Worker I.D.," and has a photo of Padre Patricio, whose last name is O'Connor, and he totally looks like an

Irish dude: pale skin and two husky-blue eyes. Quite difficult for him to pass as a Mexican.

"While I was wearing my sunglasses it worked out, but when I took them off, everybody started looking at me suspiciously," Padre Patricio says laughingly.

"Why, Father," Sonia asks still sleepy, "do you want to go work in the fields?"

"I want to know what the life of the people I serve is like," he answers nonchalantly.

Sonia shrugs.

"I can try again," the priest says putting away the card in his wallet. "Now I don't have to go to that office again."

"Next time you want to go to the fields, Carlos interjects, you should come with me." Where he works, no card is required. Carlos can take him as soon as tomorrow if he likes. But Padre Patricio has an appointment at the church in the morning.

"Can I go with you?" I venture.

Sonia and Carlos look at each other for a moment and then they both nod.

"You can sleep over tonight," adds Sonia, checking for her husband's approval.

The Garcias are extremely religious. Good people, the priest says. They go to Mass every day. Coming from Padre Patricio, it comes out almost as a warning.

"They're doing well compared to most families in Immokalee. They live in a nice house now."

Not so long ago, Carlos was working for an alarm systems company. He was making good money, but then he got laid off and went back to picking tomatoes. On the other hand, the Garcias were able to move into one of the houses reserved for farmworkers, and their expenses for rent decreased considerably.

The youngest children, Cristiano and Juan, are ill. They have muscular dystrophy. For this reason, the family receives a monthly contribution for health expenses. The children were born in the United States, and as American citizens have the right to medical assistance.

Defending Immigrant Rights 101

Padre Patricio and I walk to the RCMA, the early education center for the children of migrant workers and low-income families located on Main Street. At the center today there's a training session organized by the Florida Immigrant Coalition (FLIC)[1] and the Florida Immigrant Advocacy Center (FIAC).[2]

Padre Patricio wanted to be here. "It's good to know more about certain things," he whispers leaning toward my shoulder as I join him at a workshop. "Defending Immigrant Rights 101: Detention, Deportation and the Criminal Justice System" is the title of the seminar.[3]

The information material is being distributed in three languages: English, Spanish, and Haitian Creole. The training session today is intended for community organizers, consultants, and farmworkers' advocates so that, in turn, they will inform immigrants about their rights.

"The law, in fact, is routinely violated," Subhash (who works with FLIC) explains. "But you cannot just assume that because the police or ICE [U.S. Immigration and Customs Enforcement] are asking you a question that you have to answer them. In fact, besides your name, there are very few things that you are required to tell the police or ICE. More importantly, you should just assume that the only reason why they are asking your country of origin or your immigration status is because they are trying to deport you."

Racial profiling, in fact, is a daily reality and a constant threat for Latino immigrants.[4]

Tricky questions like "I hear an accent…where are you from?" are being asked, but not of white people who may very well be Canadian or British citizens.

Police often presume if you "look" Latino that you are undocumented. If you get caught, say, driving without a license, it's easy to be intimidated into giving crucial information, like your immigration status. In the best scenarios, when immigrants run across more lenient officers, they end up paying costly fines. During one of my visits to Immokalee, I met a woman who spent her weekends on the side of the road selling tamales to pay off her husband's fines. The man didn't have a valid U.S. license but had to drive to his workplace every day.

"When ICE raids a home," Subhash continues. "It can be a very traumatic experience. They frequently come with several officers, all armed with guns, sometimes looking like they just came back from a war. They try to trick people into opening up the door and letting them in, because they don't have a warrant.

"There are five things you must remember when ICE or the police are at your door." Subhash explains to the audience. "The first, you don't have to say anything to law enforcement except your name. You do not have to tell them your country of origin or your immigration status. Second, you don't have to open the door if they don't have a warrant signed by a judge. They quite often don't have a warrant signed by a judge, and if they don't you do not have to let them in.[5]

"Third, you don't have to sign anything if you don't understand what you are signing. If ICE is forcing you to sign a document, that document may be to give up your rights. Fourth, you should never lie to law enforcement; there is a huge difference between remaining silent and lying. One is illegal. Lastly, if you don't know what to say, tell them you will not speak to them without talking to a lawyer first.

"Ports of entry, jails, airports, train and bus stations...Greyhound now allows ICE agents to board their buses and ask people for their papers." Subhash says. "*These* are the places where people are most at risk of running into ICE."

Contrary to what many people believe, immigration law has not become more restrictive simply as a result of September 11, or after the passing of the Patriot Act and the creation of the Department of Homeland Security (DHS). Anti-immigrant legislation found new life beginning in the mid-nineties with the controversial Proposition 187, which intended to deny undocumented immigrants the basic use of social services, health care, and public education in California.[6] In 1996, the Illegal Immigration Reform and Immigrant Responsibility Act (IIRIRA) was enacted by President Clinton.[7] IIRIRA, for instance, bars admission to any person who has been without documents in the country for any period of time.[8] This piece of legislation, along with the 2006 Anti-Terrorism and Effective Death Penalty Act (AEDPA), has made deportations easier by replacing a largely discretionary system with mandatory detention and mandatory deportation. Grounds for deportation have expanded to include minor offenses. Immigrants (lawful permanent residents included) with a single marijuana conviction or a shoplifting violation become "criminal aliens" and deportable.[9] Before 1996, the suspension of the sentence was at the discretion of the immigration judge, and quite often repatriation was revoked when a person proved to have lived and worked honestly in the United States for at least seven years, or in cases of extenuating circumstances—if, for example, deportation would have caused major discomfort to the individual or to one of the members of his/her family who was a U.S. citizen or a permanent resident (usually, the children). In this way, the law protected families and specifically minors and their right to grow up with their parents.

If we are to judge from the number of immigrants that are being detained, deportations have grown exponentially since IIRIRA was passed.[10]

Traditionally, federal authorities have enforced violations of immigration statutes. 287(g) programs extended this power to local police by cross-designating officers to enforce immigration law. Even though Section 287(g) was added to the Immigration and Nationality Act back in 1996 as part of the IIRIRA, these programs have been actively implemented only in the past few years. More than half of these active partnership agreements—thirty-two out of the sixty-three on record by November 2008—are in the Southeast.[11] Twenty-seven Collier County deputies are now ICE agents.[12]

In Immokalee, too, the number of arrests has risen. In September 2006, a document released by ICE proudly announced that the FBI in collaboration with Collier County and Lee County sheriffs had arrested a record number (163) of criminal aliens, fugitives and other immigration violators. That included—what the news release didn't say—people with a speeding ticket on record, even a twenty-year-old citation. Not surprisingly, most Latinos (81 percent) don't want local police enforcing immigration laws, as a 2008 Pew Hispanic Center reports cites.[13]

The criminalization of *any* low-income Latino immigrant goes hand in hand with a new approach to the problem of "illegal immigration" that the Bush administration initiated with the passing of the Comprehensive Immigration Reform Act (H.R. 4437; S. 2611).[14] The legislation further militarized the border, criminalized undocumented immigrants, and even humanitarian assistance to immigrants (especially along the border). Congress authorized a seven-hundred-mile-long fence along the U.S./Mexico border.

The Patriot Act (2001) and the corollary creation of DHS (2003) focused on fighting domestic terrorism. Protecting the border from a possible influx of terrorists was the initial rationale behind the incorporation of the U.S. Custom and Border Patrol (CBP) within the DHS;[15] however, within a few years, the DHS policy, specifically the CBP's mission, refocused on curbing illegal immigration with a sustained expenditure of federal and state resources.[16]

As reported by the Immigration Policy Center,[17] the annual budget of the Border Patrol, once the Cinderella of the U.S. law enforcement, has increased by 714 percent since 1992. The number of Border Patrol agents stationed along the Southwest border has grown by 390 percent.[18]

In response to this harsh set of legislation and anti-immigrant feelings around the country, immigrants and civil rights supporters organized a "A Day without a Mexican" and took on the streets of Chicago, New York, Los Angeles, and many other cities on May 1, 2006.[19]

At a time when the pressure for truly comprehensive immigration reform was at its highest, the Bush administration needed to show its right-wing supporters that it was doing something to fight "illegal immigration." "Doing something" translated into performing occasional blitzkrieg operations such as workplace raids—disastrous in their human, social, and economic consequences—on the one hand,[20] and mandating an increase in the number of arrests and deportations, on the other. In fact, in a memo dated January 31, 2006, ICE raised the target goal of each team from 125 to 1,000.[21] What started with the grotesque name of Operation Return to Sender,[22] whose focus was hunting down dangerous immigrant fugitives, soon changed its original scope. ICE shifted its target from actual criminals and terrorism suspects to "ordinary status violators," with the result of criminalizing the latter while reducing the pressure on drug and human smugglers.[23]

Historically, U.S. administrative courts have processed immigration violations. Immigrants who were caught crossing the border illegally were often fingerprinted and returned to Mexico without criminal charges. Since the program called Operation Streamline (2005) went into effect, anyone caught crossing the border illegally can be charged with a misdemeanor immigration count and thus get arrested.[24] In addition, residential raids have become common with the result of terrorizing Latino communities.[25]

Meanwhile, the criminal prosecution of employers who hire undocumented immigrants is still sparse; in essence, the law only applies to the most vulnerable.[26] Additionally, hiring unauthorized workers is an employment-based immigration violation, which also results in damages for the entire U.S. labor force as it jeopardizes the competiveness of law-abiding employers;[27] the massive presence of undocumented workers is in fact detrimental for *all* workers, as it brings down labor standards.

The crackdown on "illegal" immigrants resulted in numerous arrests of unauthorized residents and "apprehensions" along the border; thus, the federal demand for beds in prisons has skyrocketed. Immigration detention centers today hold more than three hundred thousand detainees per year;[28] the number of beds have doubled in the last four years.[29] And many have expressed concern about the increased privatization of immigration centers. The average cost of detaining an immigrant is $95 per person/per day.[30] Additionally, systematic neglect of ill detainees has been documented in detention facilities run by ICE or private contractors.[31] In the recommendations for the population management of ICE, it reads: "The ideal system should create the capacity to detain and to supervise aliens *consistent with assessed risk*" (my emphasis).[32]

Another solution to the growing number of potential detainees has become, for instance, home arrest. Fancier names are used, however, for "Alternative to Detention Programs" (ATD). ICE supervises 19,160 aliens in the three ATD existing programs: Intensive Supervision Appearance Program (ISAP), Enhanced Supervision Reporting (ESR) and Electronic Monitoring (EM). ISAP, specifically, has a capacity for six thousand cases per day.[33] It is the most restrictive (and expensive) of the three programs since it utilizes telephonic reporting, radio frequency monitoring, and global position system tracking in addition to unannounced home visits, curfew checks, and employment verification.

ICE contracts both ISAP and ESR to vendors. One of these is Behavioral Interventions Inc. (BI), an agency based in Boulder, Colorado;[34] BI claims to help reduce government costs by lowering inmate population, fighting recidivism, and implementing other programs aimed to reduce prison overcrowding.[35] A much-needed service, one might think. BI offers alternatives to detention through the use of GPS tracking—the company's specialty, "while preserving the Sheriff's Office's priority—public safety," so we read on its website. The adult aliens "who joined the program" have overstayed a visa or have been denied asylum; other times, they have been found without documentation. Originally, the program was specifically directed to monitor individuals released from detention.[36] Depending on their situation, they might be given the option of either voluntarily departure or appeal under the false impression that they will get help through the ISAP program and start a naturalization process or retrieve their initial immigrant status, for instance. The ones who have family and especially children in the United States usually appeal, as well as others who fear they won't be able to come back.

After the court hearing, ICE officers are outside waiting to escort the "participants" to the BI office; here they are strapped with an ankle bracelet (HomeGuard system).[37] "The participants are always very surprised when they are escorted to the BI office," said a former ISAP Case Specialist for BI.[38] "Most of them were just attending their regularly scheduled court hearing and next thing they know, they're basically on house arrest."

ISAP consists of home guarding with an ankle bracelet or another one of the "BI electronic monitoring technologies." Participants are provided with a list of immigration attorneys and are given a strict schedule to which they must adhere. For instance, they must meet with their Case Specialist three times a week for the first thirty days; meetings occur during working hours (8 a.m.–5 p.m.), which makes it difficult for them to keep a regular job. According to my informant, participants are usually treated like criminals and are lied to because most of them inevitably end up being deported anyway.[39]

Occasionally, people win their appeals and are granted permanent residency. The rest are often tricked and turned over to ICE, my informant reports. Once their appeal gets dismissed, BI Case Specialists are informed *before* participants get officially notified.[40] Exceptions are made for citizens of Europe or Canada. "I remember one time a British guy who was a participant in the ISAP program was allowed to attend, without GPS, an FSU game and party with his friends," my informant says. The young man had previously been detained in Puerto Rico for not having proper immigrant documentation.

"No person from Latin America would have been allowed such a privilege," my informant adds.

Despite legislation becoming more restrictive, there are currently around twelve million undocumented immigrants in the United States. Doug Wilson of the ACLU reminds us that in 1990, there were only 3.5 million unauthorized immigrants in the United States.[41] Twelve million vulnerable individuals, subject to all sorts of exploitation since it takes so little for them to be deported to their countries of origin. Twelve million who are not even eligible to "get in line," as there are only five thousand green cards available yearly for less-skilled workers.[42]

◆

At the RCMA, a new speaker is showing us a typical situation. Role-playing, Subhash tells me, is the best way to explain complex issues during these training sessions. Besides, they are very practical and easy to understand regardless of participants' background.

"I have to take Tequila out," Padre Patricio whispers. So we walk toward the church where the dog is expecting us. It's a wonderful day. The sun shines up in the sky, and a positively pleasant breeze blows.

Padre Patricio introduces me to Father Hector, the parish priest of the Guadalupe Church. He is Italian, too. He comes from the city of Trento, located in the northeastern part of the peninsula.

Padre Ettore has lived in Immokalee for over ten years now. We chat a bit in Italian, while he stares at me with his big, round eyes. He is almost blind, and after the stroke he had last year, has lost part of his memory.

I'm about to ask Padre Ettore how in the world he ended up in Immokalee when he, almost reading my mind, says, giggling: "I am a mountain man...for years I have been asking myself what mysterious divine plan led me to the flat land of Florida..."

We go back in the main office. Here I meet the secretary of the parish, Santos. She is the receptionist now, and the one in charge of the administration at the church. This is the job that Angela, Paco's mother, once had, when Father Sanders was alive.

Here I see the posters of the Scalabrini and get my answer. Padre Ettore is part of the Congregation of the Missionaries of Saint Charles Borromeo, founded by Giambattista Scalabrini, a priest canonized in 1997. Created at the end of the nineteenth century to support Italian immigrants overseas and all over the world, the order has since then expanded its mission to migrants from any corner of the globe.

The Scalabrinians preach the message of Jesus Christ to immigrants and refugees, the ones most in need of solace because they live a life away from home. Likewise, Padre Ettore fulfilled his mission also by sharing the experience of migration.

As we walk outside, I see that there are men playing soccer in the fields behind the soup kitchen.

"I had them put there," Padre Patricio says, pointing to the goals and making an effort, yet not succeeding, to conceal his pride. "They played even before...but now they can have more fun, right?"

We go and see the church. ·

"We're remodeling it," he says. "It's coming out really nice." The door squeaks and the priest greets one of the workers in Spanish. "We should get the pews tomorrow," he says, to excuse the absence of seating facilities. He shows me the stained-glass windows where the Stations of the Cross are depicted. "You can tell that the person who envisioned these artworks knew of the plight of the immigrants..." Padre Patricio comments. The burdens these figures bear on their shoulders are symbols of the cross of Christ. "But you see," he points out, "the ones in the foreground are all white..."

We cross the street and venture into one of the poorest areas of Immokalee. The first home we visit is located right on Ninth Street. To get in, we have to climb a step. It's a house trailer, one of the many for which Immokalee landowners demand $700–$800 a month.

A "Merry Christmas" sign dangles on the side, although the holidays have long passed.

The priest knocks on the door.

"Georgina!* It's Padre Patricio!" he announces, almost yelling.

The woman who comes to the door is minuscule: she has straight black hair tied in a low ponytail, her traits unquestionably indigenous. Georgina welcomes us into her home literally with open arms. She smiles and continuously nods her head as she and Padre Patricio exchange pleasantries in Spanish.

We enter and we are right *in* the kitchen. Georgina invites us to have a seat. After some maneuvers, the three of us manage to fit around the table. The room, too, is miniature, without flooring yet bulging with all sorts of knick-knacks.

Georgina hands us a couple of bottles of water. Padre Patricio introduces me to her, telling her that I'm writing a book about Immokalee. He begins to speak with Georgina in Spanish, to ask her thousands of questions, with the confidence of one who asks and knows that he's always accepted, never contradicted, because his very presence, his role, engenders reverence. What's more, Padre Patricio knows how to be loved by his people. He visits these families on a regular basis, makes sure they're doing all right, helps them when and how he can.

I'm sitting in a corner next to the door; above me, at hat-height, if I wore one, a cage filled with three pigeons is mounted.

"They picked them up right in front of the house," Padre Patricio points out in a whisper.

Georgina Dolores Cortéz is from Guatemala and learned to communicate in Spanish here in Immokalee. In fact, her first language is

Acateco, widely spoken in the northern regions of Guatemala and in the southern ones of Mexico. Georgina has five kids: one of them is married with a child; the smallest, Sofia,* three, is smiling up at me from underneath the table. She looks like a petite vampire, missing the front teeth but with prominent, pointed canines. Golden, precious-stoned earrings light up her face. Now Sofia is well but last week they took her to the emergency room down in Miami due to complications with her recent liver transplant. Georgina has to take care of her kids, especially little Sofia, which means she's only able to work only once a week.

Te gusta la novela? I ask Georgina, while I nod to the small TV turned on above the refrigerator. The woman protects herself, embarrassed, seeming, if possible, even smaller.

Georgina appears pleased about Padre Patricio's visit. She smiles and nods constantly. She replies to the questions the priest, my accomplice, asks. Georgina tells us how she got to Immokalee. Georgina still remembers the day: March 10, 1995.

"I crossed the desert along with the coyote, my husband, and Juanito* on my shoulders…and I was very, very scared."

For Guatemalan immigrants, the journey to the United States is doubly risky and exhausting. They have to cross two borders: the one with Mexico and the one with the United States. I look at the picture on the fridge: it's a family portrait, Georgina with her children. Everybody smiles and looks happy. Georgina leans toward the TV and lowers the volume of the *novela*.

At that moment, Juanito comes in with a backpack on his shoulder. He is seven and a half but like the rest of his family is small and skinny, with a minute, round face that makes him look half his age. He's returning from the after-school program. Juanito is a good student, right? Padre Patricio looks at Georgina and pats Juanito's shoulder, who, in turn, lowers his eyes, shyly. He takes off his backpack and begins to fiddle with a big chain.

Padre Patricio says something I don't understand and then burst out with his signature laugh. I move the vase of flowers to better see Sofia, who, in the meantime, has started playing with Killer, the little dog that Juanito has just released from the cage hidden underneath the table and that he now controls with the help of his enormous chain. On the other end of the table, there is an additional cage on a chair. Inside, there are two little parrots. Juanito, who noticed I've been looking in that direction, lifts the cage for me, proudly, so that I can better see the birds.

We go out the back door. Padre Patricio introduces me to a couple of neighbors. They are hanging out in Georgina's yard next to an unused barbecue.

"Here is where the kids play," says the priest scanning the yard. "It's nice when all these families get together, at night or during the weekend."

We go to visit Olga,* but she's not home. We find two teachers instead, Kristy* and Pam,* of Corkscrew Elementary School. They say there was a fire a couple of days ago at Olga's place; the air conditioning short-circuited and mattresses, couch, chairs, everything, caught fire.

Kristy and Pam are making an inventory with two of Olga's children. Kristy is very angry. She just found out that Olga was paying one thousand dollars a month to the landlord. She's determined to investigate the fire.

The teachers found another trailer, a cheaper one, for Olga and her kids, just down the street. The woman, though, they say, doesn't want to move. The children can walk to school by themselves from where they live now. But the other trailer is very close. The truth, Pam says, is different: the landlord has threatened Olga, she says softly so that the kids can't hear her.

The landlord, right after the fire, sent some workers to discard the burned furniture and clean up the apartment. He had the walls repainted, and the faulty AC system replaced—to avoid an investigation on the fire, the teachers say.

The Garcia Family

The first thing I notice upon entering the Garcias's home is the smell of disinfectant. Their house, as Padre Patricio told me, is rather spacious: four bedrooms, two bathrooms, a kitchen with a big refrigerator, oven, dishwasher and microwave, dining room, and living room. Modest but dignified.

The home of the Garcias is located in a residential area, at least by Immokalee's standards. White houses, all looking alike, prefabricated, with the usual lawn and driveway in the front, not dissimilar to the ones of other lower-middle class communities in Florida.

Padre Patricio is conversing in Spanish with the Garcias. Aurelio, the oldest son, drags me to his room, the room where I will sleep tonight. Aurelio is the only healthy son, as his build and round face demonstrate. He moves and speaks constantly, excited by the idea of having guests.

Then he suddenly gets serious as kids his age do, as if part of a calculated staging. He turns around, to make sure no one is paying attention to us. He gets near, scrunches his forehead and his crew cut comes forward almost to the point of covering his eyes.

"I have to warn you about something," he says. "Sometimes my brother moans at night."

Sonia takes the pie out of the fridge.

"That's the one we bought in Naples, right?" Padre Patricio asks.

Last Monday was a holiday (Martin Luther King Jr. Day), and the priest took the Garcias to the beach. He thought it would have been the first time for the kids, but they had been there already, on a school trip. That night, also, they all went to the movies.

"It's almost five thirty!" exclaims Padre Patricio, taking a look at his wristwatch. "I gotta go." He apologizes but he can't stay any longer. He has a dinner appointment with a friend in Naples.

Padre Patricio says goodbye to everybody and heads to the door followed by Tequila. Sonia puts the cranberry pie on the table. She cuts it into slices. Aurelio arranges the vanilla ice cream on the pie over-flowing with jam. He helps the ice cream off the spoon with a finger. Now that the priest has left, something strange happens: Carlos begins to address me in English. Padre Patricio told me that only the children speak the language because they have learned it in school. "I under-stand English even though I only speak a little bit of it," Carlos smiles at me, his black eyes shining over his white teeth. I turn to Sonia. She shakes her head and lowers her eyes with that little girl's look of hers.

She understands, too, adds Carlos, only a little.

Sonia is thirty-one and has little hands. Now that Carlos has disap-peared into the other room, she begins to tell me how she got to Immokalee. Sonia speaks Spanish; I ask questions in English. When we don't understand each other, Aurelio intervenes.

"Well, back in Mexico I was engaged…" she says. "This guy had proposed when I was only fourteen. But I didn't want to commit at that time. I was so young! A few years later, I crossed. And I came to Immokalee, with my cousin. I remember that the first days I was feel-ing very lonely and lost. I didn't know anybody, I was very shy, and I still had my fiancé in Mexico…" Sonia, too, like Georgina, remembers the exact date she arrived in Immokalee: November 14, 1997. A month or so later, she met Carlos. "But he didn't like me at first," Sonia says, giggling. "It seemed like he was snubbing me." Then they got together and left for Georgia. Carlos and Sonia began to work in a couch factory; they were getting by. "That's where Aurelio was born," Sonia says laying her eyes on her oldest son. "Believe it or not, Carlos and I are not even married!"

As Padre Patricio will explain later, the Garcias are not husband and wife, despite being fervent Catholics. In fact, they don't have a visa; the priest, however, is helping them find a way to get married.

"But in all these years…" Sonia continues. "Carlos and I have been through a lot. Sad moments and happy moments. Good and bad."

Sonia gestures with her little hands while detailing the alternate periods of her life in America.

The Garcias get ready to go to the Guadalupe Church. There's a charismatic service that they hold on Fridays.

"You can come home whenever you like, but tomorrow morning the alarm is set for six thirty," Carlos warns me. "I'll leave the door open. There's nothing to steal here, anyway," he adds.

◆

I go to the Horizon Village where, time permitting, Miguel said he would show me the apartments.

We've never met but Miguel, who is the administrator, recognizes me from afar and waves. Only men live here and the arrival of a woman doesn't pass unnoticed. Miguel invites me to sit down in his office. It's Friday, payday, and the tenants of the Horizon come one after the other to pay the rent.

The Horizon Village is organized like a college dormitory. The residential complex, says Miguel, has a 192-person capacity with twenty-four units divided into four-bedroom apartments. Every apartment has two showers, two bathrooms, and four lavatories. The kitchen is shared. To live at the Horizon costs eight dollars a day.

"It's not cheap, if you consider how much they get paid." Miguel says. "But at least the sanitary conditions are decent."

According to a 2004 survey by the Shimberg Center for Affordable Housing of the University of Florida, more than two thousand migrants who live in the Immokalee area between October and May are left to meet their housing needs through the private market or through subsidized housing not specifically reserved for farmworkers. Chances are they will probably sleep on some trailer floor. "Stuck next to each other like sardines," as Paco says.

From behind the bulletproof glass window, Miguel collects rent, gives out receipts, gets asked for a dollar in change, opens the cash drawer, closes it, crosses the names off the list.

Miguel De La Cruz is a man in his sixties with thin and sharp lips that amicably stretch out into a broad smile when he greets the tenants of the Horizon. He calls them all by first name, aided by the occupants' list.

"The tenants have until Monday to pay rent," Miguel explains. "But they usually settle up on Friday evening, as soon as they get paid."

It's quiet now and Miguel comes near me.

"There is something I didn't understand over the phone…What are you writing about, exactly?" he asks.

"Well, then I cannot give you any information," Miguel deliberates in response. He raises hands and shoulders and shakes his head. "I'm sorry, but I received specific instructions not to talk to the media.

I have to get the approval of our executive director. I'm not the one responsible here. I'm only an administrator."

Miguel disappears into the other room and reemerges with a business card. Miss Serrata, that's the person you need to call.

I expected it. The Horizon Village has been built with a fund appro-
priately created by the federal government to make up for the housing
emergency of the Immokalee workers. Specifically, the Horizon is one of
the three buildings that have been built in Florida with funds from the
Migrant and Seasonal Farmworker Housing Initiative, allocated in 1999
as a result of the CIW-organized hunger strike, which attracted national
media attention.[43] At that time, the United States Department of Agriculture (USDA) allocated $20 million to provide for the housing emer-
gency; the state of Florida received $9.2 million; a third, along with other
subsidies, went to finance the construction of the male dormitory.[44]

"I arrived in the United States as a migrant worker..." Miguel begins.

But he is once again forced to stop: a new tenant is at the window.
Miguel smiles from behind the glass, joking in Spanish with the man
and a friend of his. The two guys leave. I ask Miguel if they have security problems at the Horizon.

He shakes his head and points to the cameras set up in the corners
of the ceiling.

"This place is surveilled 24/7. It wouldn't be a good idea to create
problems...And plus, did you see the police car out there? They are always around." Then he adds, warily, "Let's say that we have been lucky
so far..."

A man calls out to Miguel and he hands him ten dollars. "He is the
oldest one we have here," he says. "He has been working in the fields
since forever."

Miguel sometimes lends some money to the tenants. "The season has been bad...A couple of weeks ago that man didn't even have the money to buy food," he says.

Other times he brings them food, from the Friendship House, or from home. "Leftovers primarily, but I don't want the rumor to spread...I don't like it." He shrugs. "Life is hard sometimes. I toiled a lot. My sister...She was able to get a doctorate in Business and Administration. She now works at Keiser College in Miami. Maybe you have heard of her..." Miguel says his sister's full name. "They wrote about her in the paper and even in books, speaking of hers as 'a success story.'"

Miguel passes his big hand over his face.

"It's almost seven. I am tired. I've been up since four."

Miguel volunteers at the Friendship House. This morning he helped Monica with the annual count of the homeless.

"We found nine," Miguel says.

The questionnaire helps them understand to what extent the services provided by the Friendship House meet the needs of the people in the community.

"Sometimes we need more blankets," Miguel continues. "And then we have to let the people know that we have blankets. So if they need them, people can come and get them. This year we interviewed 162 individuals, between homeless and the so-called 'subjects at risk,' which include the guests at the temporary shelter."   .

They were 137 men, twenty-five women, of which twenty-two were African Americans, two Haitians, 127 Latinos...(significantly enough, the questionnaire grouped all of them in one category...), and eleven Whites.

"One of the questions was, 'Where did you sleep last night?' Many said in the woods, or in a car, or in the back of a store, or close to the garbage can; others, with friends, or at the Friendship House."

Miguel looks at his watch. Then he gets up. It's seven o'clock, time to go.

At the CIW I meet Gerardo. He is about to start his shift at Radio Conciencia. We walk toward a small trailer. Outside, we find the guys who run the previous program: they are part of Alcoholics Anonymous. Gerardo exchanges ideas with them on how to finance the programs without resorting to private enterprises. No commercials on Immokalee public radio.

It's cold outside, so we go into the trailer. Gerardo sets up the radio console. I ask him if he knows where Paco is. He hasn't seen our friend in a while. At that moment, Luis, the other host of the program, comes in.

Today is Friday, and Radio Conciencia features the Top 20 hits of Latin music in the United States, playing commercial music: reggaeton, the Latin rock of Manà, Christina Aguilera singing in Spanish, and so on. And the usual public service announcements.

Gerardo reminds *todas las mujeres de Immokalee* of the free English course. Starting next Sunday, the coalition will offer an English class, specifically for women. It's time to go back to the Garcias. The family returns from the church with news: we won't go to work tomorrow.

"The boss called and said, 'Monday.'"

Sonia warms up the dinner as the kids slowly take their seats around the table. Cristiano doesn't eat: he just plays with the grapes; every now and then he puts one in his mouth. They ask me where I've been and when I mention Radio Conciencia, Carlos turns up his nose. He doesn't like the CIW but he doesn't want to tell me why.

Before going into the kitchen, Aurelio drags me to a corner in the hallway. I gotta tell you something else, he says. He beckons me closer.

"My parents sometimes argue at night," he whispers. "If you hear something, just don't pay attention to them."

After dinner, Carlos disappears into the bedroom. Sonia pulls out a plastic bag full of pictures. "Do you want to see them?" asks Sonia waiting for me to nod. We sit on the couch. The kids come close too. Aurelio sits next to me; it seems that, as a first-born child, Aurelio always feels the need to be nearby, so that he can provide his commentary.

"My mom would have never imagined that one day a person from Italy would stay at our house!" announces Aurelio, teasing his mom. Sonia gives him a rap in the head; then she smiles at me, embarrassed. The inconvenient truth of children.

She begins to pass me pictures. Her sons: one after the other. Only babies first, then toddlers, progressively changing, as they grow older. The sad moments, the ones that Sonia hinted at in the afternoon, the toughest ones during Cristiano's illness, are in the pictures too, as evidenced by the IV that fed him through his nostrils. And the happy ones, the ones of their trip to Disneyworld. The entire Garcia family: in the background, the Cinderella castle at Magic Kingdom. And the kids photographed with Goofy, at Epcot Center.

"Let her go to sleep!" Carlos yells at Sonia from the other room. Sonia ignores him and continues. She keeps telling me about the happy moments. A couple of years ago they spent a week in Orlando. All expenses paid. Completely free, remarks Aurelio excitedly. One day, the "Make-a-Wish" Foundation came to interview Cristiano, they selected him, and so the entire Garcia family was able to go to Disneyworld. "Can you imagine?" Aurelio says with eyes that shine now as I'm sure did then. "They came to pick us up with the limousine!"

The day after, Aurelio drags his slippers to the living room. He has a bunch of DVDs. He fans them out for me. Pick one, he orders, still in his pajamas. Cristiano, standing by my side, suggests *Spiderman 2*. "Alright. This one," I say, mimicking Cristiano's pointed finger. "But I'll have to go soon." "Padre Patricio is on his way," Carlos announces from the other room as he hangs up the cell phone. "We are going to have breakfast together! *Sopa de pollo!*" The priest arrives after five minutes, smiling. He's definitely in a good mood. He has brought a couple of DVDs. One is a film on the life of a saint—Aurelio likes to know more about the history of the Church, Padre Patricio says—the other one, an old Mexican comedy for the parents.

We sit at the table. Carlos eats the soup with the help of a tortilla. Then he hands Padre Patricio the aluminum foil in which hot tortillas are wrapped one over the other. The priest refuses, vigorously shaking his hand.

"*Padre, no te gustan tortillas?*" (Father, don't you like tortillas?) The Garcias ask in unison.

"Oh yeah, I love them! Fact is, since I've moved here in Immokalee I gained 20 pounds!" explains the priest in defense. "It's because of the food: rich in fat and carbs!"

We start a discussion on the caloric content of tortillas. Father Patrick insists on saying that tortillas are made with lard. Sonia laughs and shakes her head benevolently, like people do with children when they say something silly. She pulls out the box of *maiz* flour and reassures the priest that the tortillas are made only with that, and a little bit of water.

But Father Patrick is not convinced and lets us eat all the excellent tortillas Sonia just made. While still tasting his *sopa de pollo*, he expertly diverts and begins to speak (in Spanish) about his trip to Italy. About its artistic wonders. Carlos asks anxiously if he has ever been to the Vatican.

"Of course!" the Father exclaims, and then resumes talking about places he's been that the Garcias have never seen.

I go back to watch *Spiderman 2* with the kids. The little one, Juan, complains; he wants his brothers to change the DVD. In fact, Alfredo Molina *is* pretty scary with his steeled tentacles.

Padre Patricio's voice comes from the other room: he's moved on to another anecdote, this one about one of his trips to Mexico. He begins to talk about Juchitán, the city in the Mexican state of Oaxaca populated primarily by indigenous people, where they still speak Zapotec. The Garcias have never heard of the place, or pretend not to, to hear what the priest has to say about it. Padre Patricio tells of the women of Juchitán, omitting the revolutionary tradition of the city and focusing on the caricatural side that has made it famous all around the world.

"*Las mujeres...*" the priest proceeds, "are big, drink tequila, and laugh coarsely," he makes the gesture to raise the elbow and mimics a laugh, like those of Mexicans in Westerns. "They are women of extraordinary force and legendary beauty, and that's why the men worship them and are subjugated to their wills."

Carlos covers Sonia's ears with his hands. Don't listen, he says. They both laugh.

◆

I look for Paco. I have left him a couple of messages on his voicemail but he's never returned my calls. He might have lost his cell phone again. Angela opens the door.

"*Hola Silvia.* I was about to go..." she says, letting me in. Angela has makeup on and is all dressed up. She is going to a wedding at the Guadalupe Church; the son of a friend is getting married. Angela looks excited. "I have never been to a Guatemalan wedding," she says.

Tina is supposed to come pick her up at any minute.

"Do you want to go?" she asks.

"Where is Paco?" I reply.

"In his room, sick," she says.

I find Paco in bed, all bundled up in the covers. I basically wake him up. He felt sick last night: stomachache. It happens to him more or less once a year, he says.

"I feel better this morning," he adds, as he's getting up. I tell Paco about what I did the day before. He gets dressed. We go outside and sit on the old bench in front of his house. Some kids are playing basketball in the opposite courts. Time slows down. As often happens, Paco and I end up talking about personal matters that are also political and political matters that are also personal. Things we decided are going to stay between the two of us.

Angela is back from Mass. She asks us if we would like to go with her to the wedding reception. "Are they going to play *marimba?*" Paco asks with shiny eyes. Angela shrugs.

I follow Paco's pickup truck. The reception is right outside Immokalee. We pass in front of Jubilation, a residential community built by Harvest for Humanity. Here, too, the houses are all alike, with a lawn and driveway, featuring the same cookie-cutter layout.

It's the American Dream that struggles to be realized in Immokalee.

We reach our destination. I park on the grassy side of the road, next to the Vasquezes' truck.

Music welcomes us as soon as we exit our vehicles. There's a strange atmosphere: no one dances, the party seems to be over already. The groom, the son of Angela's friend, is on leave for the wedding. He will go back to Iraq in a few days. His mother walks over to greet Angela and

Paco (and me, indirectly) and invite us to help ourselves.

Before us, two long tables unfurl: they are covered with aluminum trays filled with rice and beans and all sorts of meat: pork, beef, even goat. At the end of the table, a white, four-leveled wedding cake, waiting to be cut.

We congratulate the groom, a guy in his early twenties, wearing a Marine uniform and a military cap firm on his recently shorn head.

Food on our plates, we sit down; at his first forkful, Paco knocks over the entire contents of his plate. I have never seen such a messy disaster. We both laugh. Angela, on the other hand, doesn't even flinch. She seems to be quite used to certain performances of her son.

We soon leave the wedding. I ask Paco to take me to Lake Trafford. I read somewhere that last fall, due to the shallows created by drought, ancient Indian canoes have resurfaced. They are over a thousand years old and have been in the lake since then. They would crumble if anyone tried to move them. The article also said that maybe the best thing now would be for the lake to submerge them again, so perhaps they will get preserved for another thousand years.

Paco doesn't remember exactly how to get to the marina. We wander about the fringes of Immokalee until we enter an unpaved road, and almost without realizing it, we pass a NO TRESPASSING sign.

Here live the rich of Immokalee, says Paco, looking toward the houses located on the lake.

"No, this way we won't go anywhere," Paco observes. I make a U-turn. "But we are close…There's the Corkscrew Swamp here…" Paco thinks out loud.

Determined to go straight and not venture on anyone's private property, we get back onto the main road. But clearly somebody has already noticed our presence. From a perpendicular street, the one we inadvertently entered, we see a cart approaching escorted by two huge dogs who seem to bark precisely at us.

I accelerate, moderately though; after all, they seem far away, but obviously I underestimate the speed at which the two curs are now running right *towards us*. And so without even realizing it, I find one dog barking rabidly right next to me, while the other one is already skirting the car from the passenger's side, next to Paco.

"Close the window!" my friend shouts. I accelerate, unhesitant now, and concomitantly push the button with all the force I have, as if by pressing hard I would be able to make it go up faster.

Seconds seem infinite. The dog on my side seems determined to jump in the car, and I push the accelerator harder and I don't understand and even though now is the moment to act and not to ask any questions, I can't help wondering, how in the hell did we end up in this situation?

The curs finally grow smaller in the rearview window. We get rid of them. I finally turn to Paco. My heart is in my throat, and his as well, if I were to judge from his face. We both burst into hysterical laughter. We pulled it off, somehow.

Finally, we arrive at the marina. We get out of the car. There's a pleasant breeze. Before us, the water stretches out, gets lost in the inlets of the swamps and beyond. My eyes cannot circumscribe it, make it a lake. Paco points to a couple of mansions in the distance. They would like to build more over there, in the Corkscrew Swamp, but they have no permit right now, he adds thinking about something else.

There is no trace of the canoes. Maybe, I think, the lake has swallowed them already. The sun is beginning to descend toward the horizon. We stay like this for an indefinite time, to contemplate the sky and the water before us.

Paco asks me to drop him off at the Immokalee Housing Center. That's where the meeting organized by the Student/Farmworker Alliance is taking place, where he should have been two hours ago already. Paco's friends did not stop texting him while we were at the reception. I hug him and drive back to Immokalee.

◆

Padre Patricio is sitting by the computer. He is preparing the seven o'clock homily.

"Give me five minutes," he says. I asked him if he could take me to meet Olga.

"They are primarily Church books, you know…" he comments as he glimpses at me looking at his bookshelf. "Those novels…right there," the priest continues swinging in his computer chair. "They have been given to me. They are definitely *not* my favorite genre!"

"Which ones?" I ask, not understanding what he is referring to.

"Those down there…" the priest gets up and shows them to me. There are dozens of books of the *Left Behind* series.

"I don't like the apocalyptic genre. To me, it's all rubbish," Padre Patricio comments, laughing in his typical manner.

We cross the street. The sun is setting and it's getting cool. We stop at Georgina's. A woman from Naples gave the priest a Wal-Mart gift card for her. She met Georgina once and then heard about little Sofia, so she thought to give the Cortéz family a gift. Georgina says thanks, shyly.

"I know that they don't accept these gifts willingly, but what can I do? It was given to me *for* them!" Padre Patricio says as we walk toward Georgina's house.

Padre Patricio took Olga to buy groceries this morning and helped her arrange the basic furniture that the landowner bought for her. Kristy, one of the teachers at the Corkscrew Swamp Elementary, had talked resolutely with the landlord. After a couple of hours, new mattresses were in the apartment.

They are having dinner at Olga's. Here too, *sopa de pollo* with tortillas. The children are seated around the table and eat, heads down. Olga, a tiny woman with a wide, flat back, invites us to sit down and then gives us the orangey-est drink I have ever seen.

On the flowery couch sits the daughter with her baby. The girl is thirteen; her fiancé and father of the child is twenty. They ran away together last year. They went to Georgia. Olga almost called the authorities; then she asked the priest for advice. One day they came back, and Olga decided not to press charges against the young man. He doesn't have documents, so he would have ended up being deported. And the child would have grown up without a father.

Olga must have thought her daughter would be better off with a man at her side.

Farmworkers gathered in front of CIW office for El Año de los Trabajadores

Six

MARCH

It's a moonless night. I drive along Main Street passing streetlamp after streetlamp until I enter the narrow street that flows toward the little white house of the Garcias. I park next to the family's big blue truck.

I called the Garcia family on Easter. We exchanged best wishes and I asked Carlos if I could try again, the following week, to go to the fields with him. Padre Patricio is not in town: he left for South Carolina. A priest friend had asked him if he could substitute for him over the weekend. Padre Patricio reassured me that he had called the Garcia family before leaving. "They are expecting you," he said over the phone. Then he added: "You'll find Tequila over there."

Indeed, Tequila welcomes me at the door and tags along happily while I follow Carlos up to Aurelio's room. Carlos, on the other hand, looks surprised, as if he did not expect my visit at all. He stands with a vial in his hand while the dog wags its tail around me.

"Padre Patricio told you that…" I venture.

The man raises his shoulders. Then his large Mexican face opens in a smile, as if he has behaved this way on purpose, as if to mean that now the ruse is over. Carlos walks me toward the rest of his family.

In one of the bedrooms, I find Sonia; she sits on the bed, little Juan on her knees. She is fixing the vaporizer on his nose and mouth. She raises her head and smiles briefly; then she returns to take care of her child. Little Juan is slumped in her lap. Sonia tries to straighten him up, to remedy what Mother Nature didn't grant even to the last-born child.

"They have been sick for two weeks already," Aurelio finally informs me. "They caught a bad cough. They have to use the vaporizer for three hours a day," Sonia adds. I'm mortified. This explains Carlos's strange reception.

"Padre Patricio didn't tell me anything…" I think out loud.

"Padre Patricio doesn't know anything about this," Sonia says. But her voice sounds far off, covered by the vaporizer already.

In February 2005, three babies were born with congenital anomalies in Immokalee. Their mothers all worked in the fields of Florida and North Carolina for the same company, Ag-Mart, and all of them during the organogenesis stage of their pregnancy. The local papers provided extensive coverage of the story of the three women and their children in the attempt to raise awareness around the effects of pesticides in the fields. Florida turned out to have the sad national record of the highest number of pesticides used in agriculture,[1] but they were only twenty active inspectors for the more than 44,000 state farms.[2] In addition, although the Department of Agriculture investigates pesticide cases, when caught, violators are rarely fined.[3] Thus, there's no real interest in enforcing the laws on pesticide use and monitoring the health of the workers.[4] After the case of the migrants who gave birth to infants with congenital defects, an investigation was started as well as a new study to determine the effects of pesticides on farmworkers' health. No clear answer of the cause-effect relationship was found because the funds ran out and a necessary, further study to assess the effects of pesticides on human health was never performed.[5] Ag-Mart eventually settled the case, paying off the families anyway.[6]

The Garcias cannot blame the pesticides for their misfortunes: muscular dystrophy is a disease that is transmitted genetically.

Sonia switches off the aerosol machine and, cupping her hand like a spoon, begins to pat Juan's back. She turns him and turns him again as if he were a baby, shaking him gently so that the medicine can spread throughout her son's little lungs.

Carlos is in the other room: he is relaxing, toying with his cell phone.

Once finished with Juan, Sonia goes and lies down next to her husband; Cristiano, in the middle, pensively contemplates a picture card.

"What time should I set the alarm for?" I ask appearing at the door in an attempt to understand the Garcias' intentions.

"*Siete y media,*" Carlos says. He can get up later because he owns a car, knows where to go and what time he needs to be at work in the fields. Almost like a regular job.

In the meantime, Sonia has gotten up. "You'll need a long-sleeved shirt," the woman says. "To protect your skin from the pesticides and the sun."

"We'll have to work hard tomorrow. Are you ready?" Carlos says, giggling and glimpsing knowingly at his wife. I nod.

"One last thing: not a word about the fact that you're a writer and that you're writing a book and so forth, OK? You're a friend of mine who is visiting Immokalee and just wants to see what work in the fields is like. Understood?" Carlos reiterates. I nod again.

"*Tu eres comunista?*" (Are you a communist?) Sonia asks while taking refuge again in the bed next to her husband.

She catches me unprepared.

"*Pero no eres catolica.*" (But you're not Catholic.)

I reassure her as best I can but I also wonder how the otherwise circumspect Sonia could have been so direct. Maybe Padre Ettore read the article I had written for the Italian magazine and talked to them about it. Or maybe my friends at the CIW were enough to make the ultraconservative Catholic Garcias suspicious.

I close the door. The Garcias have decided that I will sleep in Cristiano's bed tonight. I lie down on the thin and boney mattress. A poster hanging in the middle of the white wall catches my attention. I get near to better look at it. Cristiano's face is mounted on the mighty body of Arnold Schwarzenegger. He is sitting on the back of a motorcycle. *Terminator 2,* as the writing on the side indicates. Cristiano's face is almost unrecognizable, painted in wrestlers' fashion: his eyes circled in white and the rest a red-and-black web à la Spiderman, Cristiano's other passion, as the trading cards on the door testify.

I turn off the light and go to bed. The springs make it unusually uncomfortable, and I almost wish the Garcias had let me sleep on the floor. The Garcias are renting one of the bedrooms to a young couple, as Aurelio will inform me the following day.

Obviously, the Garcias made sure their son would give this version of the story. The couple, in fact, seems to live autonomously in the big room that is normally Aurelio's room. In fact, that night I did not even notice their presence at the Garcias. So while I had Cristiano's room all for me, the family got divided into the two smaller rooms as follows: Carlos, Aurelio, and Cristiano slept in the big queen bed of the parents while Sonia and little Juan slept in the small bed.

But I will find out all this only the following morning.

Juan complained all night long. My alarm didn't go off, and no one woke me up; it's eight thirty already. Carlos stops me in the hallway. Let me call my boss, he says. Carlos sits in the kitchen. He makes his call, eyes to the floor, head down. I listen to him talking about me with his boss. An Italian girl...She is writing a book...Wants to see what it's like to work in the fields...I look at him, still half-asleep. Carlos hangs up.

"He says he has to ask his boss...the American farmer," he reports, in Spanish.

"Why...?" I ask Carlos.

"I thought it's always better to tell the truth," Carlos says.

His cell phone rings, and Carlos goes to the other room. This time I only hear him say OK.

"I'm sorry Silvia..." Carlos says looking down, raising his big black eyes only briefly, shamefacedly. "I am really sorry...But last Wednesday ten workers got fired and I..."

He bites his lower lip and disappears into the bedroom.

When I come back to the Garcias it's five o'clock already. I promised the kids and Sonia that I would make pizza for them. Cristiano is watching wrestling on TV.

"Did you see what he did?" he asks me as soon as I get in the room with the impetuosity of a child.

I take the opportunity to ask Cristiano why he likes wrestling so much.

"*I* don't like it," Aurelio intervenes. "It's too violent."

Cristiano ignores my question and resumes his description of the phenomenal wrestler's move the TV has just replayed and that I have missed once again.

"Do you want to go with me to Winn-Dixie to buy the ingredients for pizza?" I ask the kids.

Sonia drives the black truck in the six o'clock traffic. She asks me nonchalantly if I like to go fast with the car, and I sense her worries about letting the kids go to the store with me alone. We get back to the house and begin to roll out the dough. Within a few minutes, the kids get flour all over them. Aurelio turns out to be a skilled *pizzaiolo*. Cristiano and Juan seem to feel good: no coughing, despite the white cloud that floats all over the kitchen.

The second night I manage to convince the Garcias to sleep in their own bedrooms. As if I wasn't there. I place my sleeping bag by Cristiano's bed. "Read me a story please," he says. He picks one about Mowgli from the big book of fairytales. I lie down, my head next to the tricycle, and I begin to read. Cristiano's big, alert eyes follow the illustrations.

Into the Packing House: Six L's

The line of female workers grows under the burning midday sun. They are Haitian for the most part, some Latina, *all* women. Sorting tomatoes is an activity that requires delicate hands. And watchful eyes.

It's Saturday, and the twelve-thirty load is about to be selected at Six L's Packing Company, the biggest clearinghouse of tomatoes in Immokalee. I am waiting for the assistant manager. He will be my guide through the plant. Finally, after numerous attempts, I am about to enter the monumental building that occupies most of the right side of the street adjacent to where Paco lives.

Do you have closed shoes? An hour earlier, in another packinghouse located next to the produce market, a Mexican man I met there approaches me again, cleaning his hands with a rag. He has left behind a group of male workers in overalls who are busy repairing a car parked in front of the building. I nod without understanding.

"It's for safety," he clarifies. "It's dangerous to walk around these machines wearing sandals."

I go back to my Honda Civic, open the trunk, and slip on my sneakers. When I get back, he is maneuvering a forklift.

"You have to talk to him," he says lifting a pile of crates and simultaneously pointing to the guy who's now walking toward me.

Dominique, a tall young guy, moves in. He is the security person, apparently.

"I'm not the one in charge here," the man says right way.

"No one answers from the main offices," he fills me in while adjusting his headphones. "They are closed today."

He studies me. And reflects on the decision he has to make.

"No, no video camera, I only have my notebook," I try to reassure him. *Alright.* He eventually concedes. Dominique has me take off my earrings and hands me a white cap for my hair. These are the rules for all, visitors included.

We finally enter the packinghouse: different kinds of cucumbers and peppers are selected here. At three the sorting of peppers begins, Dominique announces. He speaks loudly to be heard over the noise of the machines.

The workers select jalapenos, the Mexican chili peppers named after the city of Xalapa in the state of Veracruz where they traditionally grow. They are working overtime because this load got here late last night. There's no time to waste. The vegetables need to be promptly selected, packed in boxes and sent to the major retailers all around North America.

Although it's Saturday and the workers have only been called a few hours ago, they still get paid minimum wage: $6.79 here in Florida. It is not much, but it is still a better-paid, easier job if compared to the one in the fields.

I stare vacantly at the jalapenos rolling horizontally over the conveyor belt, then going up, up, and eventually tumbling down. The tract is short for this type of vegetable. Dominique yells, shaking me up, and takes me to the storage room, the so-called pre-cooler where the produce gets preserved: an infinite series of crates one on top of the other form a huge Tetris. I cough as I enter the vast refrigerated storeroom.

"Cold, ah?" he laughs.

Dominique finally relaxes when he abandons me to Rebecca, at the administration offices. He has to go back to the entrance.

Rebecca, a plump white woman in her thirties, smiles behind her desk. Although I don't think she's been informed about my visit, I have the strange feeling that Rebecca has been waiting: for me or for somebody else. In any case, she's been waiting.

I sit down and Rebecca begins to give me information about the Six L's plants. I find out that there are actually three packing houses in town owned by Six L's; the one I am in, and the other two where they select tomatoes: one for the Roma and cherry tomatoes, and the big one for sorting the large tomatoes.

"We've just bought Tomato Man…" the secretary continues proudly, assuming I am aware of the operation, but then she notices my questioning look and makes sure: "You know about Tomato Man, right?" I nod, I don't want to disappoint her, and take a note—Tomato Man, I will find out, is a historic company in town—"In that plant…beginning next year…Let's keep our fingers crossed…we'll select potatoes!" Rebecca concludes, eyes teary with excitement.

I shake hands with Rebecca. Before going out, I point to some green peppers that lay on the table next to her desk, for no particular reason, if not to take a note of the peculiarity of their presence in an office, that's all—not entirely strange though if that office is located in a produce packinghouse, as I immediately reconsider.

"Ah those..." Rebecca says handling the four green vegetables. "These are the types of green peppers that are usually sorted here."

"This is a 'cubanel'...and this is the 'hungarian shot'...the 'long hot' very very hot...And the classic: the 'jalapeno,'" she explains.

"Take them," she says, handing me the vegetables.

Dominique walks me to the car. I take off the white cap and put the green peppers in it.

"Do you think I could visit the big packinghouse where they sort the large tomatoes?" I venture.

Dominique nods, unexpectedly.

"Let me call security," he says.

Then he gives me directions.

"As soon as you get out of here, you make a right and then a tight left. The packinghouse is the big building at the end of that street. You can't miss it."

And here I am, in the heart of Immokalee, in front of the imposing Six L's Packing Company warehouse. Since 1986, Six L's, founded by the six Lipman brothers, has been processing an average of fifteen million twenty-five-pound boxes a year.[7] The company has six farms and employs more than a thousand people in Immokalee between produce pickers and workers at the packinghouses. The other two big companies in town are Gargiulo Inc. and Pacific Tomato Growers, but Six L's definitely dominates in the tomato business.[8]

In this plant alone, there are 260 employees, and 1,600 twenty-five-pound boxes of tomatoes getting packed every day.

The board in the security kiosk shows the timetables of the three packinghouses.

Bell Times. Today: Roma tomatoes, cherry tomatoes, and peppers.

Dominique called the women at security. Generally quite rude with their come-back-later-when-the-manager-is-here response, now they don't look at me crossways anymore. Rather, we are quite pleasantly conversing.

"Welcome to THE packing house!" my guide says, modulating the tone of his voice as if he were a radio host.

"Hi, I'm Chris!" he gives me his hand and offers me a brief yet large smile.

Ultra-long, polish-adorned fingernails hand me a new cap and a sheet of paper. I go ahead and register my presence, writing down entrance time and reason of the visit. I thank the woman and wave at the rest of my new friends at the security kiosk.

We go toward the entrance, and Chris precedes me. He walks with splayed legs bouncing inside his large green pants, head to the ground. Chris, an African American man with a definitely New York accent, says he has lived in Florida only for a few years.

The tour begins.

"This is the packing house where we sort the large tomatoes..." Chris begins as he opens the door for me. "The tomatoes are green when they get to Six L's..."

(*Los tomates de Immokalee nacieron verdes,* El Poeta recited.)

" ...And we make them leave green! Or light pink, pink, or even red...Depending on how the buyers want them, and where they need to get…It's crucial to know how long it takes to get to their destination," Chris says, opening wide his eyes and modulating his voice.

The tomatoes actually get "gassed," in different ways, depending on where they are headed. They are treated with ethylene, the same substance that makes them naturally ripen. The doors of the warehouses where the gassing occurs remain closed for twenty-four hours: the ethylene is a hazardous gas when inhaled. But this operation is performed in another plant, Chris informs me, as if to reassure me.

The average life of a tomato once picked is four to seven days, which forces the truck carriers to drive as fast as they can: the quicker the tomatoes get to their destination, the longer their commercial life will be. Sometimes, there are trucks with generators that produce ethylene; so, after the ripening process has been temporarily blocked with the harvest, it gets reactivated, when the tomato is on its way to the market, perhaps thousands of miles away from the field where it has been picked. As a result, the tomato gets to the grocery store in the pre-arranged ripening state.

In the distance, I see yellow-colored produce rolling over the conveyor belt. "Right now we are running a specialty…" clarifies Chris, who, because of the noise, has begun to yell.

Then my guide stops, suddenly. He apologizes and disappears, cell phone attached to his ear, behind a stack of tomato boxes. I am about to take a look around, but Chris is back already, and is once again requesting all my attention.

He is now illustrating for me the differences between first-choice tomatoes ("silk tomatoes": nice big green tomatoes), second-choice ("velvet tomatoes": pink, smaller, and with some defects), and third-choice (the "cracker jacks"). These last ones end up being given away for free or sold to companies that produce ketchup or sauces.

The tomatoes grown in Florida are salad tomatoes. And fast food tomatoes.

"Hi Louise!" Chris waves at a woman—she smiles at me, so I smile back at her. Then Chris indicated the sink and the soap dispenser.

"Her job is to make sure the workers wash their hands," he explains.

Chris shows me the journey the tomatoes make inside the packinghouse. First of all, there's the cleaning: the tomatoes are bathed in a pool of water and chlorine. The temperature of the water must be at least ten degrees higher than that of the tomatoes, Chris specifies. Then he shows me the waxing machine: a steel, covered box.

I hear only the noise, every four seconds, when the wax gets sprayed. The tomatoes get brushed and finally dried. We climb up steel stairs. "The women workers sort 'the good, the bad, and the ugly,'" Chris yells pronouncing the words clearly so that I can get the reference, but without laughing, his big eyes staring at me.

Below, the women, sitting next to one another, all wearing gloves, select the good tomatoes from the bad or the ugly ones, just like Chris said. Above their capped-heads like mine, huge ceiling fans contribute to the already loud environment of the packinghouse.

Chris invites me to look at the conveyor belt, this time dotted with holes.

"The measuring machine sorts the tomatoes," Chris annotates. "The small ones are redirected to the other side. The buyers, especially the supermarkets, want homogenized produce..." The big tomatoes, for the most part, jolt as they roll over the holes, the small ones go down.

As a matter of fact, it is the machine that dictates the consistency of the tomatoes. A juicy tomato, not firm, thin-skinned, or simply too

ripe, is obviously not compatible with contemporary mechanized production practices: many tomatoes would squash and thus slow down
the process to the point of making it impossible to use the measuring
machine. That's also why tomato skins today feel like plastic.

Agribusiness, however, doesn't tell me that: it constantly strives to
associate assembly-line precision and food safety. It's modern and efficient, and it feeds the multitudes.[9]

Red tomatoes are being sorted now, Chris points out. My guide
begins to list pedantically the four sizes of tomatoes.

"We have the 5x6, the 6x6, the 6x7 and the 7x7, it depends on the
diameter. The biggest ones, the 5x6…"

Wait.

"But if the numbers refer to the size of the diameter, this should be
the small ones, right?" I ask confused.

"Excuse me, have you ever seen a pink tomato?" But Chris answers
with a question, which begs reflection.

"I was saying…" Chris continues, "The smallest ones…are generally second or third choice tomatoes and we send them to the cows! We
don't throw away anything here!"

Actually, donating or giving away the produce to the local cattle
farmers allows companies like Six L's to save a lot of money in waste
disposal costs that otherwise they would have to take on.

"Every time we run the machinery the FDA inspectors are around
to make sure everything is done according to the rules…" Chris continues as we get to his office: he has to fill out the daily run sheet.

It's a freezer in here, and I tell Chris.

"Sorry. I like it cold," he says, smiling longer this time.

Once Chris was an FDA inspector, too. That's how he found a job
at Six L's. "They were looking for a new manager," he relates.

Chris shows me the daily run sheet: insurance code, farm where the produce comes from, quantity, quality, and market definition. "This system allows us to go back and track the journey that each and every tomato has made," he explains. "Let's say somebody feels sick in California. We must be able to determine where that tomato is from and understand what went wrong."

"As you can see, it's a mess…But it's an organized mess, after all!" Chris concludes, leaning back on his computer chair.

Then Chris drags me outside. Before a huge crate of discarded tomatoes, he begins to blurt out a series of names…

"This one, for instance," he says, a bruised tomato in his hand, "This is called 'blossom rot.' This one here…" He continues picking another one. "It's a 'misshaped,' because he came out…Let's say deformed. This one over here," Chris says showing me a new one. "It's called 'rain-checked' because it has taken a lot of water and it got a sort of necklace here on top, you see?"

"You like this job, don't you Chris?" I ask him point blank.

"Oh, I love it!" he exclaims opening his arms. Then he adds: "But what do you think? I didn't know anything about tomatoes!"

Before beginning to work for the FDA, Chris had a waste management truck company. "Too stressful," he says. Within a few years in the agricultural business, he managed to land a full-time managerial job at Six L's.

When the season is over here in Florida, in June, the company moves its operations to Beaufort, South Carolina, until mid-August. After that they all go to Painter, Virginia, until October; then, come back to Florida.

Chris goes north by himself. His family stays here.

"Six L's gives me a nice, large apartment. Usually my wife takes a week off and comes up with the kids."

In June, this packinghouse is practically inactive. They fix the machinery, do some maintenance jobs, minor stuff. Most employees migrate north and go to work in Virginia or South Carolina to work on behalf of Six L's.

"They can all work twelve months a year if they are willing to move," Chris says, full of company pride.

Yet, the images of *Harvest of Shame* come to my mind. The people pressed in the trucks like beasts. The camps. What Chris doesn't say is that still today, after almost fifty years, there are trailers up north, awaiting the migrant workers. And endless fields. Not that different from Immokalee.

El Año de los Trabajadores

A stage has been set up in front of the CIW; the street has been closed to the traffic. A blue tent protects the entertainers from the pitiless early-afternoon sun. It's Sunday, and I am still in Immokalee. I couldn't miss the celebrations for *el año de los trabajadores* organized by the Coalition of Immokalee Workers.

The CIW representatives are all here. I recognize them as I walk among the many faces of the workers, mostly men, Mexican, Guatemalan, African American, and Haitian. Large and welcoming faces. Relaxed faces: today we don't work.

I see Lionel, Gerardo, and Melody; and Julia, holding Lucas's son. On the stage, there's Lucas. He speaks the language of the majority of the audience, Spanish, and invites everyone to participate in the raffle.

Then, he leaves the stage to the band, a local Mexican group. The musicians begin to play traditional songs. They all wear white cowboy hats, sky-blue shirts, and beige-colored pants.

Soon, a Haitian, white-goateed singer joins them on stage. He wears a red hat as the French do. He has on a shirt and checkered pants with suspenders. The audience laughs because the guy keeps making faces and moving like a madman, while reciting his upbeat verses in Creole.

I don't see Paco. I ask Lionel about him; he shrugs. Lionel invites me to jump over, and pass the plastic strip that marks the fictitious boundary between members and friends of the CIW and the rest of the Immokalee workers. It's for them that this type of events gets organized. They help to promote the activities and campaigns led by the coalition. And to inform the newcomers about the existence of an organization that supports the rights of migrant workers.

Here, on the side of the stage, CIW members are giving out tamales and sodas.

I spot Eduardo as well: there he is, handing a mountain dew to a *compañero*. He waves at me. He was the one who told me about this "street party."

I met Eduardo again the other day, by chance. I heard somebody calling my name. I was getting out of the car and heading toward the entrance of a medical center in town to meet Carl, Tina's husband. Eduardo was sitting at the foot of a cypress tree in the parking lot of the clinic. He had a can of beer in his hands, and a shaggy beard. At first, I didn't even recognize him. I thought he was one of the many homeless that walk the streets of Immokalee. On the contrary, Eduardo was resting in the shade of the tree after a day of work. He was simply enjoying the pleasant afternoon breeze. Just finished with work, he was waiting for his boss to come and pick him up, to get his ride back to downtown.

Eduardo works in landscaping now and earns good money, as he told me during our long chat in Miami.

"Are you hungry?" Eduardo asks.

I nod. He hands me a chicken tamale. We exchange a series of smiles. I would have had many questions to ask him, but my Spanish doesn't allow me to express myself in the past tense.

It's three o'clock. The heat is truly oppressive today; even the wind has stopped now, but there's a festive atmosphere. A new band has gotten on stage: young men, of Mexican descent, most likely Chicano, born here in Florida, or Texas, or California.

They, too, have cowboy hats on. There is a chorus girl who dances and sings along with three young fellows. She wears a white blouse tied to the waist, her belly button well exposed.

On Main Street, a crowd of people on their bikes is watching the concert from afar: hesitant about whether or not to join the party. Whenever a public event is going on, people tend to have their guard up. A police squad car is on the other side of the road. The cops show their pistols while leaning against their cars. To make sure nothing happens…

But the music has stopped. The most exciting moment of the day has come: the throwing of T-shirts and hats to the crowd. Lucas, along with two other members of the coalition, encourages the onlookers from the stage. A wave of hands rises from the audience in the attempt to snag a T-shirt or a hat. Then the lucky one rejoices, clutching the plunder close to his chest.

I see Paco, finally. I move close to him. We hug.

"I will be right back," he says.

The music goes faster, and the heat is making me feel dizzy.

But there he is: "El Poeta!" I can't believe my eyes. So long…where have you been?

Shyly, he says that he works a lot these days. I give him a hug.

Paco comes back wearing the CIW security orange vest, the same one that Gerardo has on too.

"I don't understand why there are all these cops," thinks Paco out loud, his eyes staring at the group of officers now stationed at the entrance to the street.

He sighs.

"Everything is going to be all right," I try to reassure him.

Paco convinced me to stay.

"You can sleep over if you like," he says.

His mother is in Arizona; Paco's sister just gave birth to a baby boy and Angela went to help out. Paco is noticeably happy. "I have the entire house to myself," he says. Besides, he has just started working at the Immokalee High School. He substitutes for teachers. He is on vacation these days: it's spring break.

"I went back to the Seminoles." I tell Paco, "But I haven't got a hold of any of the tribal members."

"The secretary told me to try again on Monday…to ask about Victor," I say.

Paco's eyes suddenly light up.

"Victor? That man changed my life," Paco says.

"It was he who explained to me the true origin of the name Immokalee."

Radio Conciencia has finally moved to the new building that will serve as a community center. The center is two minutes away from the old offices, right behind the Pantry. Its central position is crucial to better serve the farmworkers, many of whom live nearby since they don't own a car, and either walk or ride their bikes.

The walls of the radio room have been painted blue. The air conditioning is set below seventy, and a brand new console gives a professional look to the small community radio station.

Paco has his own program now: it's called "Roots Music." He primarily plays traditional Mexican music: *son jarocho, son huasteco, son de tierra caliente.*

In the semi-darkness, Paco moves with contrived confidence between the Mac and the console, balancing on his office chair. He puts the headphones on and gets close to the leaning microphone every time he announces a new song.

He moves as Gerardo or Luis do, trying to imitate their jovial yet firm tones, speaking the words in clear and measured Spanish. But Paco's voice, slightly shaking, betrays his lack of experience; most of all, it betrays a different character.

Paco stutters at times and has to repeat the words, but continues as if nothing happened, in an absolutely professional manner, the way he has seen his older friends do. Then I wonder if my presence is making him nervous. But I also wonder if my judgment is off; he's become like a cousin to me, a younger one you fail to see growing up.

Les celebraciones por el año de los trabajadores organizado da la Coalición de Trabajadores de Immokalee fue un éxito. Cientos trabajadores participó en esta fiesta en esta bellissima día... ("The Year of the Workers" organized by the Coalition of Immokalee Workers was a success. Hundreds of workers participated in the celebrations on this beautiful day...)

Paco takes off his headphones. "I want some yogurt," he announces just for me. I see him going out into the early night of the Pantry, his shadow heading toward La Fiesta 3, the minimarket open from early in the morning until late at night. But here he is again. He opens the door. "I forgot my wallet," he says. Paco puts on a long song now and leaves again, bouncing.

At the end of his program, Paco plays a song by the Mexican rock band Maná. I begin to tease him for it, because Maná has become a mainstream Latino band in the United States. Paco is supposed to be playing only traditional music...Suddenly, we found ourselves silent, listening to the sad lyrics of the song. It's the story of Juan, a young Mexican man who pays a coyote to cross the border. He wants to go work in San Diego or Chicago. Juan, ingenious, his heart filled with nostalgia already, shows a picture of his pregnant girlfriend to the coyote, trying to get some sympathy from him during the long and difficult journey ahead of them. Juan had promised his girlfriend he'd come back home soon. But the coyote shoots him without pity, thereby avoiding the trouble of escorting him into the United States.

Monday—Victor Billie

I go and wake up Paco. He is usually not too responsive in the morning, but he gets up without protest, saying he went to bed at six in the morning. He ended up watching *American Gangster* with his cousins.

The secretary, a young woman with straight, blonde-dyed hair, recognizes me. I call out "good morning;" she returns a nearly imperceptible nod.

"Let me see if Victor is in his office," she says, anticipating my request and dialing his number already.

No answer, she signifies by raising her shoulders and eyebrows. She hangs up the receiver, puts her elbows on the desk as if in wait for something, and finally lands her chin on the fan created by her hands.

Even this morning I won't be able to talk with anybody, I think, while staring at the secretary's white-out white fingernails.

In that moment, three men get out of the adjacent elevator: two of them head toward the door, while the other is about to go up again.

"Victor! Victor!" the secretary, without getting up, stretches out her neck in the attempt to stop our man. The elevator is about to close when Paco blocks it, promptly interposing an arm and leg between the doors.

Victor comes out of the elevator. Smiling. He looks around, positioning himself now in the middle of the scene: his legs well-grounded, the big and tense calves, the strong arms ready.

The secretary finally gets up, and begins to talk to him from the side. She waves her fake fingernails whose tips hold a dangling pen pointing now to my person.

Victor listens and nods. I stretch out a hand to introduce myself, and so does Paco. Victor beckons us to follow him. We get back, the three of us this time, into the elevator. Once upstairs, Victor shows us the room where he teaches the Seminole children after school: a little bit of language, but mostly wood carving, a craft that, Paco later tells me, Victor masters.

We get to his office. Victor has us take a seat. He wears dark sunglasses and a black T-shirt with the depiction of an Indian, a series of colorful and brief necklaces hanging over it. On the left side of his face, two long, blue-stoned earrings dangle. Victor sits down himself behind the desk.

I ask Victor to tell me about the Seminoles of Immokalee, about their relationship with the rest of the community. He begins by saying that, as for full-blood Seminoles, there are really just a few left at this point.

"My sister, Rachel…" Victor counts, helping with the fingers of his hand "…Mary, Mary's sister, Linda…Joseph and Ruth. Here in

Immokalee there are a lot of mestizos...children of Mexicans and Seminoles."

Then he explains. There are three types of Seminoles: the Miccosukee, which separated from the Seminoles in 1962, and are today only eight hundred left in number; they live south, along the Tamiami Trail—so called because it connects Miami with Tampa; then, the Seminoles recognized by the federal government; and the independent Seminoles, like him.

The independent Seminoles continue to oppose any intervention of the American government and maintain that most of Florida should be a territory free from federal control.

Victor underlines he is not part of the tribal council of the Seminoles. He only works at the reservation as a cultural educator. Besides teaching, he builds chikees, the typical huts made of cypress wood and palmetto leaves.

"And then every once in a while...I wrestle alligators!" Victor says with nonchalance. "Once we had eight alligators here. But now we have none."

Victor smiles.

"A couple of years ago a kid opened the door and they all fled." (...) "The important thing about alligators is not to feed them. You see...alligators are not pets! Fact is, they grow a lot, a foot a year, until they die," he says.

Victor substitutes for alligator wrestlers at the Okalee Village in the Hollywood reservation, "usually when somebody's sick," he says.

This attraction dates back to a time when the Seminoles were poor, confined in the swamps, forced to make a living out of paltry harvests and deal with natural catastrophes (hurricanes, primarily). Before roads were built, the Seminole Indians were practically unable to reach the cities on the coast to go find work. Thus, they developed this form of entertainment for the white men: a way to make money drawing on their knowledge of the reptile that eventually became the symbol of Florida.

"You see...the skillful wrestlers manage to flip the alligators and caress their stomachs. Then they become docile like babies...Sometimes they even end up falling asleep..."

James Billie, former president of the Seminole Tribe, still keeps the finger that an alligator bit off during an improvised show. The senior Seminole chief, once an excellent alligator wrestler, obviously must have lost his way.

"Hey Jimmy, we heard you lost a finger?" people would ask him.

"No, no, I haven't lost it at all," the chief would reply. And then he'd show the pendant on his necklace. "There it is!" Jimmy would say lifting his dead finger. It'd become a relic to show with a mixture of pride and irony.

The tradition of alligator wrestling is in decline today. Families and tourists prefer to take a boat tour in the Everglades rather than becoming spectators of this sideshow that once attracted, especially during rodeos, large, paying crowds.

Now, perhaps to revitalize this tradition, there is also an underwater alligator wrestling show at the Seminole Okalee Indian Village: the wrestler starts taming the beast when it is still under water, which makes the fight much more dangerous and thus more exciting.

But, alligator wrestling isn't the only dying tradition. Victor laments the loss of Indian customs.

"Seminole today means money," says Victor, shaking his head, hinting at the business of the casinos. "When I was in school, we didn't even learn English. We used to watch the elderly do things. That's how we would learn. We were poor back then, true, but we had a strong sense of community...I was born and raised in a 'hammock' in the Everglades.[10] Back then, if you needed help, you could always count on your neighbors. Today, I don't even know my neighbors!"

Victor begins to talk about the language and the culture of the Seminoles.

His real name, for instance, is "Tu-gua-chi," which means, "spotted tail."[11] I ask Victor to further explain his name, but Victor shakes his head.

"I can't tell you," Victor glosses behind his black sunglasses. "If I did, I'd reveal too much about my culture."

I will find out, during my visit at the Ah-Tah-Thi-Ki Musem,[12] that names belong to the deceased of the tribe and that they are traditionally handed down through successive generations. The naming ceremony occurs during the annual Green Corn Dance Festival. Every year between eight and twelve hundred participate in this rally, a big gathering of the seven Indian clans that still live in the state of Florida: the Wind, the Panther, the Big City, the Bird, the Frog, the Otter, the Wolf, and the Deer. The Corn Dance is held around mid-June, somewhere in the middle of Florida.[13]

"That's where we teach our youth how to cure themselves with plants, how our body works, how to sing songs...It's a big celebration." Victor adds, "We dance till late at night."

"The festival functions as a court, a church, and a school. All the clans get together and solve their problems according to the Seminole traditions, without having to resort to white man's laws."

Once again, I ask Victor where the Green Corn Dance takes place. He shakes his head.

"I can't tell you! You see, we Seminoles are reluctant to reveal information on our culture. Ultimately, that's why the indigenous peoples of North America have been defeated. They have revealed too much to the Europeans."

I think about the story of Squanto; wasn't he the one who taught the pilgrims how to catch eels and grow corn at the Plymouth Plantation? Since he learned English while living in Europe, he worked as an interpreter for the whites; after all, it was because of him that the settlers were able to survive in the American territory.

We continue to talk, and Victor speaks his mind from behind the desk.

They are all talking about global warming, but do you know what the real cause of terrestrial warming is? They eliminated all the plants that were supposed to keep the Earth cool! That's why. For instance, they use mercury as pesticide for the sugar cane. We got to the point that there are signs that tell you not to eat more than a fish per day. And that's because of the mercury contained in them!

They have all these pseudo-environmental programs. Like "Restore the Everglades," for example. They want to build more canals and create an overpass in certain points of the Tamiami Trail...They want to build a huge bridge, which means that they will have to dig more to put the piers...I say, leave it alone! Let Mother Nature alone! Let it be! It will work itself out.

The project Victor refers to is the Comprehensive Everglades Restoration Plan; handled by the U.S. Army Corps of Engineers together with the South Florida Water Management District, the project plans to restore, in twenty years' time the natural habitat of the Everglades and concomitantly increase the water supply along the coast.

Those who settled in southwestern Florida (in the so-called last frontier) at the end of the eighteen hundreds concentrated on the coastal regions because of the presence of the huge, hardly habitable swamp in the inner region—with the exception of the Seminoles, who were forced to retreat among the cypresses and mangroves of the Everglades.

To put a stop to the continuous floods, the Central and South Florida Project (1948) was authorized by Congress and brought about the creation of one of the most efficient water management systems in the world.[14] The environmental cost of the canalization was, however, enormous, and the Florida ecosystem was fatally damaged in the process. Also, the drainage of Lake Okeechobee led to a consistent expansion of the land available for cane sugar and thus added to the fortunes of the U.S. Sugar Corporation.[15]

Every year the Army Corps of Engineers spends $63 million in water management and control in South Florida to the advantage of the cane sugar plantations, while areas of the Everglades National Park are constantly in need of water.[16]

But Victor has some things to say about conservation practices as well.

"The Everglades National Park doesn't allow us to cut cypresses as we have done for centuries. They say the trees won't grow again. And what do they do? Every time they build a service area, or a parking lot, they cut off everything, the roots too. And there, nothing will grow again for real."

I turn to Paco. He seems half-hypnotized by Victor.

"The people of Immokalee call chickees 'palapas,'" my friend says. "What I really would like to see...I wish the people of Immokalee knew more about the Seminole traditions."

Victor nods. Paco begins to tell Victor about the community radio station; he shows him the blue T-shirt he's wearing with the Radio Conciencia logo on it. Victor says he's heard of it but he confuses it with "La Ley," the other station in town.[17]

"No, ours is community radio," Paco says. "No commercials."

"The program I have is called 'Roots Music.' I play indigenous music...The idea behind it is to preserve certain musical traditions. Sometimes we have guests..." Paco says. Then, mustering up the courage and all in one breath, he adds: "It would be great if you could come to the show."

I look at Paco and Victor exchanging phone numbers and emails. I can tell that my friend still doesn't believe that he's talking to the person who had opened his eyes years before, when he was still a student at Immokalee High. Victor was the one who spoke of the true meaning of the word *Immokalee*: "A-Mugle" in Mikasuki, *cage*.

"This is one of the books we use to teach the children about our language," says Victor, standing up and handing me a black-and-white stapled duplicate. Then he steadies himself, his legs wide open, as if to feel the ground under his feet.

On the cover are the sketched profiles of three Indians. They wear plumed hats, and the lack of color makes them appear serious and determined.

"What does it say?" I ask Victor, referring to three Indians, then reading out loud what the word between the feathers says.

I don't know, I hear Victor say.

I continue to flip through the pages, and I read another word, an extremely long one this time.

"Aheshchenehbachke."

Once. Twice.

"This means bus, right?" I ask. I point to the drawing, and the English translation below sweeps away my doubts.

Victor is silent.

I read a third word. And I raised my head, finally, in search for some sort of confirmation. I meet Victor's semi-opened mouth, and his dark sunglasses, a symbol of Seminole inscrutability. He shakes his head, his thin lips widen in a complacent smile.

"I can't read," he says. "My language is not meant to be read."[18]

I thank Victor. Paco, eyes shining, shakes hands with him.

We get back home. Paco turns on the radio.

"I am glad I came with you," he says, staring at the sheet of paper where Victor wrote his contact information.

"Are you hungry?" Paco asks. "Why don't we go to this bar bistro in Labelle?" he proposes as he hands me the flyer for the place. At that precise moment, a huge truck pulls in and parks in front of the house. Paco gets out. It's *tia* Rosita, he says. The absolute resemblance to Angela, the younger sister, confirms Paco's announcement. His aunt is petite, and her short hair almost completely white. Tia Rosita is dressed up, the red lipstick on, the jewelry well exposed. She hugs Paco and begins to talk to him quickly in Spanish. She wants Paquito to go the Consecration of the Oratory. At Ave Maria. Today is a special day. The bishop will be there too, and all the priests of the dioceses.

"Go, go with Silvia," she says.

Rosita shakes my hand, kisses me, gives me a hug. Then she opens her purse and hands Paco $50.

"The two of you go get a bite to eat at the bistro there...The Bean...The mass is at two..." Rosita takes a glimpse at her watch. "I gotta go now."

I've asked Paco a couple of times to go with me to Ave Maria, but my friend has usually found excuses. Last time I asked, he confessed that the place made him very uncomfortable. More kisses and more hugs. Tia Rosita jumps in her truck.

"I gotta go pick up a friend. I will see you there, OK?" she screams as she starts the engine.

See you there.

"I don't wanna go," Paco says monotonously, staring at the truck squealing off.

The Consecration of the Torpedo

Paco is quiet as we drive along Pope John Paul II Boulevard. I try to make him laugh: this is Paco's first real visit to Ave Maria, and I know how hard it is for him to be here. We walk to the bistro, "The Bean," the one Tia Rosita suggested. "It looks like a huge torpedo," Paco says, his eyes still aimed at the church.

There's a certain commotion going on in the Annunciation Circle, and the presence of the white van of a local TV station attests to the importance of the event for the community.

The Bishop of Venice, Frank J. Dewane, has waited for months before agreeing to the consecration of the Oratory.[19] The hearsay is that he has had hesitations about declaring Ave Maria a parish. Some say the delay is due to Monaghan's political ideas and his role—deemed excessive by the dioceses—in the development of Ave Maria town. Others say the malevolent ones have spread these rumors, that the truth is, the bishop is just a very busy man, and without his blessing no Mass can be celebrated. That's all. On the other hand, Nick Healy, president of Ave Maria University, refused to release a statement that details the communications with the dioceses. Technically, Ave Maria's canonical status differs from other Catholic universities. It's a private university in the Catholic tradition,[20] and, as such, is *not* under the bishop's jurisdiction.[21]

As a matter of fact, the Oratory has been opened to the public for a couple of months already. I visited it the previous Saturday during my second trip to Ave Maria town. Inside, its naked monumentality leaves no room to imagination: the crossing of empty metallic girders run after each other upward, a gothic web of basic geometry. No paintings are on the walls, not yet.

Before leaving, I picked up some literature. There was a brochure that caught my attention: it was about "how to become a founder of the university." The table was adorned by Ave Maria posters, among which was a big one that indicated that Tom Monaghan is the founder, yes, but only *its first one* and invites all to contribute today with a tax-deductible donation. To obtain the qualification of "founding member," $120 is needed, and, a check mark on the box under the text that reads:

> Yes, Mr. Monaghan, I want to be a Founder of Ave Maria University. I agree with you that one of the most powerful responses we can make to the current crisis of the Church is to educate new generations of Catholic leader, by building a major Catholic university dedicated to Our Lady, Seat of Wisdom. Please use my gift to help Ave Maria University become a model Catholic university. I have dedicated my level of support below. I understand that a total of $120 is necessary to become a Founder of Ave Maria University and that it can be paid over a one-year period.

From my first visit to Ave Maria, four months ago, a lot has changed. Signs now announce a soon-to-be-opened Publix. Around the main square—at Ave Maria town called "La Piazza," which sounds quite tautological to me as an Italian—there is now a store that sells bicycles, another one that sells various (religious and not) gifts, a Mexican restaurant, a Fed-Ex store, and the offices of a real estate agency, Pulte Homes. As the multiple "coming soon" signs attest, though, most of the spaces have been taken.

Given the special district status of the town, the 50–50 partnership called Ave Maria Development (Tom Monaghan & Barron
Collier Companies) has absolute authority over any private construction decisions.[22]

We go inside the Bean: here, Ave Maria–produced coffee is sold
along with pasta, panini, and shakes. We get in line after a group of
white-haired people. Paco picks up a bottle of beer from the minibar
and, half-surprised, half-amused (by the presece of alcohol), shows it
to me.

The Bean is an ultramodern spot in Starbucks style; what makes it
different are the reproductions hung on its walls: sacred arts, images of
Pope John Paul II with Mother Teresa, of the new Pope, Benedict XXIII,
and old black-and-white pictures of soldiers in front of a confessional.

We sit down in the living room area in front of a fake fireplace; a
few customers are still here: most of them have walked toward the
Church to participate in the Holy Mass. On the low internal wall that
delimits the living room is a wooden statue of Pope John Paul II, subjugated by the weight of the huge cross.

While we are eating our sandwiches, Daniel, the owner, approaches in an attempt to connect the computer to the screen over the
fireplace. At the Bean, it will be possible to follow the ceremony live, as
in other places like the library and the Student Union, where jumbo
screens have been set up for the event.

"Do you have the tickets?" Daniel asks. "Without tickets it's impossible to get in the church today…"

Paco and I look at each other; we are both thinking about the same
thing: Tia Rosita. Does *she* have tickets? She's gotta have them. Eventually, the computer screen appears over the fireplace but Daniel can't

connect the PC to the Internet. We begin to talk. Daniel lived in Italy for a year; he doesn't say what he was doing there, but he doesn't fail to remark that the idea for this bistro came to him when thinking about the Italian bars "from which the Bean obviously draws inspiration…"

I nod, perplexed, yet smiling, having never seen a bar with so much religious paraphernalia in the old country. Daniel offers me an espresso that he personally and courteously goes to prepare with his imported Italian coffee machine.

We leave Daniel to his technical problems. As we exit the Bean, I notice a reproduction of *La Domenica del Corriere* framed on the wall.[23] Padre Pio is featured in the middle. Caught by surprise, I linger with what I'm sure is a quite stupid expression on my face. So the deceased Italian priest from Pietrelcina, who became famous for his stigmata and was canonized by Pope John Paul II, made it to Florida. I doubt Paco knows who Padre Pio is; I leave the Bean and my ruminations behind.[24]

In the meantime, more than fifty people have lined up in front of the entrance of the Oratory. We pick up a missal and a bottle of water sponsored by Pulte Homes realty; then we walk toward the huge white tent that has been set up in front of the church.

Only half the seats are occupied here: it's Monday afternoon, and many people are at work. There are a lot of elderly folks and families with children. *All white*, as Paco points out. Tia Rosita is nowhere in sight. She must have had the tickets and gone inside already.

We sit down, right under the jumbo screen. After the opening song, the bishop asks to open the main door of the church. Then, he begins to bless the altar, the priests of the dioceses and those of Ave Maria, and he proceeds along the nave. He sprinkles the pews with blessed water: the community here in representation of this parish is thus blessed.

Padre Patricio comes to my mind: I wonder if he had thought about missing the consecration of the oratory when he decided to go to South Carolina. Would he have been here if he had stayed in Immokalee?

A new song begins, in Latin this time. The cameras insist on close-up shots of the choir, almost as if to freeze their mouths, which seem to remain open eternally.

"We'll listen to the homily and then we'll go, OK?" I tell my friend while leaning on his side.

Paco nods. *I* am the one who seems uneasy; yet, I want to see what the bishop is going to say. The camera lingers on a Filipino member of the choir. And now on an African American, but the long shots reveal the actual demographics of the present congregation: they are basically all white.

My expectations are frustrated, though. In the homily, the bishop talks of the Annunciation while the cameras finally reveal Tom Monaghan, in the first row.

A strong and warm wind has risen. It violently shakes the tent above us to the point that we can barely discern the bishop's words. He mentions Pope Benedict XXII and his recent reflection on the Virgin Mary, "...*the mother of all Christians, sinless, only full of Divine Grace...*"

I watch the TV set up by the sides of the tent and the firm eyes of the audience.

"...*The Church as a meeting place for us with the Living Son of God...*"

I look at the incredibly swollen veins of my hands, gesturing to Paco to check them out...

"...*This Church will survive us all...*"

...They seem about to explode.

We walk toward the perimeter of "La Piazza."

"Wow! They're giving kickboxing classes here!" exclaims Paco upon entering a gym located on Annunciation Circle. He picks up one of the brochures on the opposite table and begins to read.

A tall, red-headed guy finally comes out, all sweaty. He apologizes; he's just finished working out. He asks Paco not to judge him from his "redneck" look. They both laugh.

"Come back and check it out!" says the guy, toweling the sweat off his neck. Paco nods his head.

"I'm sure Tia Rosita was inside," Paco says as we are driving back to Immokalee. He is more relaxed now and seems in the mood for chatting. "Did I tell you that Tia Rosita's son worked on the construction of the Oratory?" he says. "I should introduce the two of you. He's obsessed with Italy!"

A farmworker in the fields at dawn in Anthony, New Mexico

Seven

MAY—RESOLUTIONS

Sí Se Puede!

Burger King eventually conceded to the requests of the Coalition of Immokalee Workers. On the day of the agreement, Democratic presidential candidate Barack Obama visits Florida in the attempt to shore up votes. Obama speaks to a galvanized crowd at the Bank Atlantic Center arena in Sunrise, a few miles west of Fort Lauderdale.

"Yes, we can!" was chanted all over the arena. Yes we can.

I had just gotten back from the Obama rally when I received news of the CIW victory. The agreement, which pertains to those growers who provide the tomatoes to Burger King, arrived after the ones with Taco Bell and McDonald's and will lead to an actual increase of 71 percent in farmworkers' salaries: from 45 to 77 cents per bucket of tomatoes. Also, the Florida Tomato Growers Exchange, which represents more than 90 percent of the farmers of the state, has announced its intention to suspend the sanctions, thus further revealing the close ties and common interests between Burger King and the state's growers. FTGE vice president Reggie Brown, however, still poses legal questions regarding the agreement and discouraged members from participating.[1]

The harvest season in Immokalee is now almost over, and it is unclear, so they say at the CIW, when these higher wages will be paid to the workers. Further qualms regarding the fulfillment of the promises made after the signing of the agreement are fostered by the traditional positions of the FTGE. Brown has repeatedly defamed the CIW by maintaining that the data on farmworkers' conditions provided by the organization are exaggerated, that the average hourly pay of a tomato picker in Florida is actually $12.46.

What Brown doesn't say is that farmworkers in the United States from Immokalee, Florida, to Anthony, New Mexico, and elsewhere are not paid by the hour but by the piece rate system. Their workdays begin before sunrise and end at sunset. They have no health insurance, no sick leave, no paid vacation or benefits. They are unwillingly exposed to a harmful cocktail of pesticides.

At this time of the year, Immokalee farmworkers are forced to travel up to three hours to get to the fields, farther and farther north. They have to follow the harvest. Most of the workers have left already for South Carolina or northern Florida.

"I'll see you tomorrow morning at four, at the gas station. Here, behind the market," yells Jesus, a Mexican crew leader, to a bunch of workers. "I'll get gas and we'll leave."

Around seven, the truck that carries the sleepy workers will get to Fort Pierce, on the east coast. Once the plants have dried out, the women and the men of Immokalee will begin to pick green peppers. Later, the "pin-hookers"[2] will come and clean the fields.

Pin-hookers work on their own; generally, they have arrangements with individual growers. They pick the remaining produce of the season and then sell it at the market the very same day. The pin-hookers clean the fields of Felda, ten miles from Immokalee, and when there's nothing left around here, they go further: to Myakka, up north, near Tampa, or to Arcadia, between Lake Placid and Sarasota, looking for the remainder of the harvest of peppers, tomatoes, melons, and watermelons. They harvest until it's not worth going anymore, considering the price of gas. When the harvest is in low water, they, too, make just a few dollars: ten or twelve for a full day of work. I try to join one of them, in a further attempt to experience work in Immokalee's fields. But the spots on the truck are even in higher demand now. I ask the crew leader if I can follow the truck with the car. He screws up his nose and walks away.

There's a quite relaxed atmosphere at the coalition offices. Julia, probably for the first time, welcomes me with a big smile. She's got a new haircut and begins to tell me about the trip to Washington where the agreement was signed, an event that will soon become legend and will be part of the glorious history of the Coalition of Immokalee Workers.

"We'd been in contact with Burger King representatives for a week. Then the news came at seven on Wednesday (May 21). At nine we were on the road already. We'd loaded the truck and the cars, trying to bring as many people as we could. We traveled all night and then we went to sign the agreement at the Capitol. It was really moving," Julia says. And even now, her small blue eyes get teary.

Lupita, too, made it this time. She went to Washington and brought her little daughter along. She had missed the celebration for victory over Taco Bell (she was in Mexico) and over McDonald's (she couldn't go as she was about to give birth), but this time she was able to celebrate along with her fellow members of the CIW.

Major U.S. news publications covered the story. Katrina vanden Heuvel in her *Nation* blog titled her post "Sweet Victory: Coalition of

Immokalee Workers Win," adding the agreement to the weekly account of the successes of the progressive movement.[3]

The news of the conclusion of the CIW campaign on Burger King arrives after weeks of scandals that have led to the firings of two big shots of the corporation: Steven F. Grover, Burger King's vice president of food safety, quality assurance, and regulatory compliance, and Keva Silversmith, Burger King vice president of communications.

The King Is under the Table: Chronicle of a Victory Foretold[4]

Following the chronological order of things, it all begins to unravel when Burger King announces its intention to stop buying tomatoes from Florida. The internal memo, signed by Steve Grover, somehow gets to the Associated Press from the address stopcorporategreed@live.com. Some time later, the same address comes up again; this time the email is signed by a certain "Kevin," who introduces himself as a student of the University of Virginia interested in organizing some protests on campus to support the CIW. Marc Rodrigues (Student/Farmworkers Alliance) becomes suspicious of the strange coincidence. Eric Schlosser, who in his book *Fast Food Nation* has documented the infiltration of London Greenpeace by McDonald's, is informed and decides to help with the search. The email is easily tracked back to the IP address. It is found that the communication did not come from Virginia but from Davie, a city twenty miles north of Miami. Marc then asks the presumed "Kevin" for a physical address to which he would be happy, he writes, to send some literature; at that point, Marc receives no answer.

A couple of months go by, and the tone of communications between Burger King and the CIW gets more and more bitter; the farmworker organization and its allies give no sign of backing down. The SFA staff then receives another email from "Kevin"; this time he's asking for the phone number to participate in the conference call scheduled in preparation for the Day of Action, the national mobilization the SFA is planning for March 31 to support the campaign against Burger King.

A few days after, a Cara Schaffer calls the CIW offices, introducing herself as a student who wants to open up a chapter of the SFA at her school, the Broward Community College. And right after, without any member of the coalition having informed her about the meeting, she asks to participate in the conference call.

Marc, suspicious again, asks Cara for her email address, promising to send her the number shortly. It turns out that Cara Schaffer is actually the president of a Pembroke Pines, Florida, security outfit called Diplomatic Tactical Services, Inc., a private investigation company specializing in the infiltration of union and grassroots groups. It turns out Schaffer does not even have the necessary license to practice in the state of Florida. Contrary to "Kevin," Schaffer participates in the virtual meeting for the Day of Action. She doesn't, however, say a word.

Meanwhile, in the parallel universe of the web, defamatory videos about the Coalition of Immokalee Workers have been posted. CIW members are called "bloodsuckers" or "libelous" and are accused of pocketing the money from the donations made to the organization and cheating people by spreading false information about Florida farmworkers. The accusations are immediately dismissed by the same Jonathan Blum, vice president of Yum! Brands, the world's largest restaurant company, holding of Taco Bell, who states: "We never paid anything directly or indirectly to the CIW,"[5] and reaffirms the integrity of the CIW representatives.

The videos that appear on YouTube are posted by activist-2008@live.com, but sometimes similar derogatory comments are found in the ones posted by surfxaholic36; like the following: "The CIW is an attack organization lining the leaders [*sic*] pockets…They make up issues and collect money from dupes that believe their story. To [*sic*] bad the people protesting don't have a clue regarding the facts. A bunch of fools!"

A letter signed by "Shaun Glass" originating from the "activist2008" email to the local paper in Fort Myers, the *News-Press*, thickens the mystery.

News-Press reporter Amy Bennett Williams begins to do some research. Soon she finds out that the email comes from the Burger King headquarters in Miami. Keva Silversmith, vice president of communications, denies the email was official, yet declares: "[…] obviously in a corporation of 900 people, you'd understand that some people get their passions aroused."[6]

Quickly, the reporter discovered that "surfxaholic36" is the online handle of Shannon Grover, daughter of the vice president of Burger King, Steve Grover. One day, Williams calls the Grovers and Shannon picks up the phone; Williams begins to ask questions about the defamatory videos, and the girl reveals: "That was my dad! My dad used to go online with that name and write about them. I don't really know much about the Coalition and Burger King stuff."

The story comes out first in the *News-Press* and then in the major national media outlets: the *New York Times*, National Public Radio, the *Nation;* Keith Olbermann on MSNBC names Steve Grover "Worst Person in the World."[7]

Magically, within a few days, the videos are gone, and Burger King reopens negotiations with the CIW. Grover and Silversmith are fired—although no official Burger King memo reveals the identity of the two company directors—and the fast food corporation signs the agreement at the Capitol, and states, through the mouthpiece of its

Senior Vice President for Global Communications Amy Wagner, that eventually the two parties have found that they had "common interests." Wagner also offers CEO John Chidsey's apologies for the negative comments expressed about the CIW.

In the meantime, the story continues in cyberspace. Shannon Grover, in fact, is thirteen and on a blog her supposed "mother" (madmom2008) accuses the reporter (Amy Williams) of having taken advantage of her daughter, exposing her "to the dangers of the web." The supposed Mrs. Grover says Williams seems "more interested in producing this type of yellow journalism, than protecting children and tomato pickers alike," and further notes in the post that "this child who as you can imagine, has not been to PR training was frightened and still recovering from this incident."

In the June issue of the *Harvard Business Review*, the father—unemployed by the time the magazine comes out—continues to give advice to corporations on how to move strategically when it comes to corporate social responsibility; in particular, writes Grover, "one of the issues I am more involved [in] with Burger King is animal welfare."[8]

Finally, although this hasn't been confirmed, the emails sent from stopcorporategreed@live.com seemed to have come from high-ranking Burger King personnel. Certain signs—the similarity of the names, the fact that he was a graduate of the University of Virginia—indicate that Keva Silversmith, the other vice president who got fired, was probably the mysterious Kevin. Plaudits to the imagination of the King.

Looking for Tomatoes, Finding Monsanto

"I was sleeping." Angela appears on the threshold of her house. "I'm really tired," she says while closing the door behind us. Paco is not home. As soon as school was over, he left with the CIW cooperative for the watermelon harvest. Angela seems sadder than usual. Che, the old dog they had, died a few days earlier. "Tina and Carl buried him over there," she says inconsolably.

I ask Angela if she wants to go to the produce market with me. After all, she was the one who first suggested I should go there and try to find someone to go with to the fields. But Angela shakes her head. She needs to rest, she says, her eyes to the floor.

◆

I walk around the fruit and vegetable counters. It's four already and oppressively hot. I ask around, trying to get near to those who, I'm assuming, are pin-hookers. Finally, two young women show me the office of the market.

"You have to talk to Elisabeth," they say in unison.

I get up on the wide stage that serves as the loading area for the crates of tomatoes and other produce. On the white, scraped door of the office the sign reads "CLOSED," repeated three times. I turn around to the women; their gestures encourage me to knock on the door. Elisabeth welcomes me in the hyper air-conditioned little room that is her office. From behind her desk, she looks at me with a suspicious air that I soon will discover as being typically Elizabeth's. She sports an eighties hairstyle: the dark blonde hair short in the front and over the ears but long in the back.

Elisabeth is in charge of the sorting and handling of all the produce that goes through the market. One of her tasks is to retain the cash share of the produce that is sold here on behalf of Mr. Salazar, the owner of the market.

She listens to my request, then says: Let me make a couple of calls. Elisabeth leans back on her chair, and I can now clearly see the T-shirt she's wearing: "Always late but worth the wait," it reads. She hangs up. Nothing. She ponders, looking down with her magnetic hazelnut eyes. She makes another call. The guy says he'll check and let her know later.

I come back the day after. Elisabeth is skillfully maneuvering the forklift among the market counters, and moving around sweaty men, dirty from the day in the fields. This time Elisabeth welcomes me with a smile, framed by her heart-shaped mouth and the two little funny side-ponytails she wears this morning.

"Listen," she says immediately, "There's this girl...She still picks tomatoes around here." Elisabeth takes a look around as to acknowledge the evident lack of privacy of the situation.

"When I'm done, I'll take you there," she says while putting the forklift into gear. "Come by my office in thirty minutes, OK?"

Elisabeth and I leave her air-conditioned office behind, and go out into the dreary and steamy heat of the dying afternoon. We walk to the area where the pin-hookers hang: they are packing eggplants, corn-cobs, peppers, and chili peppers of different shapes and colors. They stop to look at us, perhaps recognizing me as an element alien to their environment. Elisabeth calls the girl, Lucy. Lucy wears a hat with the visor turned toward her long black hair. Elisabeth explains to her in Spanish that I'm writing a book and I'd like to go to the fields, to see how tomato pickers work in Immokalee.

Lucy listens while her nimble hands continue to sort peppers. She looks askance at me. Then she stops, lights a cigarette, shakes her head.

"The inspectors, the inspectors..." she says looking at Elisabeth. And then goes back to sorting the vegetables. "Let's do this..." Elisabeth finally, says getting close to me. "Tomorrow you come here at seven thirty and we'll go to look for this guy." I give my hand to Lucy and introduce myself. I hope I'll see you tomorrow, I say. She gives a hint of a smile, and the cigarette almost falls from her lips.

The following morning, at the market, seven thirty sharp. I hand Elisabeth the coffee and the pastries I picked up at La Favorita bakery as I jump in her blue truck. She smiles in appreciation. We get on I-29 to go to Felda, a few miles north of Immokalee. The broken yellow line marks the center of the street: on the sides, there are immense, foggy fields, interrupted only by tall pine trees and rare threadbare palms. The savannah of South Florida.

Elisabeth was born and raised here. As she puts it, she spent her entire life around the area. "Up until I was twenty-five, that's all I knew: Immokalee, Naples, Lake Okeechobee..." she says. "I only took a trip to Mexico with my husband (he is Mexican) when we got married. We rented a car and drove up to the border, through Alabama, Louisiana, Texas, and then we traveled around Mexico. That was fun!"

In two weeks, Elisabeth and her fourteen-year-old daughter will go to Disneyworld.

"I haven't taken a vacation in so long..." she says. "Can you believe it? I was born and raised in Florida and I've never seen Mickey Mouse!"

"There goes Lucy!" Elisabeth nods ahead at Lucy's truck. I quickly turn around to catch a glimpse of Lucy's truck speeding in the opposite direction of the motorway.

We get on a little side road, looking for the farm where the pinhookers meet.

"You see those bushes," Elisabeth says. "Those are gooseberry plants. That is a medicinal plant, used to cure colon cancer. The gooseberries are pretty valuable: they are paid up to a dollar per pound. The landowners here don't allow anybody to pick gooseberries, but they know what's happening. So what do they do? Sometimes they wait until the pin-hookers are done and then they take away whatever they picked that day! I heard stories of people saying that they've been robbed and beaten and then left on the side of the road. That's why it's always better to go with somebody…"

Elisabeth tries to get me in a couple of farms but with no success. Something is clear to me by now: gaining permission to visit the fields in Immokalee is a tall order.

"Let's stop by my house," Elisabeth says. "I want to show you some pictures."

She turns into an unpaved side road on the right, into a wooded area and arrive in front of a slope-roofed house. A huge tractor truck is parked on the side of the building. "It's my husband's…One day he'll decide to move it…" she says.

We go in the house. "It's not the same thing but at least you can see how it works," Elisabeth says, while showing me some pictures she took; then she begins to explain: "The white plastic is put down in August when the tomatoes are planted…"

I drop by the market again later in the afternoon. Elisabeth spoke to Lucy; she seems to have changed her mind. She is going to talk to the crew leader and see if I can go with her.

"Wait for her at the Shell gas station," Elisabeth says. "When you see her blue truck, just get behind her!"

I go by Lucy's counter, just to confirm with her our appointment for the next day. She's retreated in the midst of boxes and is now slurping down a slice of watermelon. She nods at me, and smiles with the smile of a child, her blackened teeth notwithstanding.

The following morning, at seven fifteen, I'm in front of the Shell gas station. I sip my coffee, waiting to tag along behind Lucy's fast truck. I wait until seven forty-five but no sign of Lucy. At eight, I decide to drive directly to the farm. I turn at the Duda & Sons sign, as I did the day before with Elisabeth.

"You'd need all sorts of permits and authorizations…It's not that one can go like that…" a tall and bony man, wearing a pair of big, dark lenses oddly placed over his prescription glasses, said the day before.

"You should go to the research center of the University of Florida," he added then, but more to discourage rather than better direct me, as the skeptical look of the farm's receptionist confirmed.

Lucy arrives after ten minutes. I get out of my car and get close to her truck. A couple of men are loading up empty boxes. They will be filled with the produce of the day, and then later in the afternoon brought to the market to be sold. One of the two men is wearing a CIW T-shirt.

Lucy sees me and mumbles something, but I don't know if she's trying to apologize for the delay or because she forgot about our appointment. Then she sticks her head into the car window of the crew leader. I hear her asking him if he has time to show me the farm. And there I know that my adventure with Lucy is over. She won't take me to work with her as I hoped.

The crew leader delivers me to a certain Jimmy Taylor. He's the farm manager—that's how he introduces himself to me. He offers to give me a quick tour of the farm. He doesn't have a lot of time, he says. I nod. Better than nothing, I think.

"Give me ten minutes," says Jimmy walking past me.

I go back to the car, window down, waiting. I decide to follow the long-lashed receptionist's advice, and avoid making myself too visible. Her tall-and-bony boss, in particular, she reasserts, must not see me.

Jimmy Taylor comes back after a few minutes. He parks his Land Rover and nods to me from the car to get in. Jimmy has small blue eyes, framed by straight, dark-blonde hair combed so exaggeratedly forward that it looks fake. His relatively small and childlike face contrasts with the large hands thickened by years of manual, outdoor labor.

"First of all, we don't harvest tomatoes and other produce for sale here," he says warningly. "This is a laboratory farm. Monsanto owns it."

In addition to being a meeting point for local pin-hookers, the farm is indeed property of Seminis, a wholly-owned subsidiary of Monsanto Co.;[9] the company, today the largest developer, grower, and marketer of vegetable and fruit seeds in the world, posted $606 million in revenue for 2007.[10]

Jimmy begins to drive his Land Rover across the fields. But Jimmy makes it clear to me right away: "I'm only the farm manager. I'm not aware of the experiments that are being performed…"

Jimmy, too, is from here, and, like Elisabeth, lives in Felda. However, he speaks with a strong Southern accent, which makes it hard for me to understand sometimes.

He surely is no snowbird, he points out, but a Floridian with roots generations old.

"It was my great-grandfather that opened the first postal office here in Felda," he continues. "*He* gave the name to this place…"

Jimmy stops the Land Rover, takes out a piece of paper and a pen, and begins to write. On the right, out in the fields, lay a pile of rotting watermelons.

"Felix was my great-grandfather's name and Ida was his wife's," Jimmy shows me. "Take the 'Fel' from Felix and the 'da' from Ida and you get Felda. You see?"

Jimmy puts aside the piece of paper and, at least temporarily, his ancestral pride; we resume our tour.

"We have four 'doctors' that work here...They do their crossings, their experiments...They always try to develop new and better seeds that will produce the fittest plants, the ones that will resist the insecticides and the bad bacterias."

"You see, those have reacted bad, and those other ones as well," he adds as if he needed to explain what presents itself in full obviousness. I observe the string of withered tomato plants, and the ones beside, decisively healthier in their appearance. In the background, I hear Jimmy speaking of his mother's distinguished heritage.

"My other great-grandfather was Sam Thompson, the Georgian hero of the Southern Confederate Army..."

◆

"Monsanto spends more than $2 million a day in research to identify, test, develop, and bring to market innovative new seeds and technologies that benefit farmers," Monsanto spokesman Darren Wallis declared to *Vanity Fair.*[11]

Since the eighties Monsanto has enforced extreme practices of seed patenting on growers nationally. After agriculture was included in the General Agreement on Tariffs and Trade (GATT), these practices have been further commercially sanctioned at the international level.[12]

As a result of the WTO's trade liberalization policies, food prices have fallen: in the Global North, farmers have been able to take advantage of increased subsidies; in the Global South, the rising costs of production created by market monopolies have further impoverished rural communities and led small farmers into more debt. A dramatic case in point is India where thousands of peasants have committed suicide in the last few years.[13]

Conversely, Monsanto presents its biotech agribusiness as the solution to the food needs of an ever-growing world population. Poverty, however, is worsened precisely by agribusiness's practice of "enclosing" farmland, forcing millions of farmers off their land. More than 50 percent of urban population growth is due to compelled migration from rural communities further impoverished by the arrival of industrial agriculture.[14] Denying people access to food *creates* world hunger.

So it turns out that agribusiness's solution is the number one problem. In the Global South, agribusiness is destroying biodiversity by favoring monocultures. Seeds, which used to be free sources, are now commodities. As biologist and environmental activist Vandana Shiva puts it: "Feeding humanity should not depend on the extinction of farmers and extinction of species."[15]

Here lies the most astonishing, unspoken contradiction of neoliberalism, which is presumably based on the idea of a free, unrestrained market: patents are indeed instruments of control of the market itself, a crucial step in the development of monopolies.

Vandana Shiva has most notably argued that patents are actually fetters to authentic progress and limit the creativity of the scientific community, and so the development of knowledge.[16] A similar reasoning also motivated the exclusionary clauses in the Plant Variety Protection Act (PVPA).[17] The law, passed in 1970 as a result of sustained lobbying activity by the seed industry, granted a twenty-year term protection for most plant varieties and enabled holders the exclusive rights to market their

seeds; when the act was envisioned, however, Congress created two ex-
emptions to still allow for the open exchange of germplasm among researchers and the possibility for growers to save patented seeds for
replanting—the so-called Farmer's Right.[18]

Monsanto, on the other hand, claims that the practice of seed
patenting has been going on for decades, since the 1930s, at the very
least. [19] The Plant Patent Act (1930), however, protected only the "in-
ventions" of asexually propagated plants. For decades U.S. government
regulatory agencies actually opposed the rampant practice of patenting
of seeds in agriculture as these were considered forms of life of extreme
variety and, thus, non-licensable. In the eighties, however, the U.S.
Supreme Court redefined them as "widgets," thus paving the way for the
multinationals of agribusiness to take over the world's reserve of food
with their commodification of seeds.[20] Monsanto bought Seminis, understanding that whoever controls the seeds controls the food supply.[21]

After the *Ex parte Hibberd* decision (1985), the U.S. Patent and
Trademark Office began accepting applications for licensing sexually reproducing plants.[22] Monsanto then went on "a patenting spree," as the
Center for Food Safety put it; as it reported in 2005, 647 biotech plants
are held by Monsanto. The numbers are undoubtedly higher today."[23]

For ten thousand years, in pre-Monsanto times, farmers all
around the world saved their crop seeds at the time of harvest to re-
plant them the following spring. This practice has become a crime in
the new agricultural world created by Monsanto and the other corporations such as Cargill and Syngenta that today control the production
of food globally.

Once growers buy Monsanto seeds, they are perennially forced to
repurchase them from the corporation—if they don't want to be sum-
moned for violation of patent rights. Every year, an average of five hun-

dred farmers get sued by Monsanto; the company spends a total of $10 million yearly to investigate and persecute U.S. growers.[24] The practice of saving seeds has now been renamed "seed piracy" by Monsanto and its corporate allies. In addition, the corporation's agents who infiltrate communities to gather information on local farming activities are known as the "seed police"; their tactics have been described by locals with words such as "Gestapo" and "Mafia."[25] This is, admittedly, the company's tool to protect the work done by researchers to create new genetically modified seeds, which is only a way to protect intellectual property rights, Monsanto claims.[26] And to recoup the corporation's investment in research.

Thus, intellectual property (IP) laws—which originally intended "to facilitate the flow of ideas in the interest of learning" as stated in the Berne Convention Implementation Act (1988)—have been instrumentally reinterpreted as a way to financially reward inventors, so that the expansion of corporate monopolies could be both allowed and justified.[27] In the "bioserfdom" created by the "Gene Giants," genetic engineers are thus considered inventors; but truth be told, these researchers are building on the knowledge that generations of farmers have accumulated in improving and selecting seeds.[28]

Additionally, the corporation's GM seeds are developed to resist the herbicide Roundup, a Monsanto product as well, so that those farmers who use it are basically forced to buy the seeds that are resistant to the same herbicide. Monsanto has thus built a near-monopoly in the agribusiness thanks to the ease of use of the herbicide, the kill-all result obtainable with Roundup, the lowered prices applied to GM seeds and their related herbicides, and the easing of U.S. government regulation when it comes to the commercial regulation of GM seeds— all this notwithstanding the effect its products have on human health.

For instance, it's been repeatedly proven that glyphosate, the active principle contained in Roundup, is highly toxic.[29]

Monsanto was born as a chemical company; it developed from an idea of the Irish John Francis Queeny, who named the business after his wife's maiden name. Queeney began to sell saccharine and became the world's leading producer of aspirin during the First World War. In the seventies, Monsanto turned toward biotechnology and began its subsequent rise to colossus of global agribusiness.

To understand what the world of agriculture has become today, suffice it to say that Monsanto presents itself as an agricultural company. An innocent label, evoking wholesome small family-run farms, hides the reality of a monstrous empire built on numerous political ties and influential lobbyists,[30] a near-monopoly on patented seeds and the related spread of the "seed piracy" specter, as well as routine environmental and human health protection violations. For instance, dioxin was a by-product of 2,4,5-T herbicide and Agent Orange, the infamous defoliant used during the war in Vietnam; both products were made by Monsanto.[31] Additionally, Polychlorinated biphenyls (PBCs) produced by Monsanto dramatically polluted the western part of the city of Anniston, Alabama.[32]

Florida is among those states that have passed laws that require food labels to indicate whether GM technology has been used, even partially, in the production of the foods.[33] On the other·hand, Florida has also passed legislation favorable to Monsanto, thus negating the town councils' right to ban the distribution of GM crops.[34]

In Florida, Monsanto managed to neutralize the four-part exposé on a dangerous drug (rBGH or rBST) given to dairy cows, scheduled to air on WTVT, a Fox TV station in Tampa on February

24, 1997.[35] After being asked to alter their report, investigative reporters Jane Akre and Steve Wilson eventually sued the Fox station, appealing to the whistleblower laws that protect journalists from employer retaliation. Fox appealed and the case was overturned, and the reporters, to add insult to injury, had to pay $200,000 in legal fees to Fox. However, they were also recipients of several awards for their rigorous ethics, like the Goldman environmental prize. Monsanto had informed the network of its intention to pull its advertising if the report were broadcast in its initial form: among other things, the original report exposed Monsanto's outright lies about its own research on the effects of the genetically engineered bovine growth hormone (rBGH or rBST).[36]

This case has brought up some truths about contemporary culture: corporations can get away with blackmailing a media outlet in order to keep sensitive information out of the public sphere; deflecting facts and selecting a new, less controversial angle is an acceptable practice for major news networks; doing investigative journalism is either heroic or stupid, according to whom you ask.

One County under God

It happened in 1958. A terrible freeze inexorably hit the fields of Immokalee. It was a cold, cold winter forty years ago. *Miami News* reporter Howard Van Smith visited the various communities of migrant workers around Florida and wrote a series of articles that denounced the inhumane conditions they had to endure. He won the Pulitzer Prize, while the people of Immokalee got an extemporaneous intervention from Governor Leroy Collins that provided aid for the four thousand-plus people who had been starving for months.

But the general situation did not get better. Inspections became more frequent, but with substantially little change to the status quo. The exploitation of the workforce, kept in conditions of poverty or authentic slavery have historically served the interests of landlords in Florida: in Belle Glade, Palm Beach County, those who worked on the sugar cane plantations, and in Immokalee, Collier County, those who picked tomatoes were the human engines that fed the increasing food needs of the growing U.S. population.

In 1960, Edward R. Murrow with his *Harvest of Shame* brought the plague of the migrant workers into the houses of the Americans. The following year, Donald G. Grubbs in the *Florida Historical Quarterly* wrote: "Though these dilapidated shacks resemble inferior chicken coops more than anything else, none shelter livestock; the farmers of Florida are too progressive to allow cattle or poultry to be kept in such surroundings. No, these hovels are the winter residences of human beings."[37]

In 1966, the Collier County Housing Authority, the agency that today administers the male dormitory called Horizon Village, was created. Then, a group of good-willed individuals operating in the Immokalee area set as its primary goal the provision of houses to the farmworking community. As of June 2008, 641 units are part of the authority. The largest housing complex, the Farm Worker Village, is located three miles away from the center of Immokalee.

The Farm Worker Village has four sections, built between 1974 and 1991; each housing unit (611 in total) has an identical architectonic plan, although the number of bedrooms varies. With USDA (United States Department of Agriculture) low-interest loans and grants the Housing Authority has been able to keep the rents affordable—all the rents are currently under $500 a month. [38]

In response to the question, "do you still have a housing emergency in Immokalee?" Esmeralda "Essi" Serrata, executive director of Collier County Housing Authority, answers with a sigh. She also comes from a family of farmworkers: her father (Mexican) and her mother (Texan of Mexican descent) were used to migrating up north every summer. She worked in the fields up until she was sixteen and went to school in the evening. Born and raised in Immokalee, Essi lived for years in one of the houses the agency now administers.[39] That's where I meet her: at the offices located inside the Farm Worker Village. Esmeralda is a woman in her forties of robust build with long black hair that comes down her shoulders like a mantle.

"Absolutely. We still have an emergency." Essi begins. "Although agriculture is no longer the only economic activity in Immokalee, it remains the main one.[40] And people still need to have a roof over their heads…"

"Miss Serrata"—as Miguel constantly refers to her—has a personal assistant from whom she constantly requires help in the few minutes we spend at her office: make a photocopy, find a certain brochure, make another photocopy.

"Once we had a wait list for housing," Esmeralda continues. "Now we even have empty units."

Empty? Didn't she just say there was a housing emergency in Immokalee?

As for the Horizon Village, to be eligible to live at the Farm Worker Village, the primary family income needs to come from agriculture. The only crucial difference pertains to the status: only permanent residents or U.S. citizens can live in the housing complex where Esmeralda grew up. That's why there's no longer a wait list. The answer lies in this clause related to the status of immigrants.

"Collier County has always had a very clear-cut position when it came to illegal immigration," Esmeralda laments.

"In recent years we've noticed a noteworthy decrease of the Hispanic population that up to fifteen to twenty years ago made up more than 70 percent of the residents of the Farm Worker Village," she adds.

In the eighties and nineties, many Haitians and Guatemalans arrived in Immokalee and some soon obtained the status of political refugees. That allowed them to start a naturalization process; moreover, the amnesty of 1986 allowed many Mexican immigrants that had illegally entered the country to regularize their position.

Today, most people who live at the Farm Worker Village are long-time residents: primarily Creole Haitians, Mexicans, and Puerto Ricans. Those few who work in the fields own a means of transportation. Most of them work in the packinghouses.

We get in the car. Esmeralda is going to give me a tour of the housing facilities administered by the authority. She shows me the mobile homes that the nonprofit organization IHOPE (Immokalee Helping Our People in Emergency) bought from FEMA after Hurricane Wilma.

A line of white trailers rolls out to the side of an unpaved road. An old car missing a tire is parked close by, waiting to be made whole again. A stroller is abandoned on the dry grass. No one in sight.

I figure this place is uninhabited, but Essi corrects my assumptions.

"They are all at work now," she says. "The families that had to evacuate because of Wilma moved here only a few months ago. Until recently, they didn't even have a place to stay."

IHOPE, which is part of the Disaster Volunteer Network, has helped more than five hundred families (as of June 2008), both in the reconstruction and replacement of the houses damaged by Hurricane Wilma. As David Grove will inform me, Collier County has covered the costs for the installation of the mobile homes. The lot rent of a FEMA trailer costs between $225 and $275 a month plus maintenance and $100 for monthly insurance. Tenants have the option to buy the trailer and make it their new home; many do so, and pay back the organization in $250 installments, without interest. As of today, IHOPE has installed twenty-eight trailers thanks to the support of some private individuals and entities, especially churches and religious organizations. A line of FEMA trailers has been sitting by the Immokalee airport for months: they are part of a new lot that arrived in January waiting to be fixed and made available to move into.[41]

Contrary to other housing projects financed by Collier County, only one member of the family is required to have documents to request a FEMA trailer. A child born in the United States, the most common situation, will do. Although FEMA is part of the Department of Homeland Security, David says, it doesn't apply restrictive policies when it comes to immigration.

I ask David why, in his opinion, Collier County has a policy meant to discourage the settlement of undocumented immigrants in its community, or, rather, won't do anything to meet their most basic human needs, while FEMA, in line with the federal government, is willing to turn a blind eye.

"Well, FEMA's main purpose is to help whomever is in an emergency situation..." he answers, "Collier County assists prospective homeowners who are legally here."

This should not come as a surprise since the same FEMA has made use of "illegal" labor during the rebuilding of New Orleans and other Gulf Coast areas hit hard by Hurricane Katrina.[42] According to what a recent study reports, one worker out of four was actually an un-documented Latino.[43] For the reconstruction of the areas affected by hurricanes Katrina and Wilma, President Bush suspended the Davis-Bacon Act that requires contractors of federal projects to pay workers on-site no less than the locally prevailing wages and benefits paid for similar projects.[44] Additionally, the DHS decided to suspend the sanctions on employers who hire workers without documents.[45]

Historically, the federal government has been willing to condone the use of nontraditional workers to serve the economic interests of the country's industries. For instance, while many men were overseas fighting during World War Two, the U.S. propaganda machine prompted the female population to work in the factories (especially in heavy industry) as a service *and* a duty to the nation. As historian Cindy Hahamovitch has pointed out, the bracero program, launched in 1942 with the aim of bringing "arms" from Mexico in response to a purported scarcity of labor in U.S. agriculture, was primarily intended to meet growers' demand for a more submissive workforce.[46]

◆

Essi drives toward the center of Immokalee as she continues to list the problems she faces on a daily basis. "As a federal agency we have difficulties raising funds. You see, we don't even depend on the municipality, but they call us 'Collier County Housing Authority,' and this surely doesn't help…" Essi says.

"Why don't you change the name?" I object, not fully understanding. "Why not call it Immokalee Housing Authority!"

"We've talked about that," Essi says sighing. "Technically, we don't serve just the community of Immokalee, but the entire county with the subsidizing programs."[47] In this case, too, Essi confirms, only those who are U.S. citizens or hold a green card can ask for the assistance from Section 8 of the Housing Choice Voucher (HCV) Program.[48]

In 2005, the Housing Authority obtained more than nine million dollars ($4 million in loans, the rest as grants). "There was this ceremony with the showing of the big check…" Essi says sarcastically. "Nine million dollars!"

However, these are rehab funds, which means that they can only be used for remodeling existing buildings; for instance, they will go to finance the construction of the houses in section A of the Farm Worker Village, the one that was built in 1974 and that hosts 150 units.

"The idea is to demolish the one-bedroom apartments and the duplexes and then remodel the inside of the bigger units, maybe adding a laundry room," Esmeralda explains.

"As you see, we can't do anything new. Any type of urban planning has to follow the standards of the municipality to which Immokalee belongs: Collier County. That would mean building sidewalks on both sides of the road, setting up a certain irrigation system for the lawns and so forth. You can easily see that we have very different priorities here in Immokalee…"

We finally arrive at the Horizon.

"In the original project, we wanted to have a clinic and a legal office conveniently located inside the same structure," Esmeralda says pointing to a couple of rooms near the restrooms.

"Miguel is not in. He went to the Farm Worker Village," the receptionist says.

We stop in the spacious hall of the office that overlooks the courtyard of the Horizon: a wide, dry space delimited on two sides by the hallways that flow into the units and on the central side by the semi-covered laundry room.

Essi also laments the lack of recreational facilities. "It's hard to collect money to build a basketball court or even to buy some tables. People figure these things are not important..." But there's more. Four years after the opening of the Horizon, the Housing Authority is far from paying off the debt for the building of the dormitory.

"Two screws are missing here..." Esmeralda says while showing the receptionist the base of one of the windows in the hall. "Did you see it?"

The young woman appears confused: apparently, she hadn't noticed.

"Have them replaced, OK?" Esmeralda concludes authoritatively.

"Someone tried to break in," she says, thinking out loud.

We walk along the external hallway, monitored by cameras, until we get to the last unit, an empty one. Essi opens the door and I have a sudden, definite feeling of entering into a bunker. A portable TV sits on the table.

"When the tenants go away, they always leave things behind..." Esmeralda's voice resounds in the empty room. "They have to travel as light as they can...We have a storage for this stuff but what happens is that the men rarely come back to retrieve them. Well, they just don't ever come back to Immokalee."

We tour the apartment. A greenish-painted wall separates the cubicles where the workers sleep. Every cubicle has two beds, and every worker has a little closet. No windows.

"As you can see, it's a very functional structure..." Essi comments matter-of-factly.

The showers are unmercifully rudimental.

"The AC should be on 78, not on 75," Essi reproaches as we leave the bunker.

"This facade cost us at least $25,000," Essi says as she maneuvers the car out of the Horizon. If the urban decoration code imposes all these "beautifying restrictions," how do you account for the existence of ramshackled places like those I have visited in Immokalee? It's a technicality. Indeed, the urban decoration code dates back to the nineties and does not cover those houses built before then. On the other hand, the wealthy families who own most of the realties and land in Immokalee have no interest in rebuilding or even remodeling their properties. Take for example the Blockers, who are proprietors of a big furniture store and a clearinghouse just out of town (in La-belle). Gina Curtis is president and Curtis Blocker Jr. is a member of the board of directors; together, they preside over the Collier County chapter of the conservative Florida Farm Bureau, the largest agricul-tural organization, with more than 144,000 members in the nation.

The décor standards are high, and there are no incentives. The people of Immokalee, on the other hand, will still need to work in the fields and send their children to school, which practically means living in the center, if one can't afford a car. They will keep paying exorbitant rents for run-down houses because they have no choice.[49] Naples, where so many wealthy people live, and Immokalee, where so many poor people live, are part of the same county, but they are still forty miles apart from each other, and might as well be forty million.

We cut through the savannah of Immokalee, heading back to the Farm Worker Village, the clouds low in the potent Florida sky.

"In the end," Esmeralda says bitterly, "These two realities continue to coexist because they are physically separate."

The fields of Immokalee divide them.

Biking the Multitude

"It all started when I gave a bike to this guy," Padre Patricio says. "I might have been in Immokalee only for two weeks or so. The news spread and more came to see if I had more bicycles to give away. A rental shop in Sanibel donated forty bicycles to the church. Not all of them were good: actually, some of them were in real bad shape. Yet, we find a way to fix them. When the people who live in the neighborhood saw a big truck pulling in, hundreds rushed to the square in front of the church."

Fifteen minutes later the bicycles were gone. In the days that followed, more people came to visit Padre Patricio asking for more. "That was when I decided I had to create a bank account to raise money to buy more bikes," the priest says.

"A few weeks ago a couple came to visit Immokalee…" he continues.

They are members of a congregation in Reston, Virginia, where Padre Patricio served before moving to Immokalee.[50]

"The couple has been very moved by this community, so they kept asking me if they could help these people somehow. While we were visiting the run-down trailers where the immigrants live, at one point the man said: 'People deserve better!' And eureka! We found the name for it! So we put up a website and organized a fundraiser. 'Donate $40 and buy a bike for a migrant worker in Immokalee.'"

Over a weekend, $16,000 was raised for People Deserve Better.

Padre Patricio walks around the courtyard of the Guadalupe Church. The sun is still up in the sky, and the priest stops under the shade of a tree. Two worshippers are on their knees in front of the Virgin of Guadalupe. The woman has her hands wrapped around a large candle and stares at the statue of the Madonna; the man has his head tilted forward as he recites his silent prayer.

"In the end, I am in Immokalee for selfish reasons," Padre Patricio says. I look at him not understanding. He starts his walk, now careless of the blazing sun.

"I'm here because it makes me feel good...When I help the poor, the disenfranchised...I feel that I am doing the Lord's will," he adds.

Padre Patricio takes a deep breath and looks around.

"There is an abundance of life here," he says. "All these children playing in the open air and these young people working in the fields...And in all this happiness," he adds, "there's also despair and suffering."

We walk toward the Virgin of Guadalupe. The faithful have left. Padre Patricio has an interview for a documentary film. The crew is here waiting for him.

Padre Patricio adjusts his white collar, straightens out his black shirt.

"I've butterflies in my stomach," he says in Spanish. Then he laughs nervously. He's used to talking in front of hundreds of parishioners, but the camera seems to make him uneasy. The crew directs the priest to stand in front of the statue of the Virgin of Guadalupe and has him move a bit to the side to better frame the shot.

"You know, I wonder how many people will see this," Padre Patricio says while the camera operator mics him up.

"I've always thought of myself as a chubby Val Kilmer," he jokes.

We all laugh. Then the interview begins.

Padre Patricio, why does discrimination exist? Why does prejudice exist?

"Together We Are One"—mural at the Farm Worker Village

EPILOGUE

"Is it possible to have love without justice?"
—A chaplain of the migrant workers, speaking in *Harvest of Shame*

Driving southbound on SR-29 toward Immokalee, I like to linger on the signs alerting drivers to watch for panthers. The great cats are nearly extinct today. Back in the fifties, they were hunted in this area for killing cattle. Today, the Florida panther is the official state animal.

Much has changed around here, and more will.

In the last couple of years, people I met have moved away from Immokalee. Melody went back to Santa Ana, California, to be with her family and live in the community where she was born and raised. She currently works as a community outreach and early literacy coordinator at an elementary school. Melody continues to use the organizing tools and strategies she learned in Immokalee and plans to mobilize people in her community to keep supporting the CIW's Campaign for Fair Food. She holds a seat on the board of the CIW and is also a member of the SFA advisory committee. Immokalee and its people continue to live in her heart and inspire her to action. Padre

Patricio is now serving as pastor of Jesus Obrero (Jesus the Worker) Catholic Church in Tice, a poverty-saddled area in East Fort Myers, in a very poor area known as Tice. He is also a pastor of Mission San Jose in South Fort Myers, in another impoverished neighborhood called Harlem Heights; both are Spanish-speaking immigrant parishes. He still visits Immokalee regularly and enjoys spending time with its peo-ple. Tequila still has a home with the Garcias when Padre Patricio trav-els. The Garcias have not yet gotten married, but still want to. They are struggling to get the necessary documents from Mexico to obtain a marriage license in the United States. Padre Patricio is hopeful they will get them soon and is happily available to unite them in matrimony. Tricia left her position at the Guadalupe Center and is now the direc-tor of community programs at Immokalee Housing & Family Ser-vices. Most of the farmworkers I met in Immokalee still pick produce in the fields of Florida and beyond. Eduardo is now the father of a beautiful baby boy. His son will turn two soon.

New migrants come and go. And the coalition continues the strug-gle for better working conditions in the fields. Since its outset, the CIW has focused on eliminating exploitation and slavery in the plantation-scale fields of Florida. Recently, however, it has significantly widened the range of its targets. Beginning in 2008, the CIW-spearheaded Campaign for Fair Food joined forces with the sustainable food move-ment, which has traditionally focused on the development of local and organic agricultural production. Whole Foods voluntarily signed the agreement to support the "penny-per-pound" tomato program (in Sep-tember 2008), the first of its kind that the CIW struck with a super-market chain. The deal prompted the crucial convergence of the farmworkers' struggle for fairer wages and justice in the fields and the sustainable food movement, two social forces that today are striving to change the agricultural world and the food industry. Furthermore, the CIW has lately taken on Ahold, Kroger, and particularly Lakeland, Florida–based Publix, the major supermarket in the Southeast.

The SFA has also launched "Dine with Dignity," a campus campaign to prompt food giants that serve cafeterias all over the country to comply with the CIW agreement and its supplier code of conduct. Once again, there have been victories. Bon Appetit, which serves four hundred university and corporate cafés, signed, helping to open a market to Florida's small, family-scale growers. In April 2010, it was Aramark's turn. Sodexo announced at the 2009 National Conference of the Community Food Security Coalition that it intended to support the wage increase, but hasn't committed yet.[1]

After Plant City, Florida–based East Coast Brokers and Packers Inc. entered the agreement along with food service supplier Compass, in February 2010 the FTGE lifted its sanctions against growers who decided to comply with the "penny-per-pound" tomato program. The FTGE concomitantly launched a New Social Responsibility Program, which, however, didn't meet the coalition's standards. The industry-established program, the CIW maintains, is 90 percent identical to the old SAFE (or Socially Accountable Farm Employers): the main problem with both codes of conduct is the lack of worker participation. Suffice it to note that a couple of farms that complied with SAFE were implicated in one slavery case uncovered by the CIW.[2]

Chipotle was also buying from slavery-tainted farms. In order to expose the hypocrisy of Chipotle's "Food with Integrity" slogan, the Immokalee workers launched the Chipocrisy Tour. Chipotle, which made more than $1 billion in sales in 2009,[3] buys naturally raised meat, uses dairy that are free of the bovine growth hormone (rBGH), and organic and local food when feasible. The Denver-based company, however, has yet to sign the CIW agreement that would raise workers' wages.

In December 2008, Subway, the largest fast-food purchaser of Florida tomatoes, conceded too. At the time of writing, Wendy's/Arby's Group has yet to join the Campaign for Fair Food, but given the CIW's persistence and winning strategy, it is only a matter of months until it does.

But there's more. A modern-day slavery museum has been traveling the East Coast since February 2010. On exhibit are replicas of the implements used by the convicted to subjugate their victims, court rulings, photos, and media coverage of the slavery cases. The museum, which I had the opportunity to visit while attending the Farmworker Freedom March on Publix, is set up inside the cargo container of a truck resembling the one used by the Navarrete family to imprison its workers.

The latest (seventh) horrifying case of modern-day slavery was in fact brought to justice in December 2008: Cesar and Geovanni Navarrete were sentenced to twelve years in federal prison for enslaving and beating nine workers. The Navarretes locked the workers in the cargo container overnight. The enslaved men were forced to sleep on the floor with no mattresses or blankets and to urinate and defecate in one corner of the truck.

In March 2009, the CIW had reenacted the cruel practices (brutal wage theft, beating, and chaining of the workers) on the steps of the shiny Capitol building in Tallahassee. The CIW was calling for a meeting with Governor Charlie Crist—he didn't respond to the request then, but came out against exploitation in the fields and in support of the CIW shortly after.[4]

Last June, CIW cofounder Laura Germino received the 2010 Anti-Trafficking Hero award. Significantly, for the first time in ten years, the Annual Trafficking in Persons (TIP) report included the United States, and thus officially acknowledged that involuntary servitude is still a problem in this country. Secretary of State Hillary Clinton called for corporate responsibility in the food chain, and finally seemed to take notice of the work done by the Health, Education, Labor and Pension (HELP) Senate Committee and its efforts "to end a loophole in current law which enables growers to avoid taking responsibility for what happens on their fields when workers are being enslaved,"[5] as outspoken supporter of CIW struggles Senator Bernie Sanders put it.

So goes the story of this grassroots organization: what seems impossible at first—were one to judge based on the initial responses of the corporations involved—becomes a reality a few months later. Echoing Secretary of State Clinton, Germino, cofounder of Freedom Network USA, put it as follows: "it takes a whole community to fight slavery." And, as Germino herself has repeatedly pointed out, slavery occurs where degraded working conditions are the norm.

Today, in Immokalee, Florida, as elsewhere in the country, the majority of this exploited labor force is made up of immigrants, traditionally among the most vulnerable workers. Whether they are here on guest-worker visas or undocumented, low-income immigrants have very few rights, and the laws protecting them are either not enforced by the employers or unknown to the laborers.

Low wages and poor working conditions in agriculture are the legacy of a long, unbroken history of exploitation in the fields that didn't necessarily involve only immigrants; however, a comprehensive reform of the immigration system is direly needed and could improve the lives of many farmworkers.

During his 2010 State of the Union address, President Obama himself reiterated his commitment to fix "our broken immigration system."[6] In times of economic recovery for the country, the National Immigration Law Center decisively called for an immigration reform that "leads to the legalization of families and gives workers the ability to exercise their rights" and "will raise the standard of living for all workers in our country."[7]

In contrast, the Tea Party and other conservatives support an enforcement-only approach and state laws modeled after the controversial Arizona SB 1070, whose constitutionality has been questioned. The Arizona law makes it a crime to be an undocumented immigrant, thus requiring everyone (who looks nonwhite or nonforeign) to carry documents at all times and subjecting virtually anybody to immigration status checks based on a presumed "reasonable suspicion." The original SB 1070 basically legalizes a nefarious widespread practice of U.S. law enforcement: racial profiling.

Traditionally, federal authorities have enforced violations of immigration statutes. As discussed in chapter five, 287(g) programs extended this power to local police by cross-designating officers to enforce immigration law; now SB 1070 is further empowering the state over the federal government on this matter.

The introduction of the legislation came as a result of a major immigration crisis that has affected the state. Tougher enforcement along the border, conservatives claim, has lowered the number of immigrants who cross. Migration flows, however, are also affected by economic downturns, and the situation in Arizona has worsened since the routes that immigrants who are crossing take have moved from California and Texas to the Sonora Desert, a much more dangerous entry corridor.

As I write these last pages, an Arizona federal judge blocked the implementation of key provisions of the law,[8] while the legislation went into effect. In Florida, also, the Arizona law has become a campaign issue in the race for governor and two Republican legislators intend to present similar bills next year.[9]

Immigrant rights and workers' rights advocates believe comprehensive immigration reform is needed and that it will improve labor conditions for *all* U.S. workers. After all, in a free market society, if employers can get labor for less, why would they want to pay more? Basic workers' protections are eroded by the existence of "illegal" labor.

Moreover, the abuses perpetrated under guest-worker visa programs have proved that temporary admissions without the possibility to start a naturalization process are doomed to fail.[10] Whereas a hundred forty thousand employment-based legal permanent resident cards are available for qualified immigrants, there are only five thousand for less-skilled workers—those most needed by U.S. employers.[11]

This points to the hypocrisy of a system that ultimately exploits the majority of a low-wage immigrant labor force without granting the workers and their families the right to build a secure future in this country. It also invites further reflection on the issue of racism in the agricultural and food industries.[12]

They, the "dark-skinned" migrants, will keep coming. And they might end up in Immokalee, Collier County, one of the fastest-growing areas in the country[13] where within a few miles, mobile homes and run-down trailers without air conditioning or heat coexist with luxurious climate-controlled properties. The wild savannah of the preserved Corkscrew Sanctuary Swamp contrasts with the equally immense, watered golf courses that make up the landscape just a few miles west. In the middle, immense, cultivated fields.

◆

While visiting Immokalee, I wasn't able to go to the fields. This doesn't mean that it's impossible. It is, however, quite difficult. Employers who need to hide labor, environmental, and human abuses are wary of anyone who comes to document these situations.

While I was writing this book, I lived in Boca Raton, Florida. My apartment was modest, and I shared it with a nice young woman from California. Half of my monthly salary as an adjunct instructor at Florida Atlantic University was just enough to pay rent and utilities. This said, even though I was definitely not living "the good life," so to speak, after five years in the States I began to feel increasingly uneasy to be part of an inherently unjust society, if anything, because I was physically immersed in it. The Publix in my neighborhood had valet parking: without fail, a person of color—Latino, African American, or Haitian—was there at the customer service booth to park the vehicles and allow customers to have an enjoyable shopping experience.[14] A few hundred feet down the road, proceeding on US-1, is the entrance of the deluxe Boca Raton Hotel and Resort. A little bit further down are the palatial villas on the Intracoastal with their luxuriant tropical gardens: the pompous form that the American Dream takes in South Florida.

Immokalee became the place where I would go to regenerate, where I returned to look for the core of things. It was almost as if I were striving to recuperate a sense of authenticity that I felt was missing in coastal Florida.

Immokalee close, yet separate: apartheid South Florida, as Oannes defined it.

This remoteness, this invisibility, contributes to a generalized sense of disconnection (from the land and those who work it) that is also a form of alienation, and it ultimately hides the fundamental injustice on which Western societies like ours are based upon. So when farmworkers stage protests in the streets, and the invisible becomes visible again; choosing to not see then means to living in denial. And it makes us all complicit, whether we like it or not.

I feel close to the people of Immokalee. As a foreigner—a "legal alien," according to the definition of the U.S. Citizen and Immigration Services—I, too, understand what it means not to belong. Sure, distinctions are necessary. In my country, I wouldn't starve, and I'm not persecuted as member of an indigenous group either. I can freely travel and go back to Italy regularly to see family and friends. Most immigrants I met haven't seen their families and friends in years. For many of them, their parents will die, without having the possibility to hug each other once more. The experience of immigration is for most of them, even today in times of globalization and the Internet, a definite and painful separation from loved ones and the past. It was not so different for the Italians who migrated to Australia, Argentina, and the United States a century ago or so. Black-and-white snapshot: end of 1890, fields of New Jersey. Many of those migrant workers were Italian.[15]

In Italy today, people from China, Eastern Europe, and all over Africa come to look for work. Most tomato pickers who harvest the fields of Southern Italy are African. The living and working conditions of these migrants are not dissimilar to the ones of those who are held captive somewhere in the fields of Immokalee. Neither are their stories of migration: to make it to Italy, they undertake dangerous, life-risking journeys. Once in the "Bel Paese," they face discrimination. They are controlled by abusive crew leaders, here called *caporali*. They are too often victims of hate crimes. A few months ago, hundreds of farmworkers protested in Rosarno, in the southern region of Calabria, after two workers had been shot.[16] Organized crime ('Ndrangheta in this case) exploits these immigrants by robbing and abusing them, sometimes enslaving them. Recently, here too, the migrants have stood up for their rights, hoping to bring justice to the fields of Italy.[17]

All over the globe, the life of the migrant is often a risky one. For immigrants in the United States, it means making dangerous journeys to Mexico to visit their families and then leaving again to work for the gringos for two or three more years. For some of them it means coming to work in the fields of Immokalee.

The fields—immense lots of land, carefully ordered by agricultural modernity to produce crops for mass consumption, and yet, we can't go there. We cannot walk on the land where the food we eat is harvested. If anything, that says something about how alienated we have become from what we need to survive.

Immokalee: My Home, My Cage

They say that if you drink the water of Immokalee, you'll come back again and again. People say something like this about a lot of places. Places that are somewhat special. But any place is special once you make it your home. Your home, however, should never become a cage. Contrary to what people believe, a lot of immigrants would leave and go back to their home countries if they could. No one *wants* to become an immigrant. The false myth of the "happy-go-lucky" migrant fostered by exploitative farmers just doesn't hold up to reality. In recent years, Immokalee, like other communities, has seen a reduction in circular migration. In other words, immigrants tend to stay, in part, due to the lack of safe passage to Mexico and back.

Some of them are stuck in Immokalee. Like cattle in a corral, *this* has become their cage.

The stories out there are many, too many to capture and write about them all. While working with my friend Daniel Herrera on the documentary *El Green Grown Tomato,* we were driving on US-82 toward Immokalee one Sunday afternoon when suddenly Daniel stopped the car. We had to get some *chicharrones,*[18] he said. So we met Marissa.* Like many Mexicans who live around Immokalee, on the weekends Marissa parks her truck on the side of the main road and, under the direct rays of the sun, sells chicharrones to the motorists.

Daniel asked Marissa if she would do an interview with us. We would ask general questions, he reassured her: when she arrived in the States, if she has family here, what job she has, how much she earned back in Mexico. At one point Daniel asked her: what would she say to those who think that she and her family are stealing jobs from U.S. workers, and think that people like her should go back to their country? If she had one thing to say, what would she say to them?

Marissa took a deep breath and in simple and clear words gave her answer to the camera. She talked about the dangers of the journey, the desire of immigrants to improve the lives of their families, the discrimination they face here. Finally, she said: *Nos gustaria que los dejar trabajar, como todo mundo quiere: trabajar, mas que nada. Porque nos venimos a quitarle nada. [Trabajar] es lo unico que mucha gente quiere.* (We'd like to be allowed to work. This is what people all over the world want: work, more than anything else. Because we don't come here to take away anything. Work, that's what most people want.)

By then Marissa's big black eyes had become a lake of oil. She broke down as if we had just cut her open. We were struck dumb. We all became teary-eyed behind our dark glasses. Ivan, the videographer, asked Marissa for her address and promised to send her a copy of the interview. Ivan, who was born in Colombia and came to the States with his family at the age of four, hugged her repeatedly, and couldn't stop thanking her. We almost couldn't stand to leave her there, on the side of the road selling snacks on a sunny Sunday afternoon.

Had I made a difference for the people of Immokalee?

Immokalee remains a cage for many—"A-Muglé," corral, and "I-Muglé," home; at the end of the eighteen hundreds Bishop William Crane Gray named this place by choosing the transliteration that emphasized the positive side.[19]

Immokalee, a place where you arrive and then can't escape once imprisoned by cruel bosses in secluded shacks somewhere in its infinite fields. Or because you were born here, like Paco, you have to stay because, in the end, this is your home. And somebody has to stay and fight, day after day.

Maybe I haven't made much of a difference.

Yet, to see Paco meeting the hero of his youth or to listen to Eduardo who couldn't stop telling me about Mexico and his military life—because there's so much that he would like to say to the world but has hardly ever had the opportunity to do so—or to receive an email after our trip to Immokalee from one of my students who wrote that she kept thinking about it and admired the members of the CIW so much, led me to think that, after all, I was there for a reason.

As for myself, I need to thank Immokalee for having, with its very existence, made visible and real what gets hidden in the name of a decorum that is as uncivil as it is immoral. In a world where natural disasters become opportunity for profit, in which apocalypse is invoked as a solution to the problems of poverty, religious conflicts, and over-population, the idea of social justice has become too often synonymous with utopia and, for too many, of subversive pseudo-socialist plots set up by activists and progressives of various strands. I've come to realize that there cannot be real happiness in this world without social justice, and that can only be achieved if we fight for it.

Together we are one, states a mural at the Farm Worker Village, the face of a Seminole underneath. Because it does take a community to change things.

July 30, 2010
Montgomery, Alabama

CIW's Farmworker Freedom March to protest Publix
in Lakeland, Florida, April 17, 2010

NOTE ON THE METHODOLOGY

This is a work of nonfiction. The people in this book are real people I met. Without them and their willingness to participate, there wouldn't be any book. The stories have been told in the order in which they occurred, with only one exception: Melody's and Lupe's interviews (chapter three) occurred in May 2008 but have been placed earlier in the book for narrative reasons. The participants were notified of the change.

When possible, dates, times, events, and locations recounted by the participants have been reconfirmed with the use of other sources and historical records. Endnotes provide additional information and further references for the issues or situations discussed. To preserve narrative coherence, I provided updated information in the endnotes. When I inserted updated data in the text, I avoided adding the time reference—which, however, can be found in the respective note.

The conversations have been related as best as I could remember. The "protagonists" of the book have read the final draft and were active participants in the process of revising this work. As for those who had a smaller role in the book and/or I haven't been able to contact, I've tried to respect the essence of what was said or happened. Any mistakes left are my own.

In order to minimize any potentially harmful repercussions, names have been changed and pseudonyms have been used (indicated with an asterisk in the copy), sometimes at the explicit request of the person.

As for Tom Monaghan, I tried to contact and get an interview with him when I was visiting Immokalee. I had no success. I still hope one day I'll be able to have a heartfelt conversation with him.

A schoolbus used to transport farmworkers into the fields
in Anthony, New Mexico

ACKNOWLEDGMENTS

A work like this wouldn't exist without the willingness of people who opened their lives to me. Thanks go to the people of Immokalee who made this book possible. Even though pseudonyms have been used at times, you know who you are, and you should know that I am deeply grateful to you all.

I generally hate lists because I constantly misplace them; this, however, is a special one. And, *thank god*, it's printed.

Special thanks go to my guides in Immokalee: first and foremost, Paco, the not-always-dependable guide yet invaluable aid and accommodating host, and his family, especially his mother Angela; Padre Patricio, for introducing me to some of the families of Immokalee; Tricia, for her hospitality and insights; Elisabeth, at the Immokalee Farmers Market, for helping me in any way she could to get to the fields; and Oannes, who took me on a ride to Naples and showed me what he called "apartheid South Florida." Oannes passed while this book was being edited. I remember him dearly, for his wisdom and lucidity.

Also, I would like to acknowledge those who provided research assistance for this project: Marc Rodrigues and Melody Gonzalez of the

Student/Farmworker Alliance; Tom Gallagher of the Seminole Tribe of Florida; David Grove of Immokalee Helping Our People (IHOPE); Mónica Ramírez of Esperanza: The Immigrant Women's Legal Initiative–Southern Poverty Law Center; Subhash Kateel of the Florida Immigrant Coalition; Amy Bennett Williams of the *Ft. Myers News-Press;* Esmeralda "Essie" Serrata of Collier County Housing Authority; and the Collier Sheriff Department; and also those who helped me make contact with people who were somehow crucial to the realization of this book: Lee Sustar, Camilo Mejía, Cande Vazquez, Daniel Herrera, Georg Koszulinski, and Dan Gloeckner.

Special thanks also go to Camilo Mejía, Michael Martinez, Kathia Flemens, Cliff Blomgren, Daniel Herrera, Tricia Yeggy, Janalie Joseph, Jerome "J" Upshaw, Ivan Rodriguez, and Dan Bell. Your support, friendship, and encouragement greatly helped me throughout the writing and editing of the book, even when I was far away from South Florida and Immokalee.

Finally, I would like to thank Josh Diboll for helping me undertake the translation of the book into English; Sharon Smith at Haymarket Books for her work and support during the editing process; my copyeditor Dao Tran for her invaluable help; Julie Fain and Rachel Cohen at Haymarket Books for their patience; Willie Thompson, for bearing with me during the long last year of revision and helping me with editing; and my parents, Daniela Stefanacci and Claudio Giagnoni, for always being there for me, even from across the ocean.

NOTES

One: *El Día de los Muertos*

1. El Día de los Muertos (the Day of the Dead): Catholics all over the world gather with their families to commemorate deceased friends and relatives. The holiday holds special cultural significance in Mexico.
2. Among others, see Barnt, *Tangled Routes: Women.*
3. USDA, 2007 Census of Agriculture.
4. Statistics on Immokalee are from 1999; as we read on the U.S. Census Bureau website, "2006–2008 data were not available for this geography."
5. Immokalee is technically just a census-designed place. Since Immokalee doesn't have its own city government, major decisions affecting the community are made elsewhere. As pointed out later on in this work, Immokalee's status also affects the community's financial and economic welfare. The profits of farming businesses located here, for instance, don't necessarily go to benefit the community and its populace (and thus the farmworkers).
6. Guadalupe Center of Immokalee Information Packet (November 2007).
7. Various Christian denominations are represented in Immokalee, but the Guadalupe is the only Catholic Church in town.
8. According to the Coalition of Immokalee Workers website (April 2009): "Florida tomato pickers earn an average of 45 cents per 32-lb. bucket of tomatoes, a rate that has not risen significantly since 1978. As a result, workers today have to pick over twice the number of buckets per hour to earn minimum wage as they did in 1980. At today's piece rate, workers have to pick over 2 $\frac{1}{2}$ tons of tomatoes just to earn the equivalent of Florida minimum wage for a 10-hour workday, www.ciw-online

.org/101.html#facts. For additional reports about the status of the agricultural labor force in Florida, see among others: U.S. Department of Labor's 2000 report, *The Agricultural Labor Market* and Oxfam America's *Like Machines in the Fields*.

9. "Unaccompanied migrant farmworkers fall most frequently into the lowest income groups, with 81 percent earning less than $10,000 per year. Unaccompanied seasonal workers also are heavily concentrated in the lowest income groups, with half earning less than $10,000. Therefore, most unaccompanied farmworkers need single-person units or beds in larger units at rents below $250 per month. Nearly all require rents below $375 per month...Two-thirds of accompanied farmworker families need housing units with rents of $500 per month or less." Shimberg Center for Affordable Housing, "Need for Farmworker Housing," iii.

10. As Randall Sean Sellers points out in his master's thesis, the chant drew inspiration from the immigrant worker struggles of the Industrial Workers of the World of the early nineteenth century, *"Del pueblo, para el pueblo,"* 3.

11. The march was preceded by a weeklong general strike in 1995 that involved thousands of farmworkers. The work stoppage was organized to oppose a proposed wage cut and succeeded in preventing it from being implemented. After the march, beatings became rare, as crew leaders knew that now there was somebody ready to stand up and defend farmworkers' basic rights. For a more extensive account of that night, see Sellers, *"Del pueblo, para el pueblo."*

12. Radio Conciencia WCIW-LP was created by a group of farmworkers and volunteers in December 2003 during one of the so-called barn raisings organized by the Prometheus Radio Project, a national nonprofit organization committed to liberating the airwaves from the control of corporations and spreading community radio stations.

13. Thanks to the UFW's efforts, the California Agricultural Labor Relations Act that estblished collective bargaining for farmworkers was passing in 1975.

14. The UFW chapter today maintains a nominal presence in Florida. For further information about the UFW in Florida, see Sellers, *"Del pueblo, para el pueblo,"* 58–59.

15. For further information about these actions, see Sellers, *"Del pueblo, para el pueblo"* and Asbed, "Coalition of Immokalee Workers," 1–23.

16. For detailed accounts of and updates on its campaigns, see the CIW website.

17. The actual pay raise is 71 percent: from 45 to 77 cents per bucket of tomatoes.

18. To be precise, as Marc Rodrigues (of the SFA) explained to me, there's a $10 charge to get a membership card, to cover costs of the machine and the materials for making the card, but there is no fee per se to be a "member" of the CIW.

19. Radio Conciencia does not air commercials, only public service announcements.

20. In the eighteenth century, the land on which present-day Immokalee is situated was the first territory to be populated due to its higher altitude. The first settlement, ac-

cording to author Charlton Tebeau, dates back to 1872. What was known as "Allen Place" after its first pioneer, William Billy Allen, became "Immokalee" as recommended by the Bishop William Crane Gray. The first church in Immokalee was established to convert the Seminoles, but was attended primarily by the white settlers. In 1923, Immokalee became part of Collier County. To learn more about the history of the area, see Tebeau, *Florida's Last Frontier.*

21. Seventy-seven percent of Latina women say that sexual harassment is a major problem on the job. Bauer, *Under Siege,* 28. Most notably, in January 2007, Gargiulo Inc. packinghouse settled a sexual harassment case that involved one of its supervisors and four Haitian female employees who work as tomato graders. Gargiulo paid a total of $215,000 to resolve the litigation. See *U.S. EEOC et al. v. Gargiulo, Inc.*

22. Mexican soft bread covered with sugar and anise seeds.

23. Some historians claim the Virgin of Guadalupe is a syncretic icon of the Virgin Mary and the indigenous goddess Tonantzin, in other words, a product of mestiza culture. Sometimes Guadalupe is referred to as the "first mestiza." Author Judy King calls her the "common denominator" of all Mexicans.

24. In Mexican culture, the *quinceañera* is the coming of age celebration held on a girl's fifteenth birthday.

Two: Thanksgiving

1. Squanto (or Tisquantum) was a Patuxet Indian, a now-extinct tribe of the Wampanoag confederation. Kidnapped by British sea captain Thomas Hunt, he was sold in a slave market in Spain in 1614. He worked in a monastery and then escaped to England where he worked for merchant John Slaney. The latter instructed him in English; in 1619 Squanto was sent back to North America. Upon his return, he told the chief of the Wampanoag *sachem* Massasoit (also known as Yellow Father) about the size of London and England. In the meantime, the Patuxet had been wiped out by a recent epidemic, and many colonists were dying as well; so "Massasoit took pity on them. He told Squanto to teach them how to plant corn (…) and how to build a shelter." (Nies, *Native American History,* 126.) Thus, Squanto became the colonizers' teacher, interpreter, and negotiator.

2. "The Pilgrims saw Squanto as '*a special instrument sent by God for their good beyond their expectations.*'" (Nies, *Native American History,* 128.)

3. It was Massasoit, chief of the Wampanoag Indians, who first invited the settlers in October 1621 to celebrate their annual harvest ceremony—the holiday that later became Thanksgiving. Until 1873 Europeans in America celebrated Thanksgiving

in October. President Lincoln moved the holiday to November (Nies, *Native American History*, 128).

4. Today, the pardoned birds are sent to Poplar Spring Animal Sanctuary in California. Up to 2004, the spared turkeys were sent to a petting zoo at Frying Pan Park, in Fairfax, Virginia. PETA petitioned George W. Bush to stop sending the pardoned turkeys to Frying Pan Park; the animal rights organization claimed that the birds were mistreated there and not assured a peaceful retirement.

5. "The Cornerstone of New Imperialism Is New Racism," Roy writes in *An Ordinary Person's Guide to Empire* (Cambridge, MA: South End Press, 2004), 88.

6. Bishop, "Volunteers Spread Holiday"; see also the photo gallery by Lexie Swall, "About 3,000 Come to Thanksgiving Meal for Farmworkers in Immokalee Park."

7. *Harvest of Shame* was a broadcast of "CBS Reports," the news program hosted by Edward R. Murrow.

8. I transcribed this quote from the *Harvest of Shame* videocassette.

9. For a complete analysis of the Campaign for Fair Food, see "Campaign Analysis–CIW Campaign for Fair Food" at ciwonline.org. Also, read the following rebuttals to Burger King's claims at "Scholars' Statement on Rights of Farmworkers Producing for McDonald's" and "Critical Analysis of the Report."

10. Laura Germino and Greg Asbed, two Brown University graduates, have been involved with the Coalition of Immokalee Workers since the outset. As paralegals and community organizers, they helped the first workers organize themselves into what became the CIW. Laura is now the coordinator of the antislavery campaign for the Coalition of Immokalee Workers. Her husband, Greg, is also a coalition staff member.

11. In December 2008, another case was brought to justice. Cesar and Geovanni Navarrete were sentenced to twelve years in federal prison for enslaving and beating nine workers. In July 2010, another slavery operation was uncovered in Alachua County, just north of Gainesville. This case involved dozens of Haitian workers who had been illegally trafficked into the country in 2008; as reported by the *Gainesville Sun*, the victims "were denied access to their own passports and visas, effectively preventing them from going anywhere other than the farms where they were to work." Significantly enough, the three farmers (Cabioch Bontemps, Willy Paul Edouard, and Carline Ceneus) have been "charged with conspiring to commit forced labor and visa fraud." This latest case further draws attention to the abuses that often occur within the context of the H-2A program. Volyes, "Three Charged."

12. The following data about modern-day slavery cases in Florida have been retrieved primarily from the CIW website and a series of articles that came out in 1997 and 2010.

13. This has been one of the first arguments that Taco Bell and Publix representatives among others have pulled out when confronted by the CIW's requests to raise farm-

workers' wages and to abide by the participatory code of conduct compiled by the grassroots organization. John Bowe reports that Jonathan Blum, vice president for public relations of Yum! Brands, the parent company of Taco Bell, said during the Taco Bell boycott campaign: "It's a labor dispute between a company that's unrelated to Taco Bell and its workers…We don't believe it's our place to get involved in another company's labor dispute involving its employees." And on slavery in the Florida fields: "My gosh, I'm sorry, it's heinous, but I don't think it has anything to do with us (Bowe, *Nobodies: Modern American Slave*, 59). As we read on the CIW website: "For more than a year, Publix defended its decision to continue purchasing from the farms with non-sequiturs, saying it paid 'market price' for the tomatoes and refused to get involved in its suppliers' 'labor disputes,'" CIW News, "Far Too Little."

14. Bauer, *Close to Slavery*, 32.

15. Bauer, *Under Siege: Life for Low-Income Latinos*.

16. See *Luna v. Del Monte Fresh Produce* in "No Author" section of Bibliography.

17. "An elderly man cried because he wanted to leave but feared for his life, workers told authorities. When another worker tried to escape, Cuello Jr. chased him down." Zeitlin, "Slavery: Collier County's Connection." "After escaping in 1999, he bumped into Cuello, who chased him in a Chevy Suburban, yelling obscenities." Greene, "Crop of Abuse."

18. Yolanda Cuello, Abel's wife, also held an FLC license. Williams reports that there were three other cases in the Immokalee area in which relatives of barred contractors also held a license. That was not relevant in Cuello's case since he got his license back. For the record, "licensing officials were reluctant, though legally bound, to issue Cuello a new contractors license," Williams, "Labor Contractor Back."

19. Technically, Ag-Mart said Cuello "was no longer allowed in its property." Williams, "Labor Contractor Back." But see also Greene, "Crop of Abuse."

20. Romeo Ramirez cited in Cockburn, "21st Century Slaves," 18.

21. For a full report of the Ramoses' case and trial, see John Bowe's *Nobodies: Modern American Slave Labor*, 60–72 and Cockburn, "21st Century Slaves," 18.

22. Greene, "Crop of Abuse."

23. CIW News, "A Brief History of Inhumanity: Three Centuries of Forced Agricultural Labor on the Banks of the St. Johns," April 13, 2010, www.ciw-online.org/a_brief_history_of_inhumanity.html. The information is no longer available online. I tried to contact FFVA to update the information about Frank Johns but haven't gotten any response from its PR person on this matter.

24. Blackmon, *Slavery by Another Name*.

25. Bauer, *Close to Slavery*, 3.

26. About 4.5 million Mexican citizens were employed through the bracero program

between 1942 and 1964. The name "bracero" comes from "brazos," arms. "Bracero" is a manual laborer. In the United States, the term "braceros" is still often used to describe seasonal farmworkers from Mexico.

27. CIW, "Florida Modern-Day Slavery Museum," 6.

28. The sugarcane cutters' strike was relayed in Bauer, *Close to Slavery*, 5. The inhuman working conditions of cane cutters have been widely documented. Among others, see David Bacon's articles on the subject, for instance, "Be Our Guest" and Alex Wilkenson's *Big Sugar: Seasons in the Cane Fields of Florida* (1989). Sugarcane is no longer a manually harvested crop in the United States. Also, the demand for sugar and sugar-based products has dramatically diminished in the last decades due to the increase in the production of corn and especially its by-product, high-fructose corn syrup.

29. As a recent Immigration Policy Center report shows, the employment-based visa system is not responsive to employers' labor needs. Immigration Policy Center, "Breaking Down the Problems," 8.

30. The Department of State website reported "approximately 32,000 guest workers for agricultural work and another 89,000 for jobs in forestry, seafood processing, landscaping, construction and other non-agricultural industries" (Bauer, *Close to Slavery*, 1). To my knowledge, this is the most recent data available on the number of visas allotted under the H-2 program.

31. Data available at Travel.State.gov, "FY-2005 Nonimmigrant Visas."

32. "H-2A workers must get paid wages that are the highest of: (a) the local labor market's 'prevailing wage' for a particular crop, as determined by the DOL and state agencies; (b) the state or federal minimum wage; or (c) the 'adverse effect wage' rate." Moreover, H-2A workers are legally entitled, among other things, to free housing for the duration of the contract and the reimbursement for the cost of travel from the worker's home. Rarely are these provisions enforced. Also, employers must abide by the "50% rule," which requires any H-2A employer "to hire any qualified U.S. worker who applies for a job prior to the beginning of the second half of the season for which foreign workers are hired" (Bauer, *Close to Slavery*, 7). For further information about the legal rights and protections for H-2A workers, see the Travel section of the U.S. Department of State website, http://travel.state.gov/visa/temp/info/info_4578.html, accessed May 11, 2010. For a detailed investigation of the H-2 guest worker program, see Bauer, *Close to Slavery*.

33. According to the CIA, between fifty thousand and a hundred thousand women are trafficked into the United States each year. The Protection Project, U.S. Country Report.

34. Cockburn, "21st Century Slaves," 23.

35. U.S. Immigration Support, "U Visa for Immigrants."
36. The first U visa was issued in the summer of 2008, eight years after the law passed. "Through the end of 2008, 65 such visas had been issued, although about 13,300 people have filed applications. Twenty have been denied." Gorman, "U-visa Program."
37. According to the most recent statistics on hate crime (2008) released by the FBI, "Hate crimes motivated by the offender's bias toward a particular ethnicity/national origin were directed at 1,226 victims. Of these: 64.6 percent were victims of an anti-Hispanic bias. 35.4 percent were targeted because of a bias against other ethnicities/national origins." U.S. Department of Justice, *Hate Crime Statistics*, 2008. Most shockingly, on November 8, 2008, Marcelo Lucero, age thirty-seven, was attacked by a group of teenagers and stabbed to death in Patchogue, Long Island, New York. He was thirty-seven. Jeffrey Conroy, convicted of manslaughter as a hate crime, gang assault, and attempted assault against three other Latinos, was eventually acquitted of murder as a hate crime. On May 26, 2010, he was sentenced to twenty-five years in prison. See the "Times Topics: Marcelo Lucero" at nytimes.com for a full report on this tragic event.
38. Fear and distrust keep low-income immigrants from reporting crimes. According to a recent SPLC report, only 46 percent of Latino immigrants say they have confidence in the police. As discussed in chapter five, 287(g) agreements allow local enforcement to also have ICE capabilities in certain areas of the country; these agreements further discourage cooperation with local police. "In Nashville, 73 percent of Latinos surveyed said they are more reluctant to cooperate with police because of 287 (g)." Bauer, *Under Siege: Life*, 27.
39. Ibid., 26.
40. Guatemala has been battling illegal and unethical expropriation of their lands by governments in order to give them to local landowners and foreign nationals since the inception of the Liberal government (in the 1870s), which saw Mayan indigenous people as "backwards" and sought to bring progress by awarding those communal lands to foreign corporations such as the Banana Fruit Company. A Guatemalan Mayan community has been fighting for years against the mining multinational occupying part of their ancestral lands and poisoning their waters. Recently, the government ceded under pressure and halted the operations of the multinational there indefinitely. The multinational executives are refusing to answer calls about it, and the minister of energy and mines had to quit his position; this was a huge victory for environmentalists and Mayan activists. Hernández, "Cierran mina Marlin."
41. To put the amount in perspective, Bales writes, thirteen billion approximately equals how much Americans spend yearly on jeans (23). For a more thorough analy-

sis of how slavery actually affects the global economy, see Bales, *Disposable People: New Slavery*, 22–24.

42. Ibid., 232.

43. A notable exception is Mauritania, where black slaves are held by Arab slaveholders (Bales, *Disposable People: New Slavery*, 11).

44. Bales, *Disposable People: New Slavery*, 10–11.

45. An example of this new form of racism exists in Japan, where prostitutes are more likely to be Thai or Philippine or European rather than Japanese. The Japanese feel very strongly about their national identity and women in Japan are not as vulnerable as elsewhere. For instance, "Thai women are available for shipment to Japan because Thais are enslaving Thais" (Bales, *Disposable People: New Slavery*, 11). In other words, vulnerability and economic reasons are the actual motivation for enslavement of certain subjects rather than others.

46. This is just an estimate and it comes from the recently released *2010 Trafficking in Persons Report* about adults and children in forced labor, bonded labor, and forced prostitution around the world. U.S. Department of State, *2010 Trafficking in Persons Report*, 7.

47. Bales and Soodalter, *The Slave*, 3.

48. Bales, *Disposable People: New Slavery*, 11.

49. Undocumented immigrants are not eligible for Medicaid or the State Children's Health Insurance Program (SCHIP). Under the Emergency Medical Treatment and Labor Act (EMTALA-1986), however, everybody has the right to emergency medical assistance regardless of legal status or ability to pay. Childbirth is considered a medical emergency and Medicaid usually covers it—thus, the ongoing controversy around EMTALA. For more information on undocumented immigrants and health care, see the Center for Studying Health System Change website, specifically www.hschange.com/CONTENT/818/#ib1.

50. Pew Center Report, *One in 100*.

51. Ibid., 3.

52. Ibid., 11.

53. Ibid., 30.

54. Police Chiefs Guide to Immigration Issues, Project Response Publication.

55. I have to thank Professor Darren O'Byrne for this insightful reflection during the session on "Human Rights as Global Legality" that I chaired at the Global Studies Association conference in Boca Raton in May 2009.

56. Davis, *Are Prisons Obsolete?*

57. In Spanish "cimarron" means savage, rebel, writes John Mahon in his *History of the Second Seminole War* (7). "Cimarron" refers to a horse or a cow that, having departed from the group, has become self-sufficient, no longer dependent on the herd. The

word "cimarron" became "cimarrone" and then "cimallone," "seminolies," and, eventually, "Seminole."

58. The others were the Cherokees, the Chickasaws, and the Choctaws.

59. Technically, the conflicts known as the Seminole Wars were never declared as such by the U.S. government. They were seen as "a continuation of the U.S. policy of containment and relocation of Native Americans east of Mississippi." In other words, they were a result of a policy that began with the Indian Removal Act (1830) (Barrett, *American Indian History*, 506).

60. In the Second Seminole War alone, between thirty and forty million dollars were spent. John Mahon writes that it's impossible to say exactly since Congressional appropriation bills often included funds for other military conflicts. The astounding amount—forty million dollars, roughly eight hundred million in today's dollars—was spent to remove approximately five hundred warriors and their respective families.

61. See the entire *South Florida Sun-Sentinel* report "Seminole Tribe: Fast Fortune, Big Spending," and specifically the series of articles by Kestin, Franceschina, and Maines: "Seminole Tribe Is Suddenly Wealthy"; "Longtime Tribal Leader"; "Despite Its Wealth, Tribe Continues"; and Kestin, "FEMA Paid Tribe's Hotel."

62. Ibid.

63. Kestin, Franceschina, and Maines, "Longtime Tribal Leader."

64. During 1953–1964, 109 tribes were terminated and more than thirteen thousand Native Americans lost tribal affiliation. The Western Oregon Indian Termination Act of 1954 terminated sixty-seven tribes from western Oregon, including the Grand Ronde and Siletz reservations. Starting with President Kennedy, Indian self-determination was encouraged. President Johnson conclusively interrupted termination measures. The keystone of the federal government's self-determination policy was the 1975 Indian Self-Determination and Education Assistance Act. The law admitted that "prolonged Federal domination of Indian service programs has served to retard rather than enhance the progress of Indian people." (Davis, *Native America in the Twentieth Century*, 223)

65. The Hard Rock Hotel & Casino in London, now called G Casino Piccadilly, and the one in Las Vegas, bought by Morgans Hotel Group, are not part of the original agreement.

66. "Reality TV Star," CNN.com.

67. Additionally, the Seminole Hard Rock Hotel & Casino is considered a shelter for people with special needs, such as the elderly and disabled, as declared in a letter sent to FEMA by the tribe's emergency management planner in September 2006.

68. Native peoples' near extermination by the U.S. government entitles their survivors

due compensation, per federal agreements. As reported, "Council member Max Osceola Jr. told the *South Florida Sun-Sentinel* in October that the Seminoles are eligible for grants like all other tribes whether 'you have a penny in your pocket or a dollar in your pocket.'" Kestin, Franceschina, and Maines. "Despite Its Wealth."

69. Instead of "tribes," Oannes speaks of "(Indian) Nations."

70. Oannes was also director of the Yat Kitischee Native Center. In Mikasuki, "Yat Kitischee" means "respect for the place where we live."

71. Florida Public Service Commission, "Florida Public Service."

72. The former School of the Americas (SOA) renamed the "Western Hemisphere Institute for Security Cooperation" (WHINSEC) in 2001 is the U.S. Department of Defense facility now located in Fort Benning, Georgia. Thousands of Latin American soldiers and police officers have been trained over the years in SOA/WHINSEC facilities. Several of its "alumni" have become notorious for violating human rights in their respective countries (e.g., Hugo Banzer in Bolivia and Manuel Noriega in Panama).

73. Oannes Pritzker passed away in April 2010 while this book was being edited.

74. The Student/Farmworker Alliance annually organizes a conference/immersion visit usually during a weekend in September. As we read on the website, the Encuentro is an opportunity "to connect with one another, deepen our work in partnership with the Coalition of Immokalee Workers, further develop our commitment to this struggle, and increase our consciousness of the state of our world and our shared work for social justice—all in Immokalee, the birthplace of the Campaign for Fair Food and home to one of the most inspiring and successful workers' movements of our times," "2009 SFA Encuentro," www.sfalliance.org/2009encuentro.html, accessed May 13, 2010.

75. Formed in 2003 in reaction to the 9/11 terrorist attacks, Immigration and Custom Enforcement (ICE) is an investigative agency that is part of the U.S. Department of Homeland Security. ICE is responsible for enforcing immigration and customs laws, and to monitor economic, transportation, and infrastructure security. The agency currently employs nineteen thousand people (see www.ice.gov/about/index.htm). According to Section 287(g), designated officers can be authorized to perform immigration law enforcement functions. So some police officers receive ICE training in areas with a higher concentration of undocumented immigrants.

76. A tamale is a traditional indigenous food made of corn flour filled with various mixtures like cheese or chili wrapped in corn husks and steamed.

77. The case Paco refers to here was brought to justice in December 2008. It involved

the Navarrete brothers who were sentenced to twelve years in federal prison for enslaving and beating nine workers.

Three: *Luchando por Comida Justa*

1. Hughlett, "McDonald's Farmworker Raise."
2. Schlosser, "Penny Foolish." Eric Schlosser, author of *Fast Food Nation* and *Reefer Madness*, is a longtime supporter of the CIW.
3. Martin, "Burger King Shifts Policy on Animals."
4. For a critical analysis of Burger King's claims and their rebuttals, see Nissen, "Critical Analysis of the Report."
5. Here is the statement Burger King released in February 2007 as reported on the CIW website: "We have spoken to CIW representatives about our interest in recruiting interested Immokalee workers into the BURGER KING(R) system. We have offered to send Burger King Corporation recruiters to the area to speak with the CIW and with workers themselves about permanent, full-time employment at BURGER KING(R) restaurants. Burger King Corporation offers ongoing professional training and advancement opportunities around the country for both entry-level and skilled employee jobs, and we are hopeful the CIW will accept our offer." See CIW website, "Campaign Analysis-CIW Campaign for Fair Food."
6. CIW, "Coalition of Immokalee Workers, Allies to Hold Press Conference at Burger King Headquarters," press release, February 14, 2007.
7. Grech, "Fighting for a Higher Tomato Value."
8. Overtown has a 75 percent Black population. City of Miami–Planning Department, "Services: Census."
9. Power U managed to stop the Crosswinds project from building luxury condos on public land in Overtown. However, the pressure to gentrify the neighborhood and displace more longtime residents—since I-95 was built more than half the residents have had to relocate—is still there. The use of public land and resources to build luxury apartments is part of the mayor's vision for Miami to become the global city of the South. For more information about Power U projects, see their website.
10. *Road from ar Ramadi: The Private Rebellion of Staff Sergeant Camilo Mejía* by Camilo Mejía was published in the spring of 2007 by the New Press. The book was printed in paperback by Haymarket Books in the spring of 2008.
11. The National Labor Relations Act (or Wagner Act, after Robert Wagner, 1935) regulates the labor relationships between parties in the United States. It encourages col-

lective bargaining, while curtailing "certain private sector labor and management practices, which can harm the general welfare of workers, businesses and the U.S. economy." National Labor Relations Board website, National Labor Relations Act.

12. The grape boycott was one of the best organized labor actions in U.S. agricultural industry. Mexican and Filipino grape pickers in Delano, California, originally organized a walkout, which attracted the attention of César Chávez. After a series of strikes, the United Farm Workers of America decided to boycott the Schenley Liquor Company, owner of most vineyards in the San Joaquin Valley. The boycott received wide support from the national public, and eventually led to the signing of a series of contracts that granted laborers raises and other benefits.

13. The Taco Bell boycott lasted four years and ended with the joint agreement between the CIW and Taco Bell on March 8, 2003. The role of the student-led "Boot the Bell" campaign was pivotal in achieving this historic victory for Florida farmworkers.

14. For more information about the practice of boycotting in the United States, see Friedman, *Consumer Boycotts*.

15. According to statistics released by the National Labor Relations Board in 2004, employers illegally disciplined or fired twenty thousand workers per year for union activity. Half of all companies facing union organizing campaigns threatened to close down, while one-fourth fired at least one union supporter. Greenhouse, "How Do You Drive Out."

16. United Farm Workers nominally maintains an office in Florida but since 1973 it hasn't organized in the state nor does it have contracts at the moment. For a more detailed account of UFW struggles in Florida, see Sellers, *"Del pueblo, para el pueblo."*

17. Justice for Janitors was a campaign of the Service Employees International Union. The long strike of L.A. Century City janitors represented by the SEIU Local 1877 was dramatized by Ken Loach in the movie *Bread and Roses* (2000).

18. At the time of writing, the seven defendants have not been found guilty; yet, they are still incarcerated.

19. Son jarocho is a traditional musical style of the region of Veracruz, popularized by Richie Valens with "La Bamba."

20. The election of Luiz Inácio Lula da Silva to the presidency of Brazil in 2002 represented a significant change in the politics of Latin America. Although he has notably moderated his political positions, Lula, founding member of the Workers' Party in Brazil (PT—Partido dos Trabalhadores), contributed to a radical change in Brazilian politics. Since the 1964 coup d'état, presidents have been chosen by the Houses of Congress (a de facto military caucus) that elected only retired generals. Since 1984, Lula began to demand direct popular elections for the presidency by joining the "Diretas Já" (Direct [Elections] Now!). In 1989, the president was

elected by popular vote. In 2002, Lula became president of Brazil.

21. Gonzalez, *Awakening the Consciousness.*

22. La Otra Campaña (the Other Campaign) was a political action organized in the year of the General Election (2006) by the Zapatista Army of National Liberation (Ejército Zapatista de Liberación Nacional, EZLN); as thoroughly articulated in the Sixth Declaration of the Lacandon Jungle, the campaign intended to unite all the national social movements around the defense of indigenous rights and the fight against neoliberalism without engaging in the electoral process—thus the name "the Other Campaign." Subcomandante Marcos, the main spokesperson of the EZLN, traveled across the country for several months, speaking of the necessity of rewriting the Mexican Constitution according to the principles listed in the Sixth Declaration.

23. Palestinian workers in Israel and the Gaza Strip are discriminated against and thus share a history of oppression with Immokalee laborers. Arab citizens, who make up 20 percent of the population living in Israel and the Gaza Strip, have been subjected to racist policies (including the demolition of their homes, the confiscation of their land, and other repressive actions) since the state of Israel was first established (1947). International Crisis Group. "Identity Crisis: Israel."

24. Guatemala experienced the longest civil war in the Americas (1960–1996). Eduardo is referring to the techniques used by the Mexican military in fighting the Zapatista insurgence. The Mexican military hired Guatemalan captains to train its soldiers in the fight against the Zapatistas. Several Guatemalan graduates from the School of the Americas (SOA) have been found responsible for similar atrocities.

25. Several graduates of the School of the Americas (SOA) were involved in Guatemala's long civil war: Efraín Ríos Montt, former dictator and president of Guatemala (1982–83), army general and president of Congress and one of the most controversial figures of Guatemala, is considered responsible for the genocide of numerous indigenous communities and still serves as a lawmaker in Guatemala's Congress; Fernando Romeo Lucas García, who along with Montt, according to the Guatemalan Commission for Historical Clarification (CEH), is responsible for the massacre of 132,000 Mayan people; Byron Lima Estrada, who was found guilty of the assassination of human rights defender Bishop Juan Gerardi; and the top leaders of the Guatemalan intelligence agency (D-2 or G-2). "The School of the Americas and Guatemala," Nisgua.org. In 2009, the first person (former military commissioner Felipe Cusanero) was finally sentenced in Guatemala for the genocide and the disappearance of thousands of people, "Guatemala Makes Landmark," Reuters.

26. Eduardo is referring to the seven-month-long teachers' protest that occurred in 2006 and was spearheaded by the Popular Assembly of the People of Oaxaca. The protesters were demanding the removal of the state's Governor Ulises Ruiz Ortiz for violating Geneva

Conventions standards. Several people were killed and more imprisoned as the police harshly repressed the protests. In fact, the police even shot at unarmed medics who were attending to the wounded. Joshua Holland, "Updated Dispatch from Occupied Oaxaca," AlterNet.org *Peek* blog, posted October 31, 2006, www.alternet.org/blogs.peek/43643.

27. Partido Revolucionario Institucional (Institutional Revolutionary Party) is a socialist party in Mexico. The party, which is no longer a socialist party in the traditional sense, is today aligned with right-wing, neoliberal policies. The PRI, which has changed its name several times, has been in power in Mexico for over seventy years.

Four: December 8—Immaculate Conception

1. These palm trees (called cabbage palms) are an important part of the Florida landscape; the cabbage palm is indeed the official state tree of Florida.

2. With 8,500 stores all over the United States, Domino's Pizza is the second-largest U.S. pizza maker after Yum! Brands Inc.'s Pizza Hut. The thriving company registered a profit of $23.6 million in the fourth quarter of 2009. Solsman, "Domino's Pizza Profit."

3. Among others, see Whelan's "Charity and the Forbes 400."

4. Monaghan, *Pizza Tiger*.

5. Boyer, "The Deliverer."

6. Boyer, "The Deliverer." According to *Forbes*, Monaghan donated $533 of the $550 million he made in 2004. He is listed among the ones "who gave too much"; Monaghan would be ranked 260 among the wealthiest if he did not give anything away. Whelan, "Charity and the Forbes 400."

7. Tom Monaghan's activities have triggered a lot of interest. Avewatch.com is a website dedicated exclusively to monitoring Tom Monaghan's Ave Maria entities.

8. Monaghan supported Mitt Romney and then ultimately Senator John McCain in the 2008 presidential election. His financial backing, however, focused on state elections. According to rightwingwatch.org, Monaghan gave $4,600 to Tom Rooney, who ran for Congress in the 16th District in Florida. Rooney is an ultraconservative Catholic; the grandson of the Pittsburgh Steelers founder Art Rooney, his brother, Brian, is the national spokesman for Monaghan's Thomas More Law Center. "The Rise and Fall of Ave Maria," rightwingwatch.org.

9. Cited in Marchetti, "Delivering on His Word." According to the Media Matters Action Network website ("Conservative Transparency"), Monaghan is founder of Ave Maria College, Ave Maria Communications, Ave Maria Foundation, Ave Maria School of Law, Ave Maria University, Ave Maria University Inc., Legatus, and Thomas Moore Law Center.

10. Ibid.

11. Ave Maria town officially opened on July 21, 2007.

12. See Barron Collier Companies, "A New Town—Ave Maria" at their website.

13. The text of the law that makes Ave Maria a special district is available at http://web
.naplesnews.com/media/pdf/2009/avemarialaw.pdf. The *Naples Daily News* called
it a "tailor-made law." Dillon, "A Town Without a Vote."

14. In May 2009, the *Naples Daily News* ran a three-part series called "Ave Maria: A
Town without a Vote." The exposé by Liam Dillon raised questions of constitutionality around Ave Maria's government. According to the report, most of its residents
had not been informed of the special status of Ave Maria's government when they
purchased a house in the developing town. The law approved by the Collier County
Commission and then the state legislature gives developers, and not the registered
voters of Ave Maria, authority over the town. The text of the law is available at
http://web.naplesnews.com/media/pdf/2009/avemariado.pdf. Modeled after the
community development special district legislation, Ave Maria law states that registered voters can take control of the government only after a certain percentage of
land has been developed. Tallahassee attorney Ken van Assenderp tailored the law
to suit the interests of Ave Maria Development. The original memo the attorney
sent to Barron Collier Companies Vice President Blake Gable is available at
http://web.naplesnews.com/media/pdf/2009/KVAtoGable13003.pdf.

15. Dillon, "Town Without a Vote."

16. Ave Maria Development actually owns more than ten thousand acres of land within
the town and its vicinity. Dillon, "A Town Without a Vote."

17. According to the media and information center Media Matters for America, the
church will have a sixty-foot-high bleeding Jesus in stained glass. See Berkovitz,
"Tom Monaghan's Big Box Church."

18. Ibid.

19. Boyer, "The Deliverer," 88.

20. The report on Ave Maria ("Celestial City") aired on CNN on August 24, 2007. I retrieved it from YouTube (where it is entitled "The Rise of a Catholic Town: Ave Maria,
Florida").

21. Boyer, "The Deliverer."

22. Monaghan wanted to build Ave Maria University on the property of Domino's
Farms in Ann Arbor, Michigan, where the headquarters of Domino's Pizza is. On
April 15, 2002, city officials voted 5 to 2 against the rezoning request submitted by
Monaghan. By then, the entrepreneur had already arranged to have the university
built in Collier County. On November 20, Monaghan formally announced at the La

Playa Beach and Golf Resort north of Naples the construction of Ave Maria University near Immokalee. Elliott, "Ave Maria Founder."

23. Boyer, "The Deliverer," 88.

24. The Sandinista National Liberation Front (FSLN) is a socialist party currently governing Nicaragua. The Sandinistas first ruled Nicaragua from 1979 to 1990. The so-called Contras, homegrown militias financed by the CIA, created terror by attacking both state and civilian targets in Nicaragua throughout the 1980s. A good part of the Catholic Church actually sided with the Sandinistas, and espoused the principles of liberation theology. The Sandinistas galvanized leftists and social movements worldwide. The English punk rock band The Clash named one of its greatest albums after the Nicaraguan political movement (*Sandinista!* 1980). The Sandinistas came back in power in 2006 with the election of Daniel Ortega.

25. In the first Sandinista government, Father Ernesto Cardinal was minister of culture and his brother Fernando minister of education, whereas Father Miguel D'Escoto was elected minister of foreign affairs. Most people in Nicaragua, a predominantly Catholic country, sided with their Sandinista government on the occasion of the disastrous visit of John Paul II in 1983.

26. See among others by Michael Novak: *The Spirit of Democratic Capitalism* (New York: Simon & Schuster, 1982); *Will It Liberate? Questions About Liberation Theology* (New York: Paulist, 1986); *The Fire of Invention: Civil Society and the Future of the Corporation* (Lanham, MD: Rowman & Littlefield, 1997).

27. This information was updated as of October 1, 2010.

28. Florida Freedom Partnership (FFP) is a Miami-based organization that "provides a rapid-response, comprehensive support system for trafficked persons while building the capacity of the South Florida community to better understand and respond to the needs of trafficked persons," www.humantrafficking.org/organizations/319.

29. Agricultural workers are not covered by workers' compensation laws in most Southern states. When farmworkers are injured on the job, they are denied benefits. Bauer, *Under Siege: Life*, 10.

Five: January

1. Florida Immigrant Coalition's mission is to "seek equal rights for immigrants and integration into the civic and cultural life of our communities." FLIC accomplishes its mission "through coordination of immigrant organizations and community education, organizing and advocacy," http://floridaimmigrant.org/default.asp?PageNum=262.

2. Florida Immigrant Advocacy Center (FIAC) is a Miami-based "not-for-profit legal

assistance organization dedicated to protecting and promoting the basic human rights of immigrants of all nationalities," www.fiacfla.org/mission.php.

3. The training was partially based on a Deportation 101 curriculum developed by New York–based Families For Freedom (FFF). FFF is a "New York-based multi-ethnic defense network by and for immigrants facing and fighting deportation." It is an abolitionist organization whose main goal is to stop deportation of all people, www.familiesforfreedom.org/.

4. Much controversy has arisen recently around the Arizona SB 1070 as it regards constitutional rights. A class action lawsuit against SB 1070 was filed on May 17, 2010. As we read on the Legal Action Center website, Arizona's "Support Our Law Enforcement and Safe Neighborhoods Act" (SB 1070, amended by HB 2162), which "requires state and local law enforcement agencies to check the immigration status of individuals it encounters and makes it a state crime to be without proper immigration documentation," www.legalactioncenter.org/clearinghouse/litigation-issue-pages/ arizona-legal-challenges. Immigrant rights and civil rights advocates have organized boycotts of the state of Arizona and numerous actions to protest the law, which, they argue, would prevent the passage of comprehensive immigration reform. Moreover, "an enforcement-policy-only" approach to immigration that heavily relies on local and state police is doomed to fail. President Obama has expressly criticized SB 1070. Archibold, "Arizona Enacts Stringent." On July 6, the Justice Department announced the decision to file suit against Arizona on "preemption grounds," Markon, "Justice Dept. Expected."

However, as the SPLC report on Latinos in the South indicates, racial profiling has been a practice in this part of the country. Several respondents define the South as a "war zone" for immigrants. Forty-seven of the interviewees reported knowing someone who had been treated unfairly by the police. Bauer, *Under Siege: Life*, 16.

5. A warrant signed by the ICE ("an immigration warrant") does not grant the ICE authority to search someone's home. Conversely, a warrant signed by a judge or magistrate requires that there be "probable cause" to make a search or arrest. However, "no warrant is required for publicly accessible areas of a business or a workplace" ...or "for 'open fields,' such as an area of land where there is no fence. BUT warrants are required for farms or other 'agricultural operations.'" Florida Immigrant Coalition and Florida Immigrant Advocacy Center, "Defending Immigrant Rights," 63.

6. Proposition 187, the "Save Our State Initiative," was a 1994 ballot initiative designed to prohibit undocumented immigrants from using social services, health care, and public education in California. The people of California voted in favor of Proposition 187, but the initiative was then found unconstitutional by a federal court and thus never became law.

7. "IIRIRA 96—A Summary," Visalaw.com.

8. "Individuals who have been unlawfully present for more than 180 days, but less than one year, and who voluntarily depart, may not reenter the country for three years. People unlawfully present for an aggregate period of one year or more are subject to a ten-year bar. Because of such laws, even people otherwise eligible for employment-based or family-based visas are unable to adjust their status in the United States, and if they leave the country in order to get a visa at a U.S. consulate abroad, they cannot reenter the United States until the three- or ten-year period has passed. This means that unauthorized immigrants in the United States who are eligible for visas are encouraged to remain here illegally rather than risk being separated from family members for three years, ten years, or even permanently." Immigration Policy Center, "Breaking Down the Problems," 8–9.

9. "Criminal Aliens" are deported only after they have served their sentence. These convicted immigrants are detained in county jails, federal facilities, and private prisons along with the general criminal population. "Ground[s for] deportation expanded to include a broad range of minor offenses, including vast expansion of 'aggravated felony' term. This term now applies to more than 50 classes of crimes, many of which are neither 'aggravated' or 'felonies.' Most of the new deportation grounds applied *retroactively*" are. FLIC and FLAC, "Defending Immigrant Rights," 3.

10. Since all immigrants, including those seeking asylum, are required to be detained before being deported, we can use the statistics regarding detention centers to assess the number of immigrants who have been deported since the IIRIRA was passed. According to "A Broken System: Confidential Reports Reveal Failures in U.S. Immigrant Detention Centers," a report by the National Immigration Law Center, "the average number of immigrants detained tripled between 1996–2007."

11. Collier County signed the partnership agreement on August 6, 2007. For the full list of the sixty-three active 287(g) MOAs (Memorandum of Agreement) participants updated as of November 17, 2008, see the Delegation of Immigration Authority Section 287(g) of the Immigration and Nationality Act, www.ice.gov/partners /287g/Section287_g.htm (accessed July 18, 2010).

12. The first CCSOs received ICE training certification in September 2007. Collier County Sheriff's Office. As of June 30, 2010, there are thirty-six deputies with ICE training (email correspondence with Kristi Lester, public information officer apprentice).

13. The majority also disapproves all the workplace raids (76 percent), employee database check (53 percent), criminal prosecutions of employers (70 percent), and undocumented immigrants (73 percent). Lopez, and Minushkin, *2008 National Survey*, 3.

14. Proposed by Wisconsin Congressman James Sensenbrenner, the legislation passed in the House of Representatives with no debate in December 2005, full text of H.R. 4437 available at http://frwebgate.access.gpo.gov/cgi-bin/getdoc.cgi?dbname=109_cong _bills&docid=f:h4437rfs.txt.pdf. In June 2006, the Senate passed the Comprehensive Immigration Reform act (S. 2611) that includes many of the provisions of H.R. 4437, full text of S.2611 available at http://frwebgate.access.gpo.gov/cgi-bin/getdoc.cgi ?dbname=109_cong_bills&docid=f:s2611es.txt.pdf.

15. In June 2008, I interviewed Ramiro Cordero of the El Paso U.S. Custom and Border Patrol. The El Paso sector had 2,400 agents on roll. Operation Hold the Line—initiated by former CBP agent and, since 1997, Democratic Congressman for the sixteenth district of Texas, Silvestre Reyes—was still in effect. San Diego, too, had modeled its program, Operation Gatekeeper, after El Paso's Hold the Line. "Apprehensions"—that's how Cordero constantly termed arrests—he proudly stated, were in decline due to the enforcement of the tactical infrastructure, like seismic sensors, and infrared and magnetic sensors that detect tunnels—and the implementation of the border fence in the area. As a result of that, Cordero conceded, favored crossing routes for undocumented immigrants had moved west; specifically, the Arizona desert had seen an increase in the number of crossings, quite often with tragic consequences, given the harsher nature of the territory. Between 1995 and 2005 the number of deaths near the border has almost doubled, the Government Accountability Office found (U.S. GAO, *Illegal Immigration*). Cordero also admitted that only 13 percent of the "apprehensions" in the El Paso area were of criminals, mostly drug dealers. None of the arrests were for terrorism. When I asked him the question: "How many terrorists have been caught crossing the U.S./Mexico border?" Cordero's answer was, "None." In June 2008, there were 142 Border Patrol units with 14,000 active officers, 85 percent of which were concentrated along the border between the United States and Mexico.

16. Nationwide, the number of U.S. Custom and Border Patrol agents went from 9,000 in 2001 to approximately 18,332 by the end of 2008. U.S. Custom and Border Protection, *Safe Travel, Legal Trade*.

17. Immigration Policy Center, "Breaking Down the Problems," 12.

18. The annual budget of the Border Patrol grew from $326.2 million in 1992 to $2.7 billion in 2009. The number of Border Patrol agents stationed along the southwest border went from 3,555 in 1992 to 17,415 in 2009.

19. Popular pressure reached its highest point when on May 1, 2006, the Immigrant Rights March brought over one million people to the streets across the country. www.MSNBC.msn.com, "1 Million March."

20. Most notably, in May 2008 the ICE raided the AgriProcessors meatpacking plant

in Postville, Iowa, by nabbing almost four hundred employees and thus basically destroying the economy of that small community. Another example is the Howard Industries plant in Laurel, Mississippi, in which almost six hundred immigrants without documents got raided. Bazar, "Citizens Sue after Detentions."

21. Bernstein, "Target of Immigrant Raids."

22. Operation Return to Sender began on May 26, 2006, and ended on June 13, 2006. "ICE Apprehends More," Dhs.gov.

23. Much controversy has arisen lately around the actions of Sheriff Joe Arpaio of Maricopa County, Arizona; Arpaio has diverted funds from investigating crimes to focus on detecting immigrants without documents. For examples, see the special report "Investigating Sheriff Joe Arpaio" by the *Phoenix New Times*.

24. Hsu, "Immigrant Prosecutions Hit."

25. For a collection of stories of ICE abuses, see Bauer, *Under Siege: Life*, 16–24.

26. "Fewer than 100 owners, supervisors or hiring officials were arrested in fiscal 2007, compared with nearly 4,900 arrests that involved illegal workers," according to Hsu's "Immigrant Crackdown Falls" report. In a news conference on November 6, 2007, Homeland Security Secretary Michael Chertoff said: "The days of treating employers who violate these laws by giving them the equivalent of a corporate parking ticket—those days are gone" (Hsu, "Immigrant Crackdown Falls"). However, a few months later, T. J. Bonner, president of the National Border Patrol Council, declared, "Criminalizing illegal immigration while turning a blind eye to employers who provide the jobs that lure migrants makes for good election-year politics but poor policy." (Hsu, "Immigration Prosecutions Hit")

27. Electronic employment verification programs (such as E-Verify) have been proven faulty and can't provide effective solutions to the problem of undocumented labor. E-Verify, for instance, is "a voluntary system, except where state laws require businesses to register to use E-Verify, as well as a few other exceptions in which the federal government has made E-Verify mandatory. There have been multiple attempts to expand E-Verify and make it mandatory for all employers…E-Verify is an extremely controversial program because of the high probability for database errors, misuse of the system by employers, and the burden it imposes on the Social Security Administration (SSA). Furthermore, E-Verify does not even identify unauthorized workers effectively. Some unauthorized workers are erroneously confirmed as authorized to work because E-Verify cannot identify counterfeit, stolen, or borrowed identity documents. And E-Verify cannot identify unauthorized workers when employers who knowingly hire them simply do not run their workers through the system, or when work is performed 'off the books' in the un-

derground economy." Immigration Policy Center, "Breaking Down the Problems," 15.

28. In small communities across the country, the construction of these structures is good news in a suffering economy as they employ hundreds of people. A case in point is Farmville, Virginia. The center was built to accommodate Virginia's growing number of undocumented immigrants with criminal charges. Sieff, "Immigrant Detention Center."

29. Think Progress Staff, "Consequences of Enforcement."

30. Kolodner, "Immigration Enforcement Benefits."

31. For examples, see Priest and Goldstein. "System of Neglect" and Hernandez, "Lethal Limbo for Migrants."

32. Ibid., 18.

33. Schriro, "Immigration Detention Overview." Stats refer to 2009.

34. As of June 19, 2010, the following BI offices have Pretrial Services Programs: Broward County, Florida; Maricopa County, Arizona; and Philadelphia, Pennsylvania.

35. As we read on the company's website, BI claims "Broward County's Pretrial Services Division helps divert criminal defendants from pretrial incarceration, thereby keeping beds open for serious offenders."

36. So we read in the "Memorandum to Field Office Directors," Subject: Eligibility Criteria for Enrollment into the Intensive Supervision Appearance Program (ISAP) and the Electronic Monitoring Device (EMD) Program. The document was retrieved through the Freedom of Information Act www.ice.gov/doclib/foia/contracts/acb4c0008orderacl4d0270bi.pdf (accessed September 26, 2010).

37. The monitoring system consists of the ankle bracelet device and a connected unit that is plugged into the participants' homes. The unit communicates with the ankle device and results show up on the case specialist's computer. If the participants are not home when they are supposed to be, then the case specialist on call is contacted and will have to locate the participant.

38. My informant worked for BI as an ISAP case specialist for over a year between 2007 and 2008.

39. My informant reports: "Sometimes I'll think about some of the humble, kind, hardworking people who were in the program. I remember this one Guatemalan indigenous man who worked at Sun Citrus (or some other citrus plant) in Indiantown and he was always so compliant and careful to work only when he had a valid work permit. It makes me so sad to think that the participants thought I was really helping them when in reality I was only baiting them for deportation."

40. My informant recalls several cases in which participants whose appeal had been dismissed were tricked to come by the BI office to sign some paperwork and *la migra*

(ICE) was there to take them to a deportation center; in other cases, ICE agents would go to the participant's home to arrest them.

41. Immigration Policy Center, Special Report. "Breaking Down the Problems: What's Wrong with Our Immigration System?" October 2009, 12.

42. U.S. employers' labor needs are not met by the current immigration system. 140,000 employment-based green cards are available for qualified immigrants. Immigration Policy Center. "Breaking Down the Problems," 8.

43. "Farmworkers End Hunger," *USA Today*, January 19, 1998; "3 Fla. farmworkers give up hunger strike after Carter plea," *Washington Post*, January 19, 1998; Navarro, "Florida Tomato Pickers Take on Growers." At the end of 1997, the CIW organized a long hunger strike that focused the attention of national media on the conditions of Immokalee's tomato pickers. CIW members Roberto Acevedo, Abundio Rios, Antonio Ramos, Domingo Jacinto, Pedro Lopez, and Hector Vasquez fasted for almost a month. As Sellers reports: "Lopez described his participation in terms of a *cargo* (a responsibility to the community), a notion that has its roots in parts of Guatemala and Mexico" (84). The hunger strike ended thanks to the direct intervention of former President Carter. For more details about the hunger strike and the history of the CIW, see Sellers, *"Del pueblo, para el pueblo."*

44. Collier County Housing Authority, "At a Glance."

Six: March

1. Lantigua, "Why Was Carlitos."

2. The number of inspectors has been raised to thirty after the recent cases of children born with congenital diseases were reported. Calvert, Alaron, and others, "Case Report: Three Farmworkers."

3. "Between 1993 and 2003, Florida inspectors found 4,609 violations of pesticide regulations, but only 7.6 percent resulted in fines." Lantigua, "Why Was Carlitos."

4. In California, for instance, there is a separate agency dedicated to the regulation of pesticide use, the Department of Pesticide regulation, which is part of the Environmental Protection Agency (EPA), and is independent from the Department of Agriculture. Lantigua, "Why Was Carlitos."

5. Calvert, Alaron, and others, "Case Report: Three Farmworkers." Ag-Mart has a history of pesticide violations: in Brunswick and Pender County, North Carolina, the Department of Agriculture issued the largest number of state pesticide law violations to Jeffrey Oxley, Ag-Mart's farm manager. The violations refer to the use of pesticides in 2004 and 2005. More recently, the New Jersey Department of Envi-

ronmental Protection fined Ag-Mart $931,000 for violations. New Jersey charged Ag-Mart with "hundreds of violations that include denying state environmental inspectors access to facilities, losing track of a highly toxic insecticide, failing to properly ventilate areas during pesticide use...and using forbidden mixtures of pesticides." Lantigua, "Ag-Mart Fined $931,000."

6. After the case of Carlos "Carlitos" Candelario, the child born with Pierre Robin syndrome, without arm or legs, the Florida Department of Agriculture and Consumer Services investigated Ag-Mart, since the women had all worked in farms controlled by the company. Ag-Mart was found responsible for more than eighty-eight violations due to the use of pesticides. The company eventually ended up paying only $8,500 of the $111,200 requested by the prosecution. Carlitos's parents received a life-long compensation for the medical expenses of their child—even though scientifically, no direct link between the pesticide exposure and the cases of neonatal deformities had been shown. The etiology of human birth defects is still unknown. Stapleton, "Deal Ensures Lifetime." Yet, it is known that pesticides are harmful to human health. For instance, regulations state that workers should be kept far from the fields for a set time after the spraying of pesticides. There is no evidence that Ag-Mart had used this precautionary measure. The information related to pesticide exposure is based on the data provided by the same company, so they could easily be falsified or be inexact, to say the least. Furthermore, according to what the mothers of the children born with congenital anomalies reported, there were no places where they could wash their hands on the job nor were they required to wear gloves. Although there is no data available regarding the manifestation of certain symptoms during the gestational period of their pregnancy, a medical checkup during the different phases of their pregnancy might have helped identify and track back nausea and other symptoms to the exposure to pesticide rather than to the pregnancy. "The findings...support the need for epidemiologic studies to examine the role of pesticide exposure in the etiology of congenital anomalies," we read in the conclusion of the research on the three cases. "Fact is that we ran out of funds," laments Hugo Leon, one of the researchers at the Collier Health Development in Naples who participated in the report. Calvert, Alaron, and others, "Case Report: Three Farmworkers."

7. See the Six L's website at www.sixls.com.

8. Lykes Brothers and Consolidated Citrus have control over the production of citrus.

9. For a discussion of this point and others related to biotech agriculture, see, for example, the chapter titled "A New Sort of Tomato" in Pringle, *Food, Inc.: Mendel*.

10. The "hammocks" are little islands modeled by the slow water streaming in the immense swamps of the Everglades.

11. My phonetic transcription.

12. The name Ah-Tah-Thi-Ki literally means "place where one learns." The Seminole museum is located around Clewiston, Florida, south of Lake Okeechobee.

13. The Corn Dance Festival falls during the so-called small moon of June when the constellation of the Pleiades reappears at the horizon. The green corn is planted four months earlier and it's ripe in time for the celebration.

14. See the Comprehensive Everglades Restoration Plan, "Development of Central and South Florida (C&SF) Project."

15. In June 2008, the state of Florida announced the acquisition of the U.S. Sugar Corporation for $1.75 billion. The plan was that within six years the U.S. Sugar Corporation would give the 187,000 acres north of Everglades to the state. Many have interpreted the operation as the bailout of a company unable to keep up with a competitive, globalized market. The price of sugar—whose harvest is almost completely mechanized in Florida—has gone down as a result of the competition with companies whose production is located in other countries where labor is cheaper. However, to truly complete the restoration project, the state will need an additional 40,000 acres still in the hands of the Cuban American Fanjul family, owner of Florida Crystal, the other U.S. giant in the sugar industry. Criticism came also from the Miccosukee Tribe, which sued the state as it claimed the plan was diverting money from other, more important projects. Since then, the proposed purchase has been downsized twice due to the economic crisis that badly hit Florida. In April 2009, Governor Crist announced the purchase of only 72,500 acres for $530,000 with an option to buy the remaining land by 2019. Cave, "Florida Buying Big"; Walsh, "Florida Deal for Everglades"; Cave, "Everglades Restoration Plan."

16. Kimbrell, *Fatal Harvest Reader: The Tragedy*, 141.

17. La Ley WAFZ plays mainstream Latin music and is part of the Glades Media Company.

18. It had been a crime for the Seminoles to learn how to read and write, and those who were discovered had to defend themselves in court.

19. The consecration of Ave Maria occurred on March 31, 2008. Dewane also visited the Ave Maria campus prior to that. His predecessor, Bishop John J. Nevins, was at the temporary campus in North Naples for the initial public announcement of Ave Maria in 2002. According to the *Naples Daily News*, "Ave Maria's quest for church status has been going on since 2004." "Editorial: Ave Maria Oratory."

20. "Ave Maria Oratory," Catholicnewsagency.com.

21. According to the Ave Maria University website, AMU received accreditation from Southern Association of Colleges and Schools on June 24, 2010. "SACS membership covers both the campus in Ave Maria, Fla., and the branch Latin American

Campus in San Marcos, Nicaragua." June 24, 2010, www.avemaria.edu/news/ 496.html, accessed July 9, 2010.

22. See Dillon, "Town Without a Vote."

23. The "Domenica del Corriere" (my translation: "Sunday Courier") was a popular weekly magazine in Italy that ran between 1899 and 1989.

24. Pio di Pietrelcina (1887–1968) was an Italian priest who is now venerated for his stigmata. A vast industry of religious paraphernalia has been created and pilgrims from all around the world come to San Giovanni Rotondo where the monastery of Padre Pio is located.

Seven: May—Resolutions

1. Martin, "Burger King Grants."

2. A "pin-hooker" is somebody who buys something in order to resell it quickly.

3. Vanden Heuvel, "Sweet Victory: Coalition."

4. Most of the following section is based on research work done by *Ft. Myers News-Press* reporter Amy Bennett Williams.

5. 2007 letter to Burger King quoted in Bennett Williams, "From April 12."

6. Ibid.

7. See a transcript of the April 28 show at http://www.msnbc.msn.com/id/24369344/.

8. Grover, "Getting Sound Advice."

9. In 2005, Monsanto Co., the St. Louis–based corporation specializing in agricultural biotechnologies, bought Seminis for $1.4 billion. "Monsanto to Buy Seminis," *St. Louis Business Journal.*

10. Revenues increased to $800 in 2009. Seminis sells its seeds in more than 160 countries; see the Seminis website at http://us.seminis.com/about/default.asp. The company controls more than 40 percent of the U.S. and 20 percent of the global fruit and vegetable seed market. Barlett and Steele, "Monsanto's Harvest of Fear."

11. Quoted in Barlett and Steele, "Monsanto's Harvest of Fear." The research costs have gone up to $2.6 million today according to what is stated in the Monsanto video responses to the documentary *Food, Inc.* These videos are no longer up on the Monsanto website, but the written responses are at www.monsanto.com/food-inc/Pages/ default.aspx.

12. The GATT, created in 1948, operated for over forty years as a multilateral treaty regime on a provisional basis. Up until 1994, the "GATT rounds" produced a series of international tariff agreements; in 1994, this cooperation mechanism was transformed into GATT and soon after led to the creation of the World Trade Organization (WTO),

the international organization that now promotes free trade, and also comprises the Council for Trade-Related Aspects of Intellectual Property Rights (TRIPS Council). The Agreement of Agriculture (AoA) was the treaty that included the sector in the WTO. AoA has been criticized since it has reduced tariff protection for small farmers and thus harshly penalized the Global South. For more information about the AoA and its impact on farming, see Hoda, and Gulati, *WTO Negotiations on Agriculture*.

13. For years the Indian government and scientific research have denied the relationship between the suicides and the increasing poverty and indebtedness of small farmers. To understand the dramatic consequences of the advent of agribusiness in India, a nation of one billion people, suffice it to say that two-thirds of the population supports itself through farming. Shiva, "Suicide Economy of Corporate Globalisation."

14. Kimbrell, *Fatal Harvest Reader*, 8.

15. Shiva, "Suicide Economy."

16. Shiva, *Biopiracy: Plunder of Nature*.

17. The 1970 PVPA allowed its holders to use the patented variety for research and agricultural purposes. See the text of the law (revised in 2005) in its entirety at USDA, "Plant Variety Protection Act." www.ams.usda.gov/AMSv1.0/getfile?dDocName =STELDEV30027.

18. Center for Food Safety, "Monsanto vs. U.S. Farmers," 24. This right was abolished in 1994 with an amendment to PPVA that prohibited the sale of all seeds without permission of the variety owner.

19. See, for example, the Monsanto page "Food, Inc. Movie " in response to the claims made in *Food, Inc.* about seed patenting at www.monsanto.com/food-inc/Pages/default.aspx.

20. The first patent of living organisms (technically, a bacterium) dates back to 1980: *Diamond, Commissioner of Patents and Trademarks v. Chakrabarty*, 447 US 303—Supreme Court 1980. In 1985, the Patent and Trademark Office (U.S. PTO) decided the *Ex parte Hibberd* case that sexually reproducing plants (read, living organisms) are patentable. After this decision, the U.S. PTO began accepting applications for licensing these plants. In 2001, *J.E.M. Ag Supply v. Pioneer Hi-Bred International* confirmed the legality of the patenting of sexually reproducing plants by stating, "there is no 'positive repugnancy' between the issuance of utility patents for plants and PVP coverage for plants," http://scholar.google.com/scholar_case?case =2332797136716120967&hl=en&as_sdt=2&as_vis=1&oi=scholarr.

21. Shand, "Intellectual Property: Enhancing."

22. In 1987, The U.S. PTO ruled that animals are patentable as well.

23. Center for Food Safety, "Monsanto vs. U.S. Farmers."

24. Ibid., 24.

25. Bartlett and Steele, "Monsanto's Harvest of Fear." Also, it's worth noting that a sim-

ilar corporate rhetoric has been recently used by the music industry. In response to file-swapping and digital downloading, the music business adopted similar labels to criminalize its very consumer base: music fans. "The degree to which the music industry projected terms such as *piracy* and *theft* onto consumers tended to deflect attention from its own less than ethical practices," Garofalo argues (478). Likewise, the music industry has historically served it own interests (signing artists for life to one-sided contracts, for example); hypocritically camouflaging them as defense of the artists' intellectual property rights. However, as further noted by the Berne Convention Implementation Act (1988): "The constitutional purpose of copyright is to facilitate the flow of ideas in the interest of learning…[T]he primary objective of our copyright law is not to reward the author, but rather to secure for the public the benefits for the creations of authors" (quoted in Garofalo, 475). For a further investigation on this point, see Garofalo, *Rockin' Out: Popular Music.*

26. Center for Food Safety, "Monsanto vs. U.S. Farmers."

27. Monsanto posted on its website a series of short video responses to the documentary *Food, Inc.* One of them, titled "Why Are Seeds Patented?" (which is no longer available) is quite telling. Accessed July 12, 2010, www.monsanto.com/foodinc/ seeds_patents.asp. The video is supposed to rebut the "statement/suggestion" made in the film that "the ability to patent plants and living organisms came into being only in the 1980s." In the video, a non-threatening-looking Key Magin, soybean product manager for Monsanto explains, in the manner of an elementary school teacher, how the practice of patenting seeds has been going on since the 1930s, but fails to acknowledge the pivotal changes that the more recent U.S. Supreme Court rulings have triggered. Significantly enough, Magin says that patents give the creators of "a new plant variety or biotech trait the opportunity to commercialize that new invention and get a return in their investment of both time and money that went into developing it." Then she moves on to a comparison. She takes two DVDs that look identical: one is a copyrighted movie (seemingly, the very same *Food, Inc.*) and the other one, a blank DVD, she says. One required an investment of money, work, and creativity; the other did not. Then she shows two soybeans and continues with her parallelism. The video also doesn't say that farmers are basically forced to use Monsanto seeds once they buy Monsanto herbicides as only Monsanto seeds are resistant to said products. Finally, through its mouthpiece, Monsanto claims that its biotech agriculture is the way to feed the ever-growing world population, thus failing to acknowledge both overproduction of certain crops (namely, corn) that are not used to feed people and the amount of food that gets regularly wasted in the Global North. On the other hand, by presenting Monsanto's solution as the only viable one, Magin ignores the years of research that other organizations like the Land Institute have put into developing a non-industrialized, sustainable system to perpetuate agriculture productivity (the "Natural Systems

Agriculture"). On the Land Institute's research see, for instance, Jackson, "Farming in Nature's Image," 65–75. Jensen, "Where Agriculture Meets Empire."

28. Peter Pringle notices that biotech companies prefer the term "engineering" as they want people to associate food production with assembly-line precision not with "genetic gardening" experiments. Contrary to Medellian crossbreeding practices, the idea of engineering evokes predictability and, thus, safety. Pringle, *Food, Inc.*, 58; Shand, "Intellectual Property: Enhancing," 240–48.

29. Scientists are calling for banning the release of Roundup-tolerant GM crops worldwide due to the high toxicity of glyphosate. Institute of Science in Society, "Death by Multiple Poisoning."

30. In 2009–2010, Monsanto was listed among the top industry contributors to federal candidates and parties with $230,000; the corporation is a number one client when it comes to lobbying activities ($2,460,000). See the Center for Responsive Politics website. The political ties with the biotechnological corporation are well known: Judge Clarence Thomas was an attorney for Monsanto; former Secretary of Defense Donald Rumsfeld was on the Board of Directors of Searle, the pharmaceutical subsidiary of Monsanto; former Secretary of Health Tommy Thompson received $50,000 during his campaign for governor of Wisconsin; and the list goes on. Judge Clarence Thomas voted in favor of patenting living organisms. Monsanto claimed that the U.S. Supreme Court case actually favored a rival corporation. In fact, the real competition is not horizontal (among corporations) but vertical. In other words, it is meant to maintain the privilege of a few wealthy. Thus, legislation favors a system, not a specific corporation.

31. Monsanto has a long history of environmental violations. Dioxin was a by-product of the 2,4,5-T herbicide made by Monsanto. Almost one hundred cancer suits against the company have been recently filed by residents of Nitro in West Virginia where the herbicide was produced. Dickerson, "Nearly 100 More Cancer." The factory also manufactured the infamous Agent Orange, whose by-product was also dioxin. The U.S. military used Agent Orange to defoliate jungles during the Vietnam War. The Vietnamese government claims that millions of nationals have been exposed to the poisonous defoliant. In 2004, the Vietnamese Association of Victims of Agent Orange (VAVA) was formed and filed a class action lawsuit against Monsanto and other manufacturers of Agent Orange. Fawthrop, "Agent Orange Victims."

32. "U.S. EPA Fact Sheet Anniston." Polychlorinated biphenyls (PBCs) produced by the Monsanto facility dramatically polluted the western part of the city of Anniston, Alabama. In 1997, Solutia was formed as a divestiture of Monsanto. In 2003, Solutia filed for bankruptcy. Today, there's "no control relationship between Monsanto…[and] Solutia," as we read on the corporation's website. The Monsanto plant, which closed in 1971, dumped its toxic residue in an open-pit landfill and engaged in other hazardous

environmental practices. When in the nineties the toxicity of PBCs become common knowledge, Monsanto settled residents' claims for $550 million with more than 21,000 Anniston residents and later took on the clean-up operations for the area (still ongoing). See www.monsanto.com/who_we_are/monsanto_relationships.asp. Barlett, and Steele, "Monsanto's Harvest of Fear."

33. Lasker, "Federal Preemption and State."

34. Mascarenhas and Busch, "Seeds of Change."

35. Lately, Monsanto has campaigned in the United States to remove labels that indicate that cows have been treated with artificial growth hormones. It's worth noting that Europe has banned rBGH.

36. Among others, see the documentary *The Corporation* (2003) by Abbot and Achbar; and Smith, "Monsanto Forced Fox." For a deeper analysis of Monsanto and GM foods, see also Smith, *Seeds of Deception*.

37. Grubbs, "Story of Florida's Migrant," 2.

38. Data updated to July 2010. E-mail correspondence with Esmeralda Serrata.

39. "I grew up in Farm Worker Village—my parents were farmworkers and I also worked in the fields up until I was sixteen years of age. After high school I went to work and also went to school during the evening and earned my bachelor's degree in business administration...went to Edison Community College and then to Hodges University (formerly International College). I came to work at the Housing Authority in 1988 as a temporary clerk and was eventually hired full time as a secretary. I worked myself up the ladder to then being the new executive director in 2002." E-mail correspondence with Esmeralda Serrata.

40. The other emerging sectors are construction and landscaping for men, and social work and service for women.

41. As of July 2010, all the trailers have been set on lots and are occupied.

42. For a further investigation on the abuse of workers in the Post-Katrina reconstruction, see Browne-Dianis, Lai, Hincapie, and Soni, *And Injustice for All*; and Fletcher, Pham, Stover, and Vinck, *Rebuilding After Katrina*.

43. Bauer, *Under Siege*, 6–9. Regardless of their status, 80 percent of the workers in New Orleans reported wage theft. See also Bauer, *Close to Slavery*.

44. Edsall, "Bush Suspends Pay."

45. Employers who hire workers without employment authorization are subject to sanctions (penalties) as of the 1986 Immigration Reform and Control ACT (IRCA). In the aftermath of the storm, the Bush administration through the Department of Homeland Security suspended for at least forty-five days sanctions against employers who hired workers who could not present documents normally required by federal immigration law; in addition, the U.S. Occupational Safety and

Health Administration suspended enforcement of health and safety measures on the job. Rasell, "New Orleans: Jobs."

46. Hahamovitch argues that it wasn't so much the actual scarcity of the labor force in agriculture that motivated the creation of the "Emergency Farm Labor Supply Program," but rather it was "political[ly] expedient" to create guest worker programs as "the nation's most powerful growers were demanding the preservation of [a] cheap, plentiful, and complacent labor force" (Hahamovitch, "The Politics").

So it was in response to the increased discontent among U.S. farmworkers who had become unwilling to perform backbreaking tasks at Depression-era wages that the federal government signed a deal with Mexico to import foreign cheap labor. In addition, legal barriers were constructed against domestic migrants who could have fulfilled the need for an agricultural workforce in areas of the country that were, due to the war and newly built industrial factories, experiencing a dearth of labor. Significantly, Hahamovitch notes, the loudest protests regarding a shortage of labor came from those Southern farmers who were paying workers the least. In 1941, the typical farmworker was making an average of 12 cents an hour in the South, whereas wages averaged 31 cents an hour in the Northeast.

47. The Housing Authority provides rental assistance to more than three hundred families who only pay 30 percent of their annual adjusted income. Data updated to July 2010. E-mail correspondence with Esmeralda Serrata.

48. The Collier County Housing Authority in addition has 641 units of farm labor housing (Farm Worker Village and Collier Village) funded through loans and grants from the USDA. The Housing Authority also administers a Housing Choice Voucher Program through HUD that assists 440 families and a Tenant Based Rental Assistance Program in partnership with the County funded through the HOME Program. (Information taken from the brochure produced for the opening of the Horizon Village).

49. There are nonprofit organizations in Immokalee that help provide farmworkers with their housing needs. Immokalee Housing & Family Services (IHFS) is one of these. IHFS's mission is "to provide decent, safe and affordable rental housing with supportive educational and social programs for farmworkers and other low income families." See IHFS's website at www.ihfservices.org/.

50. Specifically, the church is the St. John Neumann Catholic Church in Reston, Virginia.

Epilogue

1. On August 23, 2010, Sodexo signed the Fair Food agreement with the CIW. See CIW, "Sodexo and Coalition of Immokalee Workers."

2. Amy Bennett Williams, "Immokalee Family Sentenced."

3. Lohan, "One Company Thinks."

4. Barry Estabrook, "Politics of the Plate."

5. CIW News, "Statement of Sen. Bernie Sanders."

6. "Remarks by the President," January 27, 2010.

7. Immigration Policy Center, "Real Enforcement with Practical Answers."

8. For example, see Immigration Policy Center, "Real Enforcement with Practical Answers."

9. Billeaud and Myers, "Judge Blocks Parts."

10. Miguel and Staats, "Florida Legislators Want."

11. Bauer, *Close to Slavery*.

12. Immigration Policy Center, "Breaking Down the Problems," 8.

13. While I was editing this book, I attended the U.S. Social Forum in Detroit. The city is a clear example of resegregation and its consequences in terms of accessibility to fresh, clean, and healthy food. Detroit's population is half the size it was back in the 1950s—more than 80 percent of those who still live in the city are African American (most Whites have relocated to suburbs). The last major supermarket chain left in 2007, and all that remain are fast-food chains and a few restaurants. Despite the remarkable efforts of community organizers to develop gardens to provide fresh produce to the inner-city population, Detroit remains a "food desert" in the poorest big city of America surrounded by some of its wealthiest suburbs.

14. The county ranks seventh in the States for population growth: in 1960, it had 16,000 inhabitants; growing to 86,000 in 1980. Today, it counts more than 350,000, not including 150,000 additional winter residents, thereby confirming southwestern Florida's long-time moniker the "last frontier."

15. Publix's slogan is "where shopping is a pleasure." One store manager in Montgomery, Alabama, used the expression in quotation marks and claimed I was "harassing customers." I was handing out flyers in the attempt to raise awareness around the labor conditions of Immokalee workers and point to Publix's refusal to comply with the CIW agreements. Significantly enough, she used the word "fair" to justify Publix policy about flyering. I couldn't help but say that what's not *fair* is to allow the exploitation of farm workers by buying tomatoes from growers that exploit them (as Publix still does).

16. Among others, see Hahamovitch, *Fruits of Their Labor*.

17. "Rosarno, immigrati in rivolta," *La Repubblica*.

18. Burleigh, "African Immigrants in Italy."

19. Fried Latin American specialty made of pork rinds, often eaten as snacks along with *arepas*.

20. Tebeau, *Florida's Last Frontier*, 195.

BIBLIOGRAPHY

Articles, books, reports, pamphlets, and the like with individual or organizational authors

Archibold, Randal C. "Arizona Enacts Stringent Law on Immigration." *New York Times,* April 23, 2010. www.nytimes.com/2010/04/24/us/politics/24immig.html (accessed July 5, 2010).

Asbed, Greg. "Coalition of Immokalee Workers: *¡Golpear a Uno Es Golpear a Todos!*" In *Bringing Human Rights Home,* Cynthia Soohoo, Catherine Albisa, and Martha Davis, eds., vol. 3, 1–49. Westport, CT: Praeger, 2008.

Bacon, David. "Be Our Guest." September 27, 2004. http://dbacon.igc.org/Imgrants/2004guests.html (accessed July 23, 2010).

Bales, Kevin. *Disposable People: New Slavery in the Global Economy.* Berkeley and Los Angeles: University of California Press, 2004.

Bales, Kevin, and Ron Soodalter. *The Slave Next Door: Human Trafficking and Slavery in America Today.* Berkeley and Los Angeles: University of California Press, 2009.

Barlett, Donald L., and James B. Steele. "Monsanto's Harvest of Fear." *Vanity Fair,* May 2008. www.vanityfair.com/politics/features/2008/05/monsanto200805 (accessed July 11, 2010).

Barnt, Deborah. *Tangled Routes: Women, Work and Globalization on the Tomato Trail.* 2nd ed. Lanham, MD: Rowman & Littlefield Publishers, 2008.

Barrett, Carole, ed. *American Indian History.* Pasadena, CA: Salem Press, 2003.

Bauer, Mary. *Close to Slavery: Guestworker Programs in the United States.* A Report by the Southern Poverty Law Center. March 2007. www.splcenter.org/get-informed/publications/close-to-slavery-guestworker-programs-in-the-united-states.

————. *Under Siege. Life for Low-Income Latinos in the South.* A Report by the Southern Poverty Law Center. April 2009. www.splcenter.org/get-informed/publications/under-siege-life-for-low-income-latinos-in-the-south.

Bazar, Emily, "Citizens Sue after Detentions, Immigration Raids," *USA Today,* June 24, 2008. www.usatoday.com/news/nation/2008–06–24-Immigration-raids_N.htm (accessed July 21, 2010).

Berkovitz, Bull. "Tom Monaghan's Big Box Church." Media Transparency, July 7, 2005. http://mediamattersaction.org/transparency/?storyID=76 (accessed December 15, 2007).

Bernstein, Nina. "Target of Immigrant Raids Shifted." *New York Times,* February 3, 2009. www.nytimes.com/2009/02/04/us/04raids.html (accessed July 18, 2010).

Billeaud, Jacques, and Amanda Lee Myers. "Judge Blocks Parts of Arizona Immigration Law." Associated Press, July 28, 2010.

Bishop, Katy. "Volunteers Spread Holiday Treats with Those Less Fortunate." *Naples Daily News,* November 22, 2007. www.naplesnews.com/news/2007/nov/22/about_3000 _come_thanksgiving_meal_farmworkers_immo/ (accessed September 7, 2010).

Blackmon, Douglas A. *Slavery by Another Name: The Re-enslavement of Black Americans from the Civil War to World War II.* New York: Anchor Books, 2009.

Bowe, John. *Nobodies: Modern American Slave Labor and the Dark Side of the New Global Economy.* New York: Random House, 2007.

Boyer, Peter J., "The Deliverer." *New Yorker,* February 19 & 26, 2007, 88–93, 100, 102, 104, 105, 108, 111.

Browne-Dianis, Judith, Jennifer Lai, Marielena Hincapie, and Saket Soni. *And Injustice for All: Workers' Lives in the Reconstruction of New Orleans,* Washington, DC: Advancement Project, 2006. www.advancementproject.org/sites/default/files/publications/workersreport.pdf.

Burleigh, Nina, "African Immigrants in Italy: Slave Labor for the Mafia." January 15, 2010. www.time.com/time/world/article/0,8599,1953619,00.html (accessed September 7, 2010).

Burns, Allen F., *Maya in Exile: Guatemalans in Florida.* Philadelphia: Temple University Press, 1993.

Calvert, Geoffrey M., Alaron, A. Walter, and others. "Case Report: Three Farmworkers Who Gave Birth to Infants with Birth Defects Closely Grouped in Time and Space—Florida and North Carolina, 2004–2005." *Environmental Health Perspectives* 115 (May 5, 2007): 787–791.

Cave, Damien. "Florida Buying Big Sugar Tract for Everglades." *New York Times,* June 25, 2008. www.nytimes.com/2008/06/25/us/25everglades.html (accessed July 8, 2010).

————. "Everglades Restoration Plan Shrinks." *New York Times,* April 2, 2009. www.nytimes.com/2009/04/02/us/02everglades.html (accessed July 9, 2010).

Chen, Michelle. "Driven by Globalization, Today's Slave Trade Thrives at Home and Abroad." *In These Times,* June 18, 2010. www.inthesetimes.com/working/entry/6119/driven_by_globalization_todays_slave_trade_thrives_at_home_and_abroad/ (accessed June 23, 2010).

Coalition of Immokalee Workers. *Florida Modern-Day Slavery Museum: An Examination of the History and Evolution of Slavery in the Florida Fields,* February 2010.

Cockburn, Andrew. "21st Century Slaves." *National Geographic.* September 2003.

Davis, Angela. *Are Prisons Obsolete?* New York: Seven Stories Press, 2003.

Davis, Mary B., Joan Berman, Mary E. Graham, and Lisa A. Mitten. eds. *Native America in the Twentieth Century: an Encyclopedia.* New York: Garland Publishing 1996.

Detention Watch Network. "Deportation 101. A Community Resource on Anti-Deportation Education and Organizing," revised May 2010. www.familiesforfreedom.org/files/Deportation101Manual-FINAL%2020100712-small.pdf (accessed July 24, 2010).

Dickerson, Chris. "Nearly 100 More Cancer Suits Filed against Monsanto." *West Virginia Record,* August 26, 2009. www.wvrecord.com/news/220760-nearly-100-more-cancer-lawsuits-filed-against-monsanto (accessed July 11, 2010).

Dillon, Liam. "A Town Without a Vote: Now and Forever." *Naples Daily News,* May 9, 2009. www.naplesnews.com/news/2009/may/09/town-without-vote-now-and-forever/ (accessed July 9, 2010).

———."A Town Without a Vote: Taxation without Representation?" *Naples Daily News,* May 10, 2009. www.naplesnews.com/news/2009/may/10/town-without-vote-taxation-without-representation/ (accessed July 10, 2010).

———. "A Town Without a Vote: Residents' Control Hinges on Trust." *Naples Daily News,* May 11, 2009. www.naplesnews.com/news/2009/may/11/town-without-vote-residents-control/ (accessed July 10, 2010).

Domino's Pizza Inc. Company Profile. http://finance.yahoo.com/q/pr?s=DPZ (accessed June 6, 2010).

Donahue, Bill. "Hail Mary." *Mother Jones,* March/April 2007. http://motherjones.com/politics/2007/03/hail-mary (accessed July 9, 2010).

Edsall, B. Thomas. "Bush Suspends Pay Act in Areas Hit by Storm." *Washington Post,* September 9, 2005. www.washingtonpost.com/wp-dyn/content/article/2005/09/08/AR2005090802037.html (accessed July 17, 2010).

Elliott, Marci. "Ave Maria Founder Tom Monaghan Is a Man of Faith, Plans and Action." Catholic Education Resource Center, April 13, 2003. www.catholiceducation.org/articles/catholic_stories/cs0039.html (accessed July 3, 2010).

Estabrook, Barry. "Politics of the Plate: Harvest of Hope." *Gourmet,* March 31, 2009.

www.gourmet.com/foodpolitics/2009/03/politics-of-the-plate-tomato-workers-support (accessed January 18, 2011).

Fawthrop, Tom. "Agent Orange Victims Sue Monsanto." Corpwatch.org, November 4, 2004. www.corpwatch.org/article.php?id=11638 (accessed July 11, 2010).

Fletcher, Laurel E., Phuong Pham, Eric Stover, and Patrick Vinck. *Rebuilding After Katrina: A Population-Based Study of Labor and Human Rights in New Orleans*, Berkeley and Los Angeles, CA: International Human Rights Law Clinic, Boalt Hall School of Law, UC, 2006. www.law.berkeley.edu/clinics/ihrlc/pdf/rebuilding _after_katrina.pdf.

Friedman, Monroe. *Consumer Boycotts: Effecting Change through the Marketplace and the Media*. New York: Routledge, 1999.

Galarza, Ernesto. *Stranger in Our Fields*, 2nd ed. Washington, DC, 1956.

Garofalo, Reebee. *Rockin' Out: Popular Music and in the U.S.A.* 5th Edition. Upper Saddle River, NJ: Pearson Prentice Hall, 2010.

González, Juan. *Harvest of Empire: a History of Latinos in America*. New York: Viking, 2000.

Gonzalez, Melody. "Awakening the Consciousness of the Labor Movement: the Case of the Coalition of Immokalee Workers" (undergraduate thesis, University of Notre Dame, 2005). www.sfalliance.org/resources/Gonzalez2005.pdf (accessed September 7, 2010).

Gorman, Anna. "U-visa Program for Crime Victims Falters." *Los Angeles Times*, January 26, 2009. http://articles.latimes.com/2009/jan/26/local/me-crimevisa26 (accessed July 23, 2010).

Grainger, Sarah. "Guatemala Makes Landmark Civil War Conviction," Reuters, September 1, 2009, available at www.nisgua.org/news_analysis/index.asp?id+3508.

Grech, Dan. "Fighting for a Higher Tomato Value." "Marketplace Morning Report," American Public Media, November 30, 2007. http://marketplace.publicradio.org/display/web/2007/11/30/fighting_for_a_higher_tomato_value (accessed May 14, 2010).

Greene, Ronnie. "Crew Boss Accused of Abuse Gets Owner's OK." *Miami Herald*, August 31, 2003. www.miamiherald.com/2003/08/31/56970/crew-boss-accused-of -abuse-get.html (accessed June 22, 2010).

———. "A Crop of Abuse." *Miami Herald*, September 1, 2003. www.miamiherald .com/2003/09/01/56983_p2_a-crop-of-abuse.html#ixzz0raB1iOIj (accessed June 22, 2010).

———. "Advocates Don't Feel Labor Department Is Ally." *Miami Herald*, September 2, 2003. www.miamiherald.com/2003/09/02/57002/advocates-dont-feel-labor -department.html (accessed June 22, 2010).

Greenhouse, Steven. "How Do You Drive Out a Union? South Carolina Factory Provides a Textbook Case." *New York Times*, December 14, 2004.

————. "Tomato Pickers' Wages Fight Faces Obstacles." *New York Times,* December 24, 2007. www.nytimes.com/2007/12/24/us/24tomato.html (accessed July 2, 2010).

Grover, Steve. "Getting Sound Advice on Social Initiatives." *Harvard Business Review,* June 2008. http://hbr.org/2008/06/getting-sound-advice-on-social-initiatives/ar/1 (accessed July 10, 2010).

Grubbs, Donald H. "The Story of Florida's Migrant Farm Workers." *Florida Historical Quarterly* 40 (October 1961): 2.

Hahamovitch, Cindy. *The Fruits of Their Labor: Atlantic Coast Farmworkers and the Making of Migrant Poverty, 1870–1945.* Chapel Hill: University of North Carolina Press, 1997.

————. "The Politics of Labor Scarcity: Expediency and the Birth of the Agricultural 'Guest Workers' Program." *Center for Immigration Studies.* www.cis.org/Agricultural .GuestWorkersProgram-LaborScarcity.

Hernández, Manuel. "Cierran mina Marlin; se va el Ministro de Energía y Minas." SigloXXI.com, June 24, 2010. www.sigloxxi.com/nacional.php?id=13661

Hernandez, Sandra. "Lethal Limbo for Migrants." *Los Angeles Times,* June 1, 2008. www .latimes.com/news/opinion/commentary/la-op-hernandez1–2008jun01,0,3747284 .story?track=rss (accessed August 30, 2010).

Hoda, Anwarul, and Ashok Gulati. *WTO Negotiations on Agriculture and Developing Countries.* Baltimore: Johns Hopkins University Press/International Food Policy Research Institute, 2007.

Hsu, Spencer S. "Immigrant Crackdown Falls Short." *Washington Post,* December 25, 2007. www.washingtonpost.com/wp-dyn/content/article/2007/12/24/AR2007122402025 .html (accessed July 18, 2010).

————"Immigrant Prosecutions Hit New High." *Washington Post,* June 2, 2008. www .washingtonpost.com/wp-dyn/content/article/2008/06/01/AR2008060102192.html (accessed July 19, 2010).

Hughlett, Mike. "McDonald's Farmworker Raise Fought by Growers." *Chicago Tribune,* November 6, 2007. http://articles.chicagotribune.com/2007–11–06/business/ 0711050555_1_tomato-pickers-florida-tomato-growers-exchange-tomato-farmers (accessed August 26, 2010).

Immigration Policy Center. Special Report. "Breaking Down the Problems: What's Wrong with Our Immigration System?" October 2009. http://immigrationpolicy.org/ special-reports/breaking-down-problems-whats-wrong-our-current-immigration -system (accessed July 28, 2010).

International Association of Chiefs of Police. "Police Chiefs Guide to Immigration Issues." July 2007. www.theiacp.org/Portals/0/pdfs/Publications/PoliceChiefs GuidetoImmigration.pdf (accessed July 23, 2010).

Jackson, Wes. "Farming in Nature's Image: Natural Systems Agriculture." In *The Fatal Harvest Reader: The Tragedy of Industrial Agriculture,* edited by Andrew Kimbrell.

Washington: Foundation for Deep Ecology in collaboration with Island Press, 2002. 65–75.

Jensen, Robert. "Where Agriculture Meets Empire." Alternet, July 1, 2003. www.alternet .org/story/16306/where_agriculture_meets_empire/?page=entire (accessed July 12, 2010).

———. "The Anguish of the Age: Emotional Reactions to Collapse." Commondreams.org, June 22, 2010. www.commondreams.org/view/2010/06/22–4 (accessed July 30, 2010).

———. "Coping with Collapse Emotionally." Countercurrents.org, July 8, 2010. www.countercurrents.org/jensen080710.htm (accessed July 3, 2010).

Kestin, Sally. "FEMA Paid Tribe's Hotel Tab." *South Florida Sun-Sentinel,* November 29, 2007. www.sun-sentinel.com/news/local/southflorida/sfl-semfemasbnov2 9,0,5744648.story (accessed May 1, 2010).

Kestin, Sally, Peter Franceschina and John Maines. "The Seminole Tribe Is Suddenly Wealthy, but Little Oversight Means Potential Abuses." *South Florida Sun-Sentinel,* November 25, 2007. www.sun-sentinel.com/news/local/southflorida/ sfl-semday1newsbnov25,0,5727424.story (accessed June 21, 2010),

———. "Longtime Tribal Leader Collects a Big Salary, but Owes a Fortune to IRS and Tribe." *South Florida Sun-Sentinel,* November 27, 2007. www.sun-sentinel.com/ news/local/southflorida/sfl-semmaxsbnov27,0,7576205.story (accessed May 1, 2010).

———. "Despite Its Wealth, the Tribe Continues to Get Lots of Federal Help." *South Florida Sun-Sentinel,* November 29, 2007. www.sun-sentinel.com/news/local/ southflorida/sfl-semgrantspnnov29,0,7811979.story (accessed June 21, 2010).

Kimbrell, Andrew, ed. *The Fatal Harvest Reader: The Tragedy of Industrial Agriculture.* Washington, DC: Foundation for Deep Ecology in collaboration with Island Press, 2002.

———, ed. *Fatal Harvest: the Tragedy of Industrial Agriculture.* Washington, DC: Foundation for Deep Ecology in arrangement with Island Press, 2002.

Klein, Naomi. *The Shock Doctrine: the Rise of Disaster Capitalism.* New York: Metropolitan Books, 2007.

Kolodner, Meredith. "Immigration Enforcement Benefits Prison Firms." *New York Times,* July 19, 2006. www.nytimes.com/2006/07/19/business/19detain.html (accessed July 21, 2010).

Lantigua, John. "Why Was Carlitos Born This Way?" *Palm Beach Post,* March 16, 2005. www.palmbeachpost.com/localnews/content/local_news/epaper/2005/03/13/s1a _carlitos_0313.html (accessed July 6, 2010).

———. "Ag-Mart Fined $931,000 in New Jersey." *Palm Beach Post.* January 30, 2009. www.palmbeachpost.com/hp/content/state/epaper/2009/01/30/0130agmart.html (accessed July 7, 2010).

Lasker, Eric. "Federal Preemption and State Anti-'GM' Food Law." *Legal Backgrounder.*

20, No. 60 (December 2, 2005). www.wlf.org/upload/120205LBLasker.pdf (accessed July 20, 2010).

Lester, Kristi, e-mail to author, July 1 and July 7, 2010.

Lohan, Tara. "One Company Thinks They've Created Fast Food with a Conscience—Are They Right?" Alternet, February 9, 2010. www.alternet.org/food/145593/one _company_thinks_they've_created_fast_food_with_a_conscience_—_are_they _right/ (accessed July 30, 2010).

Lopez, Mark Hugo, and Susan Minushkin. *2008 National Survey of Latinos: Hispanics See Their Situation in the U.S. Deteriorating; Oppose Key Immigration Enforcement Measures.* Washington, DC: Pew Hispanic Center, September 2008. http:// pewhispanic.org/files/reports/93.pdf (accessed July 18, 2010).

Mahon, John. *History of the Second Seminole War, 1835–1842.* Gainesville: University Presses of Florida, 1985, 1967.

Marchetti, Domenica. "Delivering on His Word." *Chronicle of Philanthropy,* October 7, 1999. http://philanthropy.com/free/articles/v11/i24/24000101.htm (accessed June 28, 2009).

Markon, Jerry. "Justice Dept. Expected to Sue Ariz. on Immigration, Citing 'Preemption Grounds." *Washington Post,* July 6, 2010. www.washingtonpost.com/wp-dyn/ content/article/2010/07/06/AR2010070600061.html?hpid=topnews (accessed July 6, 2010).

Martin, Andrew. "Burger King Shifts Policy on Animals." *New York Times,* March 28, 2007. www.nytimes.com/2007/03/28/business/28burger.html (accessed June 6, 2009).

———. "Burger King Grants Raise to Pickers." *New York Times,* May 24, 2008. www.nytimes.com/2008/05/24/business/24farm.html (accessed July 15, 2010).

Mascarenhas, Michael and Lawrence Busch. "Seeds of Change: Intellectual Property Rights, Genetically Modified Soybeans and Seed Saving in the United States." *Sociologia Ruralis* 46 (2006): 122–138.

Mejía, Camilo. *Road from ar Ramadi: The Private Rebellion of Staff Sergeant Camilo Mejía.* Chicago: Haymarket Books, 2008.

Miguel, Tracy X. "Poll: Push Resumes for AgJobs Bill to Allow Farmworker Illegals to Stay." *Naples Daily News,* July 10, 2010. www.naplesnews.com/news/2010/jul/10 /push-resumes-agjobs-bill-allow-farmworker-illegals/ (accessed July 30, 2010).

Miguel, Tracy X., and Eric Staats, "Florida Legislators Want Bill Modeled after Arizona Illegal Immigration Law." *Naples Daily News,* July 12, 2010. www.naplesnews .com/news/2010/jul/12/florida-legislators-want-adopt-arizona-illegal-imm/ (accessed July 30, 2010).

Monaghan, Tom (with Robert Anderson). *Pizza Tiger.* New York: Random House, 1986.

Muñoz, Jorge Luján, ed. *Historia General de Guatemala.* Guatemala: Asociación de

Amigos del País, 2005, Fundación para la Cultura y el Desarrollo, 1993–1999.

Navarro, Mireya, "Florida Tomato Pickers Take on Growers," *New York Times*, February 1, 1998.

Nies, Judith. *Native American History: A Chronology of the Vast Achievements of a Culture and Their Links to World Events*. New York: Ballantine Books, 1996.

Nissen, Bruce. "Critical Analysis of the Report *Economic Impact: Tomatoes in Florida, Report 1*" Center for Reflection, Education and Action. www.ciw-online.org/Nissen _report.html (accessed July 24, 2010).

Novak, Michael. *The Spirit of Democratic Capitalism*. New York: Simon & Schuster, 1982.

———. *Will It Liberate? Questions About Liberation Theology*. New York: Paulist, 1986.

———. *The Fire of Invention: Civil Society and the Future of the Corporation*. Lanham, MD: Rowman & Littlefield, 1997.

Ohlemeier, Doug. "Updated: Florida Tomato Industry Changes Position on Farmworker Pay." Thepacker.com, February 16, 2010. http://thepacker.com/Florida-tomato -industry-changes-position-on-farmworker-pay/Article.aspx?oid=988203&fid= PACKER-ALL-NEWS&aid=683 (accessed July 29, 2010).

O'Neill, Richard, Amy, *International Trafficking of Women to the United States: A Contemporary Manifestation of Slavery and Organized Crime*, April 2000. www.cia.gov/library/center-for the-study-of-intelligence/csi-publications/books -and-monographs/trafficking.pdf (accessed July 28, 2010).

Oxfam America. *Like Machines in the Fields: Workers without Rights in American Agriculture*. Boston: Oxfam America. 2004.

Pew Center on the States. *One in 100: Behind Bars in America in 2008*. February 28, 2008. www.pewcenteronthestates.org/report_detail.aspx?id=35904 (accessed June 19, 2010.)

———. *Public Safety, Public Spending: Forecasting America's Prison Population 2007–2011*. February 14, 2010. http://www.pewcenteronthestates.org/report_detail.aspx?id=32076 (accessed June 19, 2010.

Philpott, Tom. "Another Win for the Coalition of Immokalee Workers." Grist.org, May 2, 2009. www.grist.org/article/2009-05-01-immokalee-win/ (accessed July 29, 2010).

Preston, Julia. "Ruling Against Arizona Is a Warning for Other States." *New York Times*, July 29, 2010. www.nytimes.com/2010/07/29/us/29immig.html?_r=1&hp (accessed July 29, 2010).

Priest, Dana, and Amy Goldstein. "System of Neglect." *Washington Post*. May 11, 2008. www.washingtonpost.com/wp-srv/nation/specials/immigration/cwc_d1p1.html (accessed July 19, 2010).

Pringle, Peter. *Food, Inc.: Mendel to Monsanto—the Promises and Perils of the Biotech Harvest*. New York: Simon & Schuster, 2003.

Rasell, Edith. "New Orleans: Jobs, Workers, and Barriers to Economic Equity." United

Church of Christ. www.ucc.org/justice/advocacy_resources/pdfs/gulf-coast-initiative/
New-Orleans-Jobs-Workers-and-Barriers-to-Economic-Equity-small.pdf (accessed
July 17, 2010).

Robinson, M. *Justice Blind? Ideals and Realities of American Criminal Justice.* Upper Saddle
River, NJ: Prentice-Hall, 2002.

Roy, Arundhati. *An Ordinary Person's Guide to Empire.* Cambridge, MA: South End
Press, 2004.

San Martin, Nancy. "Farm Labor Suppliers Plead Guilty to Charge of Enslaving
Workers." *South Florida Sun-Sentinel,* May 12, 2010. http://articles.sun-sentinel
.com/1997–05–12/news/9705110153_1_labor-camps-illegal-immigrants-servitude
(accessed May 10, 2010).

Schlosser, Eric. *Fast Food Nation: The Dark Side of the All-American Meal.* New York,
NY: Perennial, 2002.

———. "Penny Foolish." *New York Times,* November 29, 2007. www.nytimes.com/
2007/11/29/opinion/29schlosser.html.

Schriro, Dora. "Immigration Detention Overview and Recommendations." October 9,
2009. www.ice.gov/doclib/091005_ice_detention_report-final.pdf (accessed July
21, 2010).

Sellers, Randall Sean. "'Del pueblo, para el pueblo': The Coalition of Immokalee Workers
and the Fight for Fair Food," (Master's diss., University of Texas at Austin, 2009).
www.sfalliance.org/resources/Sellers2009.pdf (accessed May 1, 2010).

———. "Chipotle Challenge: Time to Back Up 'Food with Integrity.'" Grist.org,
December 11, 2010. www.grist.org/article/steve-ells-will-you-accept-the-chipotle
-challenge (accessed July 30, 2010).

Serrata, Esmeralda, e-mail messages to author. July 15–17, 2010.

Shand, Hope J. "Intellectual Property: Enhancing Corporate Monopoly and Bioserfdom." In
Kimbrell, Andrew, ed. *The Fatal Harvest Reader: The Tragedy of Industrial Agriculture.*
Washington: Foundation for Deep Ecology in collaboration with Island Press, 2002.

Shimberg Center for Affordable Housing, University of Florida. "The Need for Farmworker Housing in Florida," September 10, 2004. http://flhousingdata.shimberg
.ufl.edu/docs/04RMS_FarmworkerHousing.pdf (accessed July 17, 2010).

Shiva, Vandana. *Biopiracy: The Plunder of Nature and Knowledge.* Boston, MA: South
End Press, 1997.

———. "The Suicide Economy of Corporate Globalisation." Countercurrents.com, April
5, 2004. www.countercurrents.org/glo-shiva050404.htm (accessed July 17, 2010).

Sieff, Kevin. "Immigrant Detention Center in Va. Would be Mid-Atlantic's Largest."
Washington Post, July 18, 2010. www.washingtonpost.com/wp-dyn/content/article/
2010/07/17/AR2010071701416.html (accessed July 19, 2010).

Smith, Jeffrey. *Seeds of Deception: Exposing Industry and Government Lies about the Safety of the Genetically Engineered Foods You're Eating.* Fairfield, IA: Yes Books; White River Junction, VT: Distributed by Chelsea Green Publishing, 2003.

———. "Monsanto Forced Fox TV to Censor Coverage of Dangerous Milk Drug." Huffingtonpost.com, April 13, 2009. www.huffingtonpost.com/jeffrey-smith/monsanto -forced-fox-tv-to_b_186428.html (accessed July 14, 2010).

Solnit, David, ed. *Globalize Liberation: How to Uproot the System and Build a Better World.* San Francisco: City Lights Books, 2004.

Solsman, Joan E. "Domino's Pizza Profit More Than Doubles on Sales, Margin Growth." *Wall Street Journal,* March 2, 2010. http://online.wsj.com/article/ SB10001424052748703807904575097213409089500.html (accessed July 2, 2010).

Stapleton, Christine. "Deal Ensures Lifetime of Care for Carlitos." *Palm Beach Post,* April 17, 2008. www.palmbeachpost.com/search/content/state/epaper/2008/04/17/w1a _CARLITOS_AGMART_0417.html (accessed July 6, 2010).

Swall, Lexie. "About 3,000 Come to Thanksgiving Meal for Farmworkers in Immokalee Park." *Naples Daily News,* November 22, 2007. www.naplesnews.com/photos /galleries/2007/nov/22/about_3000_come_thanksgiving_meal_farmworkers_immo/ (accessed July 22, 2010).

Tebeau W., Charlton, *Florida's Last Frontier: The History of Collier County.* Coral Gables, FL: University of Miami Press, 1966.

Think Progress Staff. "The Consequences of Enforcement Without Reform." Alternet, June 4, 2008. www.alternet.org/immigration/87027/?page=2 (accessed July 19, 2010).

Vanden Heuvel, Katrina. "Slavery in the Union." Nation.com, Editor's Cut Blog, January 29, 2008. www.thenation.com/blog/slavery-union (accessed July 10, 2010).

———. "Invasions of Privacy." Nation.com, Editor's Cut Blog, May 11, 2008. www.thenation.com/blog/invasions-privacy (accessed July 17, 2010).

———. "Sweet Victory: Coalition of Immokalee Workers Win." Nation.com, Editor's Cut Blog, May 23, 2008. www.thenation.com/blog/sweet-victory-coalition -immokalee-workers-wins (accessed July 10, 2010).

———. "Victory for Tomato Picker's Fight Against Burger King." Nation.com, Editor's Cut Blog, May 29, 2008. Reposted on Alternet. www.alternet.org/story/86619/.

Volyes, Karen. "Three Charged with Human Trafficking on Alachua County Farms," Gainesville.com, July 6, 2010. www.gainesville.com/article/20100706/ARTICLES/ 100709714/1139?Title=Three-charged-with-human-trafficking-on-Alachua- County-farms (accessed September 25, 2010).

Walsh, Mary Williams. "Florida Deal for Everglades May Help Big Sugar." *New York Times,* September 1, 2008. www.nytimes.com/2008/09/14/business/14fanjul.html (accessed July 8, 2010).

Whelan, David. "Charity and the Forbes 400." Forbes.com, September 24, 2004. www .forbes.com/2004/09/23/cz_dw_0923philan_rl04_print.html (accessed July 2, 2010).

White, Douglas, and Robert D. Stroh. *The State of Florida Housing 2009*. University of Florida. www.shimberg.ufl.edu/pdf/SOFH_2009.pdf (accessed July 17, 2010).

Williams, Amy Bennett. "Labor Contractor Back Despite Conviction." *Ft. Myers News-Press*, December 9, 2005. Retrieved through email communication with Amy Williams. July 5, 2010.

———. "From April 12: Tomato Pickers Feeling Spied On." *Ft. Myers News-Press*, July 5, 2008. www.news-press.com/article/20080704/NEWS01/107050001 (accessed July 10, 2010).

———. "Immokalee Family Sentenced for Slavery; Each Navarrete Boss Gets 12 Years in Prison." *Ft. Myers News-Press*, December 20, 2008. www.sanders.senate.gov/newsroom.news.?id+517f1da1-8900-40ee-b650-B3acd6ff8efe (accessed on January 18, 2011).

Zeitlin, Janine. "Slavery: Collier County's Connection." *Naples Daily News*, January 29, 2006. www.naplesnews.com/news/2006/jan/29/modernday_slavery_reaches_immokalee_farm_fields_pr/?print=1 (accessed June 22, 2010).

———. "Labor Camps Kept Workers in Servitude with Crack Cocaine." *Naples Daily News*. September 23, 2006. www.naplesnews.com/news/2006/sep/23/labor_camp_owner_hawking_crack_cocaine_homeless_ad/?local_news (accessed June 19, 2010).

Articles and online materials with no author

"1 Million March for Immigrants Across the U.S." msnbc.msn.com, May 1, 2006. www.msnbc.msn.com/id/12573992/ (accessed July 18, 2010).

"3 Fla. farmworkers give up hunger strike after Carter plea," *Washington Post*, January 19, 1998.

"Ave Maria Oratory Dedication Delayed by Bishop." Catholicnewsagency.com, January 23, 2008. www.catholic.org/national/national_story.php?id=26543 (accessed July 17, 2010).

Barron Collier Companies, "A New Town—Ave Maria," www.barroncollier.com.

"Bishop Ought to Teach Us Why Status Still in Limbo." *Naples Daily News*, editorial. January 18, 2008. www.naplesnews.com/news/2008/jan/16/editorial-ave-maria-oratory/ (accessed July 9, 2010).

Center for Food Safety, "Monsanto vs. U.S. Farmers." www.centerforfoodsafety.org/pubs/CFSMOnsantovsFarmerReport1.13.05.pdf (accessed July 9, 2010).

City of Miami–Planning Department, "Services: Census," 2004, www.miamigov.com/Planning/pages/services/Census.asp (accessed July 14, 2010).

Coalition of Immokalee Workers, "Coalition of Immokalee Workers, Allies to Hold Press Conference at Burger King Headquarters," press release, February 14, 2007.

Coalition of Immokalee Workers website. "Campaign Analysis—CIW Campaign for Fair Food." www.ciw-online.org/images/BK_Campaign_Analysis.pdf (accessed July 24, 2010).

———. Farmworker Facts and Figures. www.ciw-online.org/101.html#facts. April 2009.

———. CIW News, "A Brief History of Inhumanity: Three Centuries of Forced Agricultural Labor on the Banks of the St. Johns," April 13, 2010, www.ciw-online.org/a_brief_history_of_inhumanity.html.

———. CIW News, "Far Too Little, Far Too Late," April 12, 2010, www.ciw-online .org/too_little_too_late.html#jump (accessed April 6, 2010).

———. CIW News, "Statement of Sen. Bernie Sanders," www.ciw-online.org/Sen _Sanders_on_Slavery_Verdict.html.

———. CIW News, "Sodexo and Coalition of Immokalee Workers Sign Fair Food Agreement," www.ciw-online.org/ciw_sodexo_joint_release.html.

———. "Florida Modern-Day Slavery Museum: An Examination of the History and Evolution of Slavery in Florida's Fields," www.ciw-online.org/freedom_march/ MuseumBookletWeb.pdf.

Collier County Housing Authority, "At a Glance," brochure.

Collier County Sheriff's Office. Press release, September 19, 2007. www.colliersheriff .org/index.aspx?recordid=22858&page=1929. "Death by Multiple Poisoning, Glyphosate and Roundup." Institute of Science in Society. Press release November 2, 2009. www.i-sis.org.uk/DMPGR.php (accessed July 17, 2010).

"Conservative Transparency: People: Thomas S. Monaghan," Media Matters Action Network, July 2, 2010, http://mediamattersaction.org/transparency/people/Thomas_S _Monaghan/roles (accessed September 30, 2010).

Comprehensive Everglades Restoration Plan, "Development of Central and South Florida (C&SF) Project," www.evergladesplan.org/about/restudy_csf_devel.aspx.

"First, They Took on Taco Bell. Now, the Fast-Food World." Associated Press. New York Times, May 22, 2005. query.nytimes.com/gst/fullpage.html?res=9E04EEDA1539 F931A15756C0A9639C8B63&sec=&spon=.

Florida Immigrant Coalition and Florida Immigrant Advocacy Center. "Defending Immigrant Rights 101: Detention, Deportation and the Criminal Justice System." January 25, 2008. Immokalee, Florida.

Florida Public Service Commission, "Florida Public Service Commission Denies Determination of Need for Proposed Power Plants in Glades County," news release, June 5, 2007, www.psc.state.fl.us/home/news/index.aspx?id=273.

"Guatemala Makes Landmark Civil War Conviction." Reuters, August 31, 2009. www.reuters.com/article/idUSN31457710 (accessed July 2, 2010).

"ICE Apprehends More Than 2,100 Criminal Aliens, Gang Members, Fugitives and

Other Immigration Violators in Nationwide Interior Enforcement Operation." Department of Homeland Security press release, June 14, 2006. www.dhs.gov/ xnews/releases/press_release_0926.shtm (accessed July 18, 2010).

"IIRIRA 96—A Summary of the New Immigration Bill," Visalaw.com–The Immigration Law Portal, www.visalaw.com/96nov/3nov96.html (accessed September 1, 2010).

Immigration Policy Center, "Real Enforcement with Practical Answers." http:// immigrationpolicy.org/sites/default/files/docs/REPAIR_Summary_050310.pdf.

Institute of Science in Society, "Death by Multiple Poisoning, Glyphosate and Roundup." Press release, November 2, 2009. www.i-sis.org.uk/DMPGR.php (accessed July 17, 2010).

International Crisis Group. "Identity Crisis: Israel and its Citizens," *Middle East Report* 25 (March 4, 2004), web.archive.org/web/20080709020917/http://www.crisisgroup .org/home/index.cfm?id=2528&l=1 (accessed September 30, 2010). Document13

Legal Action Center: www.legalactioncenter.org/clearinghouse/litigation-issue-pages/ arizona-legal-challenges.

Luna v. Del Monte Fresh Produce (Southeast), Inc. U.S. Dist. N.D. Ga. Dec. 9, 2009. http://scholar.google.com/scholar_case?case=18102581304156590222 (accessed July 20, 2010).

National Immigration Law Center. *A Broken System: Confidential Reports Reveal Failures in U.S. Immigrant Detention Centers.* 2009. www.nilc.org/immlawpolicy/arrest-det/A-Broken-System-2009-07.pdf (accessed January 16, 2011).

National Labor Relations Board, National Labor Relations Act, www.nlrb.gov/about _us/overview/national_labor_relations_act.aspx.

Network in Solidarity with the People of Guatemala. "The School of the Americas and Guatemala," www.nisgua.org/themes_campaigns/impunity/The%20School%20of %20the %20Americas%20and%20Guatemala.pdf.

"Obama Declares Commitment to Reform." National Immigration Law Center press release, January 28, 2010. www.nilc.org/immlawpolicy/CIR/cir031.htm (accessed July 20, 2010).

The Protection Project, U.S. Country Report, www.protectionproject.org/sites/default/ files/file/activities/tacap/US/trafficking/us%20country%20rpt.pdf (accessed June 29, 2010).

"Real Enforcement with Practical Answers for Immigration Reform (REPAIR) Proposal Summary." Immigration Policy Center, May 3, 2010. http://immigrationpolicy.org/ sites/default/files/docs/REPAIR_Summary_050310.pdf (accessed July 30, 2010).

"Reality TV Star Anna Nicole Smith Dies at 39," CNN.com, February 8, 2007, http:// articles.cnn.com/2007-02-08/entertainment/anna.nicole.collapses_1_anna-nicole

-smith-dannielynn-hope-howard-k-stern?_s=PM:SHOWBIZ (accessed September 24, 2010).

"Remarks by the President in the State of the Union Address." January 27, 2010. www.whitehouse.gov/the-press-office/remarks-president-state-union-address (accessed January 18, 2011).

"The Rise and Fall of Ave Maria." Rightwingwatch.org, September 2, 2009. www .rightwingwatch.org/content/rise-and-fall-ave-maria (accessed July 25, 2010).

"Rosarno, immigrati in rivolta, centinaia di auto danneggiate." *La Repubblica.* January 7, 2010. www.repubblica.it/cronaca/2010/01/07/news/rosarno_immigrati_in_rivolta _centinaia_di_auto_danneggiate-1872028/ (accessed September 7, 2010).

Scalabrinian Missionaries of St. Charles Borromeo. "The Scalabrinian Missionaries." www.scalabrini.org/index.php?option=com_content&view=article&id=45&Itemid =230&lang=en.

"The School of the Americas and Guatemala." Nisgua.org, www.nisgua.org/themes _campaigns/impunity/The%20School%20of%20the%20Americas%20and %20Guatemala.pdf (accessed July 2, 2010).

Sidney A. Diamond, Commissioner of Patents and Trademarks, v. Ananda M. Chakrabarty, et al. 447 US 303 Supreme Court 1980. http://scholar.google.com/scholar_case ?case=3095713882675765791.

"Times Topics: Marcelo Lucero," nytimes.com, updated June 4, 2010, http://topics.nytimes.com/topics/reference/timestopics/people/l/marcelo_lucero/index.html?s=ol dest& (accessed September 30, 2010).

Travel.State.gov, "FY-2005 Nonimmigrant Visas Issued," http://travel.state.gov/pdf/ FY2005_NIV_Detail_Table.pdf.

U.S. Census Bureau website. http://factfinder.census.gov/home/saff/main.html?_lang=en.

U.S. Custom and Border Protection. *Safe Travel, Legal Trade: U.S. Customs and Border Protection Fiscal Year 2009–2014 Strategic Plan,* January 12, 2010. www.cbp.gov/ linkhandler/cgov/about/mission/strategic_plan_09_14.ctt/strategic_plan_09_14.pdf (accessed July 19, 2010).

U.S. Department of Justice—Federal Bureau of Investigation. *Hate Crime Statistics, 2008.* November 2009. www.fbi.gov/ucr/hc2008/documents/victims.pdf (accessed July 23, 2010).

U.S. Department of Labor. *The Agricultural Labor Market—Status and Recommendations.* Washington, DC: U.S. Department of Labor, 2000.

U.S. Department of State. *2010 Trafficking in Persons Report.* June 14, 2010. www.state .gov/documents/organization/142979.pdf (accessed July 23, 2010).

USDA 2007 Census of Agriculture. www.agcensus.usda.gov/Publications/2007/Full

_Report/Volume_1,_Chapter_1_State_Level/Florida/index.asp (accessed April 7, 2010).

USDA, "Plant Variety Protection Act," www.ams.usda.gov/AMSv1.0/getfile?dDocName =STELDEV30027.

U.S. EEOC et al. v. Gargiulo, Inc., SPLC website, www.splcenter.org/get-informed/case -docket/-us-eeoc-et-al-v-gargiulo-inc> Gargiulo Consent Decree (April 24, 2006), http://www.splcenter.org/sites/default/files/Gargiulo_consent_decree.pdf, and Amended Complaints (January 22, 2007) www.splcenter.org/sites/default/files/ Gargiulo_amended_complaints.pdf.

"U.S. EPA Fact Sheet Anniston PCB Site Anniston, Calhoun County, Alabama." August 2002. www.epa.gov/region4/waste/npl/nplal/annpcbfsaug02.pdf (accessed July 17, 2010).

U.S. Government Accountability Office, *Illegal Immigration: Border Crossing Deaths Have Doubled Since 1995; Border Patrol's Efforts to Prevent Deaths Have Not Been Fully Evaluated,* GAO 06 770, August 2006, http://www.gao.gov/new.items/d06770.pdf.

U.S. Immigration Support, "U Visa for Immigrants Who Are Victims of Crimes," www.usimmigrationsupport.org/visa-u.html (accessed August 31, 2010).

Videos

The Corporation. Mark Achbar, and Jennifer Abbott. Big Picture Media Company. 2003, DVD.

Food, Inc. Robert Kenner. Magnolia Pictures, Participant Media, and River Road Entertainment. 2008, DVD.

Harvest of Shame. CBS News Productions. 1960, VHS.

"The Rise of a Catholic Town: Ave Maria, Florida." Posted August 27, 2007. www .youtube.com/watch?v=pyiTlLEfxHs (accessed June 7, 2010).

Websites

Alliance for Fair Food: www.allianceforfairfood.org

American Civil Liberties Union (ACLU): www.aclu.org

Avewatch.com "Investigative Journalism on Tom Monaghan's Ave Maria Entities": http://avewatch.com/

Barron Collier Companies: www.barroncollier.com

Behavioral Interventions: www.bi.com/about; and specifically, www.bi.com/sites/all/
    themes/BI/pdf/casestudy/BrowardCoFL.pdf

Center for Responsive Politics: www.opensecrets.org/industries/indus.php?ind=A07

Center for Studying Health System Change: www.hschange.com

Coalition of Immokalee Workers: www.ciw-online.org

Economic Development Council of Collier County: www.enaplesflorida.com

Families for Freedom: www.familiesforfreedom.org

Florida Freedom Partnership: www.humantrafficking.org/organizations/319

Florida Immigrant Advocacy Center (FIAC): www.fiacfla.org

Have It Your Way Foundation: www.haveityourwayfoundation.org

Immigration Policy Center: http://immigrationpolicy.org

Iraq Veterans Against the War: www.ivaw.org

The Land Institute: www.landinstitute.org/

Legal Action Center: www.legalactioncenter.org/clearinghouse/litigation-issue-pages/
    arizona-legal-challenges

Monsanto Company: www.monsanto.com

National Immigration Law Center: www.nilc.org

The Packer: http://thepacker.com

Phoenix New Times: www.phoenixnewtimes.com/arpaio

Power U: www.poweru.org

Scalabrinians; Missionaries of St. Charles Borromeo: www.scalabrini.org

Seminis: http://us.seminis.com/about/default.asp

The Seminole Tribe of Florida: www.semtribe.com

Six L's: www.sixls.com

Student/Farmworker Alliance: www.sfalliance.org

United States Department of Agriculture–National Agricultural Statistics Service:
    www.
    nass.usda.gov/QuickStats/PullData_US.jsp